PAST TIME

PAST
TIME

Baseball as History

JULES TYGIEL

OXFORD
UNIVERSITY PRESS
2000

OXFORD
UNIVERSITY PRESS

Oxford   New York
Athens   Auckland   Bangkok   Bogotá   Buenos Aires   Calcutta
Cape Town   Chennai   Dar es Salaam   Delhi   Florence   Hong Kong   Istanbul
Karachi   Kuala Lumpur   Madrid   Melbourne   Mexico City   Mumbai
Nairobi   Paris   São Paulo   Singapore   Taipei   Tokyo   Toronto   Warsaw

and associated companies in
Berlin   Ibadan

Copyright © 2000 by Jules Tygiel

Published by Oxford University Press, Inc.
198 Madison Avenue, New York, New York 10016

Oxford is a registered trademark of Oxford University Press

Library of Congress Cataloging-in-Publication Data
Tygiel, Jules.
Past time: baseball as history/Jules Tygiel
p. cm.
Includes bibliographical references and index.
ISBN 0-19-508958-8
1. Baseball—United States—History—19th century.
2. Baseball—United States—History—20th century.
I. Title.
GV863.A1 T94 2000
796.357'0973 21—dc21   99-040106

Book design by Adam B. Bohannon

9 8 7 6 5 4 3 2 1
Printed in the United States of America
on acid-free paper

For Charlie and Sam

Contents

Introduction

This is a collection of essays about American history. I say that lest this be mistaken for a book about baseball. This would be a natural misconception. Baseball, after all, appears in its title. Each of its chapters revolves around baseball. The purpose of this book, however, is not to examine developments or events in the sport, but rather changes occurring in American society. The narratives rarely venture onto the field but concern themselves more with the broader baseball experience: how fans received and processed their baseball information; how they witnessed the games; what baseball symbolized in different eras; and how each generation reinvented the national pastime to fit its own material reality and ideological perceptions.

Many historians will recognize the subtitle, *Baseball as History*, as a play on Warren Susman's seminal collection of essays, *Culture as History*. "Each age has its special words, its own vocabulary, its own set of meanings, its particular symbolic order," wrote Susman. "A careful study of the conventions, the unassuming everyday acts, the rhetorical devices in speech and song, the unconscious patterns of behavior, all help to uncover . . . those fundamental assumptions that such cultures share."

Baseball, a constant in American life since the 1850s, reveals much about these "fundamental assumptions." I do not subscribe to Jacques Barzun's unfortunate and oft-quoted adage, "Whoever wants to know the heart and mind of America had better learn baseball." Remarkably, people with a total ignorance of baseball have written many fine books on American society and culture. Nor do I wish to over-intellectualize the game, ascribing hypothetical meanings to rudimentary phenomena. Nonetheless, baseball, with its long, rich, well-documented history remains a powerful vehicle for exploring the American past.

If there is a unifying theme in these chapters, it is that, while the game of baseball itself has changed minimally since its origins, the context and format in which Americans have absorbed and appreciated the game have dramatically shifted. In 1998 Americans embraced the exhilarating quest by Mark McGwire and Sammy Sosa to break Roger Maris's single-season home run record. They did so in an environment markedly different from that in which Americans in 1961 followed Maris's pursuit of Babe Ruth's record and even further removed from the world of Ruth himself. When Ruth set his first home run records in the early 1920s, he did so in an age in which major league baseball was played in a few cities in the Northeast and Midwest and daily newspapers remained the dominant source of information. By 1927, when Ruth established sixty home runs as a benchmark, the news could be relayed instantaneously to fans via the radio. Within days they could see the feat in a newsreel. Thirty-four years later, baseball had begun its westward expansion and a horde of newsmen from a variety of media descended on Maris, challenging his powers of concentration as he approached Ruth's sacred record. Millions of fans, many with mixed emotions, watched Maris dethrone Ruth, as it happened, on television.

The 1998 "media circus" dwarfed that which surrounded Maris. Americans rejoiced in the friendly McGwire-Sosa competition in a multitude of ways undreamed of by earlier generations. Twenty-eight cities in all regions of the nation and two cities in Canada now hosted major league teams. That Sosa hailed from the Dominican Republic gave the rivalry an international flavor. Fans throughout the United States, Canada, and the Caribbean followed the chase on network and cable television and on the Internet, discussed it in e-mail chat rooms, and read about it in national newspapers beamed to local communities via satellite. In each era, different levels of technology facilitated different levels of involvement and shaped the manner in which people responded.

I have organized these essays chronologically, but they need not be read in any particular order. Each stands alone as a separate inquiry into a particular age. The articles are designed to be suggestive, rather than definitive. Although I have done a substantial amount of primary research, the core analysis rests on secondary sources, the vast outpouring of writing on baseball history that has appeared in the 1980s and 1990s. I hoped to steer clear of two of the dominant themes in recent baseball writing: a heavy focus on the business side of the game and the ethereal, rhapsodic celebration of baseball and its special essence. These essays, with their emphasis on communications, team relocation, social mobility, and economic issues of supply and demand have drifted further into the realm of business than I had intended, but they nonetheless, I believe, approach these subjects from a fresh angle. I also make no grand claims for baseball beyond the obvious: that since its origins in the 1850s it has reflected broader changes in society and maintained a special place in American culture.

I am deeply indebted to my fellow historians, amateur and professional, scholarly and popular, who have offered new insights into the game and on whose work I have heavily relied. My fellow members of the Society for Baseball Research (SABR), both through their publications and SABR-L discussion list, have added significantly to my understanding of the game. John Thorn and Peter Palmer's *Total Baseball*, to which I am honored to contribute, was an irreplaceable source of information at every phase of this work. Unless otherwise noted, all information on attendance and player statistics is derived from *Total Baseball*.

My agent, Peter Ginsberg at Curtis-Brown, made this book possible. Dave Kelly at the Library of Congress and Scot Mondore at the Baseball Hall of Fame provided invaluable research assistance. Steve Appel helped out during a research trip to Cooperstown. Richard Zitrin, Ben Rader, John Thorn, Ron Story, Jeff Sammons, Don Spivey, Bill Issel, Barbara Loomis, Martha Tygiel, and Luise

Custer all critiqued portions of the manuscript. Bill Kirwin published earlier drafts of chapters one and two in *Nine: A Journal of Baseball History and Social Policy Perspectives*. I tested many of these ideas in "The History and Literature of Baseball," a course that I team-taught with the inimitable Eric Solomon. Both Eric and the students added greatly to my knowledge. I am, as always, grateful to my colleagues in the History Department at San Francisco State University for their collegiality and support. I also wish to thank Albright College, where I spent a delightful year as the National Endowment for the Humanities Visiting Professor as I completed the manuscript.

This is my third and final book written under the editorship of Sheldon Meyer, who has retired after almost a half-century of distinguished work at Oxford University Press. I thank Sheldon for his wisdom, kindness, patience, friendship, and support over the past two decades.

I thank my son Sam for developing an interest in baseball and making my springs and summers (and falls and winters) more enjoyable. As those who know him are well aware, my son Charlie cares less for baseball, but he enriches my life in innumerable other ways. Most of all, I thank my wife, Luise Custer. I cannot imagine a better and more loving traveling companion on life's unpredictable journeys.

I began work on *Past Time* during 1993 at a particularly foreboding moment in baseball history. Storm clouds were gathering, foretelling the onset of a major tempest: the devastating strike that resulted in the cancellation of the 1994 World Series. I conceived this book as an escape from these events, an inquiry into what was right about baseball, rather than an exposé about what was wrong with it; an examination of why baseball had appealed to different generations of Americans and how it had fit into and represented the fabric of their lives. I complete this book at a more upbeat moment. Although problems abound as salaries continue to rise and the imbalance between high- and low-income teams threatens its competitive structure, baseball, on the strength of a remarkable 1998 season, has largely recovered from the effects of the last strike.

Technological developments during the past five years have given us even more wondrous ways with which to access and enjoy the game. Above all, like the generations before us, we can still take ourselves to the ballpark, buy peanuts and cracker jacks (and garlic fries), suspend the present, and move past time, to bask in the unparalleled pleasures of "the old ball game."

PAST TIME

The National Game

Reflections on the Rise of Baseball in the 1850s and 1860s

In November 1860 popular lithographers Currier & Ives depicted the results of the most significant presidential election in the nation's history in a most unusual fashion. The firm issued a print featuring the four leading contenders for the presidency—Unionist John Bell, northern Democrat Stephen A. Douglas, southern Democrat John Breckinridge, and Republican Abraham Lincoln—as baseball players. The three losing candidates each held baseball bats emblazoned with their political positions—"fusion," "non-intervention," and "slavery extension." Lincoln, holding a ball, his right foot planted firmly on "home base," fittingly held a long rail, labeled "equal rights and free territory." Each of the men discussed the outcome of the election using baseball jargon. Bell wondered "why we three should strike 'foul' and be 'put out.'" Douglas muses, "I thought our fusion would be a 'short stop' to his career." Breckinridge, shown slinking back to Kentucky with his fingers sealing his nostrils, complains "that we are completely 'skunk'd,'" a popular term for a rout or shutout. Lincoln warns his defeated opponents that should they choose to challenge him again, "You must have 'a good bat' and strike a 'fair ball' to make a 'clean score' & a 'home run.' " Currier & Ives entitled its editorial cartoon: THE NATIONAL GAME. THREE "OUTS" AND ONE "RUN."[1]

This print appeared at the very moment that the United States stood on the edge of defining for itself the meaning of terms like "nation" and "national." The "national game" illustrated here is not really baseball, but politics. Three years earlier, most Americans would have found this metaphor undecipherable. But Currier & Ives, a New York-based firm with a national clientele, felt confident that in 1860 its patrons not only would recognize the baseball imagery, but would understand the baseball language and be familiar with the notion that baseball had been anointed "the national game." Thus, the cartoon captures not just the profound political challenge confronting the United States, but also the extent to which a fledgling pastime had captured the imaginations of a significant segment of the American populace.

The question of why baseball appealed to the American people has evoked both treacly flights of romantic fancy as well as more serious scholarly analysis. Amherst College Professor Allen Guttmann attributes baseball's triumph, in part, to "the place of baseball in the cycle of the seasons." Yale President Bart Giamatti, shortly before he became baseball commissioner, lyrically explained, "The game begins in spring, when everything else begins again, and it blossoms in the summer . . . and then as soon as the chill rains come, it stops and leaves you in the fall alone." Philosopher Michael Novak invokes the "mysticism of baseball numbers," while Guttmann adds "the tendency of baseball toward extremes of quantification." Others have proposed theories of rural nostalgia, the folk-hero factor, and baseball as a compensatory mechanism for the travails of industrial life.[2]

Yet these explanations have a curiously ahistorical flavor. They describe values and attributes that Americans have grafted onto baseball after it became embedded in our culture. In 1860, when Currier & Ives felt comfortable in portraying baseball as "the national game," there was no clearly defined baseball season; statistical computations were in their barest infancy; few players or writers invoked rural imagery in their depictions; individual players remained anonymous rather than heroic; and industrial life had yet to cut the wide swath it would in the latter third of the nineteenth century. The key to baseball's appeal, therefore, rests not in the false nostalgia of the twentieth century, but in the culture of the United States in the years immediately preceding the Civil War.

The half-decade before the 1860 elections witnessed the clear elevation of the modern version of baseball in the consciousness of the influential mid-Atlantic states and, to a great extent, the nation as well. From the 1830s through the late 1850s Americans played an assortment of ball and bat games. Each city and region boasted its own variation. In New England, Philadelphia, and areas of Ohio and Kentucky, residents played versions of townball, in which squads of various sizes (up to fifteen men on a side) played on a square field with no distinction for foul territory and recorded outs by "plunking" base runners with a thrown ball. One out retired the side, and a fixed number of runs, usually 100, won the game.[3] One correspondent reported playing bat and ball games at midwestern barn raisings.[4] In many urban centers cricket flourished among British immigrants. In New York, the Knickerbocker game, which replaced the square with a diamond and "plunking" with the tag and force play, increasingly predominated in the 1850s.

Yet until roughly 1855 these games (other than cricket, which had been brought from England with a higher degree of organization), while growing in popularity, appeared on a largely ad hoc basis. A handful of clubs structured regular practices and mostly intramural games. Most participants played ball games more informally. Games rarely pitted teams from rival regions, cities, or communities.

The next few years, however, featured both a startling explosion of organized baseball clubs, most playing the New York version of the game, and a growing assertion that baseball was now our national pastime. In 1855 the New York City area boasted a dozen clubs. The following year expansion began in earnest. *Porter's Spirit of the Times*, one of the first newspapers devoted to covering sporting events, reported that baseball players had converted every grassy lot within ten miles of New York into playing fields. Brooklyn, asserted the *Spirit*, was emerging as the "city of baseball clubs." The *Spirit* and the *New York Clipper* that year began to refer to baseball as the "national game." On December 5, 1856, the *New York Mercury* coined the phrase "the national pastime."[5]

These assertions might well be dismissed as wishful hyperbole. After all, the version of baseball being celebrated in 1857 was not a national, but a New York pastime. Even the *Spirit* qualified its initial 1856 designation, calling baseball "the National game in the region of the Manhattanese." In January 1857, when the first "national" convention of baseball clubs created a National Association of Baseball Players, all fourteen clubs represented came from New York and Brooklyn. As the *New York Clipper* noted after the second convention in 1858, the association was "a mere local organization, bearing no *State* existence even—to say nothing of a *National* one." A writer in *Harper's Weekly* in 1859 protested, "We see no evidence that . . . base-ball . . . is so generally practiced by our people as to be fairly called a popular American game."[6]

But the aptly named *Spirit of the Times* and others who asserted the national character of the new game had tapped into a deeply felt sentiment. Several commentators have argued, with considerable supporting evidence, that the wish to create a "national game" stemmed from, in Melvin Adelman's words, a "desire upon the part of Americans to emancipate their games from foreign patterns."[7] The *Spirit* called for a game "peculiar to the citizens of the United States, one distinctive from the games of the British like cricket or the German *Turnverein*." The *New York Times* in an 1857 article entitled "National Sport and Their Uses" argued that "To reproduce the tastes and habits of English sporting life in this country is neither possible nor desirable."[8]

The concept of nationalism, however, expresses not only distinctiveness from others but defines the disparate elements that unify a country. Improvements in transportation and communication in the antebellum era had begun to create a more truly national culture and fueled the ongoing sectional controversy over the meanings of federalism and republicanism. Indeed, this type of nationalism lay at the core of the political debates rending the United States in the 1850s. Northern soldiers fought for "union," a concept in which the needs of the nation transcended those of its component parts. Before the Civil War, the union, Carl Degler argues, was not yet a *nation*. American nationalism remained incomplete. The southern threat of secession challenged the assumptions of nationhood, threatening to fragment the United States, as James McPherson writes, "into several petty, squabbling autocracies" undermining the American experiment in democracy.[9]

This conviction did much to shape the demand for national attributes, particularly in the northern states, which facilitated the spread of baseball during the pre–Civil War years. Even by 1860, when the Currier & Ives cartoon appeared, baseball, particularly the New York version, had indeed become a more national pastime. The game had largely supplanted townball in both Massachusetts and Philadelphia. Baseball appeared in California and New Orleans in 1859. In 1860 the Brooklyn Excelsiors toured Philadelphia, Baltimore, and upstate New York, spawning new baseball clubs in their wake. Washington, D.C., and Lexington, Kentucky, also welcomed baseball in 1860, as did several cities in the Midwest, including St. Louis, Chicago, Milwaukee, Detroit, and Cleveland. Players in these cities adopted the rules published and printed by the National Association.[10] Songs like "Baseball Fever," "Baseball Polka," and, in 1861, the "Home Run Quick Step" celebrated the increasingly popular game.[11]

Ironically, throughout the 1850s, the British sport of cricket had a broader popularity than baseball. Cricket clubs appeared in at least twenty-two states and more than 125 cities and towns. At least in its organized forms, it attracted more participants, greater attention in the press, and larger crowds to its showcase events. In 1858, landscape architects for New York's new Central Park dubbed the land allocated for ball games the Cricket Ground, much to the chagrin of enthusiasts for the newer game. This has led several historians to posit a rivalry between the two games for the sporting soul of America, wherein "baseball vied with cricket for supremacy" and Americans ultimately "rejected" cricket, which "lost out" to baseball. Some engage in the dubious exercise of explaining how baseball appealed more to the American "character" or "spirit" than cricket. Others note the advanced institutional standardization of cricket, transplanted intact from England, and the unwillingness of British-American cricket players to adapt the game to make it more palatable to an American audience.[12]

This interpretation, however, misreads the tenor of the era. Cricket was rarely more than an immigrant game, one used, as George Kirsch points out, to allow the English community "to preserve its own ethnic identity."[13] Its popularity stemmed from the predominance of British immigrants in America among the white-collar and skilled occupations that employed most of those who participated in organized sports. There is no evidence that native-born Americans, who had always played indigenous varieties of ball and bat games, or non-British immigrants ever evinced much interest in cricket in any place other than Philadelphia, where the game had its greatest popularity. When crossovers occurred and choices had to be made, it was more likely to be the British-born cricketers, like Henry Chadwick and Harry and George Wright, who abandoned the immigrant game for that of their adopted homeland, rather than the other way around. Both games benefited from the same social forces that made organized sports possible in the 1850s, and baseball clearly borrowed from the institutional, statistical, and linguistic traditions of cricket. Nonetheless, baseball and cricket developed separately, rather than in any true competition with each other. Cricket remained contentedly confined to the British community, leaving a clear field for baseball to develop in its own manner.

The form that it assumed was the "Knickerbocker" or "New York" variation on townball. Both nineteenth-century commentators and some recent historians attributed the triumph of the New York game in the 1850s to its uncannily intuitive adherence to the American "temperament" or "character." In 1866 Charles A. Peverelly called it "a game which is peculary suited to the American temperament and disposition," a sentiment echoed in the *Spirit of the Times* in 1867, which hailed it as "the pastime which best suits the temperament of our people." Twenty years later Mark Twain invested baseball as, "The very symbol, the outward and visible expression of the drive and push and rush and struggle of the raging, tearing booming nineteenth century."[14]

The fundamental difference between the New York game and most versions of townball and cricket lay in its configuration into a diamond, rather than a square or oval. In both townball and cricket the ball could be hit in any direction. The New York version of baseball designated a fair territory within the baselines established by the diamond, giving greater order and direction to the game. Indeed, the baseball diamond has assumed a mystical quality in the hands of romanticists. Allen Guttmann notes that, among team games, the movement in baseball is "uniquely circular" and wonders, "Is it wholly accidental that the four bases correspond numerically to the four seasons of the year?" Michael Novak writes, "To circle the bases is to traverse 360 feet, the precise number of degrees in a circle." The distance of ninety feet between the bases, contends Novak, repeating a frequently held fallacy, "leaves an almost exact balance between runners and fielders . . . another two feet in either direction might settle the issue decisively between them."[15] (In reality, any similar distance would produce a similar balance.)

Several recent commentators have performed metaphorical gymnastics to shoehorn the baseball diamond into the nineteenth-century American soul. David Lamoreaux sees the diamond as "an almost physical analogue of the country, an abstraction of the idea of the continent as it appeared to Americans in the mid-nineteenth century." The infield/outfield division parallels that between civilization and wilderness, with the infield "an abstract symbol of the civilized portions of the country." The outfield, "with its theoretically illimitable reach . . . suggests the frontier." Warren Goldstein, on the other hand, sees the diamond as an allegory of nineteenth-century urban life. "The game was a constant play of safety and danger," writes Goldstein, not unlike the daily journey through hostile urban neighborhoods. The tour around the bases required a passage through a territory "patrolled by the opposition," where one "could be put 'out' for the slightest error of skill or judgement," in order to return home safely. Novak envisions this same circuit as a "voyage" of "Yankee Clipper ships blown silently across the sparkling seas, sails creaking in the wind (the canvas that covers the diamond when it rains) . . . the silence and isolation of each sailor at his post, encircling the world for trade."[16]

Stephen Gelber argues that baseball, appearing in "the formative years of modern business" alongside large factories and commercial enterprises, replicated the environment of the new urban workplace. "The highly structured, sequential nature of baseball" duplicated the modern urban work experience. Thus, baseball "mark(ed) the transition from individual to corporate values . . . subsuming the individual into the collective." Goldstein agrees that the "baseball world had never been very far removed from the world of work," but places its appeal within antebellum artisan culture, with its emphasis on manliness, self-control, and self-discipline, rather than the incipient corporatism stressed by Gelber.[17]

Melvin Adelman compares baseball to cricket, in which a batter may hit indefinitely until put out. Adelman contends that "Baseball's structure expressed the American notion of individualism, with its emphasis on independence, self-reliance and equality," articulating the "American commitment to equal opportunity as each batter is afforded roughly the same number of at bats regardless of success." Novak carries the American analogy even further. Baseball, writes Novak, "born out of the enlightenment and the philosophies so beloved of Jefferson, Madison, and Hamilton," is "designed as geometrically as the city of Washington . . . orderly, reasoned, judiciously balanced . . . a Lockean game, a kind of contract theory in ritual form." Novak likens baseball to the U.S. Constitution, integrating a system of checks and balances, with the umpire as judiciary, the batters as executives, and the fielders "a congress checking the power of the hitters."[18]

Yet one need not dip into the murky depths of metaphor to explain baseball's appeal. The sudden expansion and acceptance of the New York game reflect several factors, not the least of which was the emergence of an increasingly national culture. The spread of the railroad and telegraph facilitated the spread of ideas and activities throughout the country. As George Kirsch has pointed out, the centrality of New York City in this emergent national culture helped to spread the game. The city's sporting weeklies, like *Spirit of the Times*, which enthusiastically promoted baseball, gained a limited but increasing circulation in other major cities. Businessmen traveling to New York, like George Beam who introduced baseball to Baltimore, discovered the game and brought it back to their home cities, while itinerant and migrating New York businessmen became missionaries for the game, founding clubs wherever they settled.[19]

Furthermore, the argument that baseball, the "New York" game in particular, suited the American or modern urban industrial character stands reality on its head. It would be more correct to say that the men who shaped baseball in the 1850s and 1860s fashioned it in their own image. As Adelman has noted, the originators of the game embraced the modern, rational, scientific worldview that had grown prevalent in mid-nineteenth-century America.[20] The appeal of the New York game lay not in its inherent attributes, but in the ability of its originators to incorporate emerging social attributes into the evolving game. Beginning in the 1840s, these athletes and, in the 1850s and 1860s, their supporters in the press consciously attempted to create a sport that suited their modern sensibilities. They replaced the chaos of townball—with its large teams, plunking, indefinite directional and time boundaries, and too frequent side changes—with a more ordered, rational variation. Limiting play to nine men on each side, imposing a diamond with foul lines radiating outward and confining play within that area, fixing the length of a game at nine innings, and replacing the "one out–all out" rule with a variation of three outs to allow more sustained play all reflected conscious decisions designed to make the game more attractive to those who played it. Baseball did not appeal to Americans, as many have suggested, because it took less time to play than cricket or townball. The architects of the game deliberately adopted an out and inning structure designed to compress play into the time available for games.

Nor were the New York arbiters averse to incorporating the best from other variations. At the early conventions of the National Association, delegates repeatedly debated rule changes designed to improve baseball. Fundamental elements of the game, like the distance between the pitcher's mound and home plate, the numbers of balls and strikes, and the meaning of a foul ball, would not be resolved for decades. In the 1880s baseball would incorporate overhand pitching from the Massachusetts game. The original New York game that spread through the nation in the late 1850s allowed players to be put out by catching the ball on a bounce. Both Massachusetts townball and cricket required the more difficult skill of catching the ball on the fly. Suggestions to adopt the fly rule were heard at the first national convention in 1857 in order to make the game "more manly and scientific." The debate over the fly rule lasted several years before the measure was ultimately adopted in 1863.[21]

The terms "manly" and "scientific" reflect the rhetoric of nineteenth-century modernism. Yet, there was nothing inherently manly or scientific about catching a ball on a fly (at least when compared to other athletic feats) or about the game of baseball. Players imbued the game with these desirable attributes so as to justify their participation and to make it more attractive to similarly minded men. Sportswriters and baseball publicists shared a similar worldview and described the game accordingly. By invoking this language, they gave the game of baseball a modern ethos.

These changes in the game largely reflected the desires of the players. Yet, it is surprising, given the absence of commercialized or for-profit matches in the 1850s, how prominently the concept and needs of spectators figured into these deliberations. As Harold Seymour argues, "The long process of rules refinement . . . was to make the game increasingly palatable to spectators." Part of the appeal of the Knickerbocker diamond configuration stemmed from its attractiveness to observers. The clear definition of fair and foul territory allowed those watching to get closer to the action without interfering with the course of play. Henry Chadwick, in defending the fly rule in 1860, invoked the demands of the fan, commenting, "Nothing disappoints the spectator . . . as to see a fine hit to the long field caught on the bound in this simple childish manner."[22] The growing demand for reports on baseball on the part of participants and nonparticipants alike led to expanded newspaper coverage. The first book catering to the baseball fan, *Beadle's Dime Base Ball Player*, appeared in 1860.

Yet, in the late 1850s and even the early 1860s spectators were not generally paying customers. Although sports entrepreneurs had charged for access to horse races, cricket matches, and prize fights for several decades, no record exists of an admission fee required at a baseball game until a New York–Brooklyn all-star contest in 1858. The need to recoup rental fees for the Fashion Course racetrack, rather than the quest for profit, led to a tariff variously reported as between ten and fifty cents. The practice of charging those wishing to attend games did not begin in earnest until 1862, when William H. Cannemeyer demanded a ten-cent fee to watch clubs at play at Brooklyn's new Union Grounds.[23] Others, particularly in the post-Civil War years, sought to emulate his success. By this time a ready baseball public had appeared without the lure of widespread commercial inducements.

The years immediately following the Civil War would witness, in the words of the *Chicago Tribune* in 1866, "the arrival of the Age of Baseball." The *Paterson (New Jersey) Press* described a baseball "frenzy" in the city. The nearby *Newark Advertiser* added in 1868, "People have baseball on the brain to an extent hitherto unequaled." The *Spirit of the Times* noted in 1867 that "Of all out of door sports, base-ball is that in which the greatest number of our people participate either as players or as spectators." Another national periodical conservatively estimated that 2,000 organized baseball clubs graced the nation that year. California alone boasted as many as 100 clubs.[24]

Baseball became a symbol of reunification. The *New York Clipper* in 1866 asserted that "the (baseball) fraternity should prove to the world that sectionalism is unknown in our national game." *Clipper* reporter Henry Chadwick, one of the most ardent advocates of a national game with standardized rules, expressed fears of regional variations leading to "four or five distinct styles of playing base ball," in which case "the term 'National Game' would have become a misnomer."[25]

By this time the leading clubs in many cities had evolved into professional teams, paying top players to represent them against other professional squads. These games, increasingly played before paying audiences, attracted large crowds. Harold Seymour estimates that 200,000 spectators attended games in 1868. The following year, the Cincinnati Red Stockings, the nation's first openly professional team, toured the nation. *Outing* magazine reported that 179,000 fans paid to see the Red Stockings play.[26]

Thus, by 1870 baseball's architects and promoters had invented a sport and established an ethos surrounding it that held a broad appeal to nineteenth-century Americans. They had rationalized the ball and bat games of preindustrial society and endowed the resulting amalgam with the language of modernism emphasizing order, science, and manliness. Baseball had become embedded in the culture on several levels: as a popular pastime for boys and men; a spectator sport; a centerpiece of national and local periodical reporting; a profession and form of entrepreneurial commercialized leisure; and increasingly as a source of national pride. The Civil War had defined the United States as a nation. In its aftermath, baseball truly reigned, as Currier & Ives had prematurely crowned it in 1860, as the "national game."

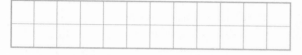

The Mortar of Which Baseball Is Held Together
Henry Chadwick and the Invention of Baseball Statistics

During the late nineteenth century, in the midst of a tour of England by American baseball players, a distinguished elderly gentleman approached one of the visiting athletes. The Englishman, Edwin Chadwick, was one of the most famous men in Great Britain. For almost a half-century he had reigned as that nation's "sanitary philosopher," the architect of its public health laws. In 1889 he would receive knighthood for his efforts. But on this day, Edwin Chadwick was concerned with celebrating the achievements of his younger American half-brother, Henry. Henry Chadwick, he reportedly boasted to the ballplayer, had "invented" the game of baseball. "Then you are the brother of a great man, Sir," responded the American.[1]

Edwin Chadwick's familial pride notwithstanding, no one, of course, not Abner Doubleday, or Alexander Cartwright, or Henry Chadwick, actually "invented" baseball. There is, however, more than an element of truth in the elder Chadwick's assertion. For Henry Chadwick, more than any other individual, created the game of baseball Americans have since celebrated and enjoyed. He invented not so much the game on the field, although through his continuous presence on the rules committee he significantly influenced its evolution. Rather, by his development of the box score, tabular standings, the annual baseball guide, the batting average, and most of the common statistics and tables used to describe baseball, Chadwick invented the game's historical essence. The ways in which Americans would absorb and analyze baseball from the late nineteenth century to the present emerged largely from Chadwick's vision, innovation, and reforming passion. In his lifetime, Chadwick was hailed as "Father Baseball." For more than a half-century, as a reporter for many of the major New York metropolitan newspapers and editor of, first, *Beadle's Dime Base Ball Player* and, later, the *Spalding Baseball Guides*, he was the most influential person in reporting the game and recording its early progress. He bequeathed to us a substantial archive of writings. Yet baseball historians have paid surprisingly little attention to Chadwick. There are no biographies, no major articles about him—only scattered accounts of his role in the rise of baseball in various histories of the sport.[2] The work of Henry Chadwick, however, and particularly his inspired decision to use statistics to chronicle and popularize baseball, illuminate not only the formative years of the national pastime, but the nation itself in the antebellum and post-Civil War eras.

Henry Chadwick was born in Exeter, England, in 1824. His grandfather, Andrew, an associate of John Wesley, had devoted his life to the promotion "of measures for the improvement of the condition of the population."[3] Henry's father, James, was a prominent figure in regional intellectual and cultural circles. A follower of Thomas Paine and a staunch adherent of the French Revolution, James Chadwick became an outspoken journalist and advocate of radical causes. At the time of Henry's birth James edited the *Western Times* in Exeter.[4] Half-brother Edwin, the product of an earlier marriage and twenty-four years older than Henry, had long since set out on his own.

In 1837, when Henry was twelve, James moved his second family to the United States and settled in Brooklyn.[5] Henry found America, and particularly its sporting activities, much to his liking. As a boy in England he had played rounders. Tall and athletic, he now became a skilled cricket player. He frequently accompanied friends to the playing fields of Hoboken, New Jersey, where he occasionally indulged in local variations on rounders, like townball. But Chadwick found these games juvenile and uninspiring. He particularly disliked the practice of "soaking" then prevalent in American baseball. "I remember getting some hard hits in the ribs, occasionally, from an accurately thrown ball," he later recalled with distaste.[6] James Chadwick encouraged his son to become a music teacher, but Henry was more attracted to his father's profession. As early as 1844, at age nineteen, he wrote articles for the *Long Island Star*. Four years later, he married and began to earn his living as a reporter, specializing in cricket and other sports coverage for a variety of New York and Brooklyn newspapers.[7]

In 1856 Chadwick rediscovered baseball. "On returning from the early close of a cricket match, I chanced to go through the Elysian Fields during the progress of a contest between the noted Eagle and Gotham Clubs," recalled Chadwick twelve years later. "The game was being sharply played on both sides and I watched it with deeper interest than any previous base ball match that I had seen. It was not long before I was struck with the idea that base ball was just the game for a national sport for Americans." From that day on, asserted Chadwick, he devoted himself to promoting and improving baseball.[8]

Meanwhile, Edwin Chadwick's career had blossomed in spectacular fashion.[9] In 1834, three years before Henry departed for America, Edwin had become a secretary to the royal commission on the reform of the poor laws. During the next decade Edwin Chadwick revamped the British system of administering poor relief. Like many reformers on both sides of the Atlantic, Edwin relied heavily in his work on the accumulation of accurate statistics. His 1842 *Report on the Sanitary Condition of the Labouring Population of Great Britain* became a sensation in England. A landmark of social research, the 1842 *Report* featured voluminous quantitative data supporting the opinions of doctors and public health officials. The primary author of the Public Health Act of 1848, Edwin became the Commissioner of the Board of Health from 1848 to 1854.

There is no evidence that the Chadwick brothers, separated by two and a half decades and later thousands of miles, had much contact during Henry's youth and adolescence, but Henry clearly followed, and gloried in, his brother's career.[10] In addition, through his radical father, young Henry was exposed to the same social ideals that had propelled his brother into the field of reform. These ideals meshed well with intellectual and political trends in antebellum America. As in England, urbanization led to growing concern about the impact of city life on American society and morality. Fears of crime, intemperance, prostitution, and vice inspired innumerable reform movements.[11]

Antebellum reformers worried about these most visible forms of urban pathology and also about the latent evils of the emergent order. City living exposed its residents to immorality, offered temptations that appealed to people's passion rather than reason, and also threatened their health. Severed from the invigorating countryside and bound by sedentary occupations, city-dwellers, especially young males, faced the prospect of physical as well as spiritual degeneration.

With the notable exception of the antislavery issue, on which Chadwick, who was married to a Virginian, apparently made no commentary, Chadwick fully embraced, and at times defined, the spirit and language of reform. In the middle decades of the nineteenth century, American health reformers and sportswriters evolved what Melvin Adelman has called a "new sports ideology" that justified baseball and other pastimes for their utilitarian benefits for the troubled urban social order.[12] Chadwick was a prime architect of this ideology. He publicized baseball as "a moral recreation" that would exert "a powerful lever . . . by which our people could be lifted into a position of more devotion to physical exercise and healthful out-door recreation."[13] Baseball, he wrote, merited "the endorsement of every clergyman in the country . . . (as) a remedy for the many evils resulting from the immoral associations [that] boys and young men of our cities are apt to become connected with."[14]

Chadwick's writings reverberated with the rhetoric of American reform. He sought to make baseball more "scientific" and "manly." He extolled team sports for their emphasis on "order" and "discipline." As Warren Goldstein notes, Chadwick's model baseball club constitution, first published in 1860, suggested fines for "profane language," "disputing the decision of the umpire," and "refusing obedience to the captain," offenses that exhibited a player's lack of self-control.[15] He continually favored strategies that emphasized displays of skill, control, and intellect over those reliant on unbridled power. "The true estimate of good pitching," he wrote in 1868, "is based on the chances offered fielders for outs. Striking out simply shows inferior batting, not superior pitching. . . . [A pitcher] would be more effective were he to depend less on mere speed."[16] Twenty years later he hailed the reduction in the number of called balls necessary for a walk from five to four, because "it would moderate the dangerous speed in delivering the ball to the bat."[17] Chadwick repeatedly rejected reliance on the home run over more "scientific" strategies for scoring.

Chadwick's passion for reform was most evident in his crusades against gambling and alcohol. Upon Chadwick's death, his friend and patron, Albert Spalding, celebrated the sportswriter's struggle with the "gambling and the pool-selling evils" as his greatest contribution to the game.[18] Chadwick repeatedly called for "prohibition planks" in player contracts. "The two great obstacles in the way of the success of the majority of professional ball players are wine and women," he wrote in 1889. "The saloon and brothel are the evils of the base ball world at the present day."[19] As Edwin Chadwick once joked, "While I have been trying to clean up London, my brother has been keeping up the family reputation by trying to clean up your sports."[20]

Chadwick's "ardent nature," bludgeoning language, and endless pontification were not always welcome. Chadwick dismissed those who disagreed with him "as old fogy individuals" and termed their arguments "absurd." "He made enemies by the hundreds; he received the personal abuse of unscrupulous newspapers and their correspondents," eulogized Spalding. In 1876 the *Chicago Tribune* dismissed him as the "Old Man of the Seas . . . a dead weight on the neck of the game." Even Harry Wright, who shared most of Chadwick's visions of sportsmanship, accused Chadwick of writing too much about "suspicious play" and "crooked players." Furthermore, chided Wright, Chadwick "also uses words he doesn't understand."[21]

But if Chadwick's zealous commitment to social reform offended his detractors, it also fed his inclination toward statistical analysis. As in England, antebellum social reformers were among the foremost adherents of statistical research. As early as 1816 prison, temperance, and school reformers in Boston and Philadelphia published statistical surveys to bolster their demands for reform. Temperance advocates in the 1830s compiled statistics of drunkenness and published almanacs detailing the dimensions of the problem. Antislavery advocates increasingly relied on numbers to sustain their arguments. As historian Patricia Cline Cohen has noted, "The statistical champions of the mid-nineteenth century were fairly clear about what they regarded as the effects of quantification on social thought. Enumeration focused concern on an issue, accurately described its dimensions and suggested the proper course of action to be taken."[22]

These statistical arguments found an ever more responsive and sophisticated audience. During the first half of the nineteenth century Americans were, as one English traveler noted in the 1830s, a "guessing, reckoning, and calculating people." According to Cohen, Americans in the Jacksonian and antebellum periods became a numerate people, "as things once thought of solely in qualitative terms became subject to quantification." The rise of a market economy, requiring more people to be competent in arithmetic, and the spread of mass education gave the public a growing familiarity with numbers.[23]

Statistical manuals and almanacs grew popular. In part the attraction of these almanacs stemmed from the same fervor that led Chadwick to envision the emergence of a "national sport for America." By statistics, wrote George Tucker in 1847, "we can trace the progress of society and civilization; or in other words measure a nation's moral and religious improvement; its health, wealth, strength, and safety." Newspapers, pamphlets, and journals included statistical sections. By the 1830s businessmen regularly employed double-entry bookkeeping, while pediatric advice manuals included tables of neonatal weights. The end of the decade marked the founding of the American Statistical Society.

This fascination with numbers was not a peculiarly American trait. A European historian has described the 1830s and 1840s as an "era of enthusiasm" for statistics.[24] Other industrializing nations like England, Prussia, and France demonstrated a greater sophistication in their collection and application of data and most of the major breakthroughs in mathematical theory occurred in Europe. But, as Cohen notes, "What struck foreign travelers in America was the extent to which ordinary inhabitants had incorporated and internalized a tendency to measure, count, and calculate." Thus, a compiler of statistics, "assured of an audience that would understand his numerical message and accord it a superior credibility, had only to choose the exact form his data would take."[25]

"It was not long . . . after I had become interested in baseball that I began to invent a method of giving detailed reports of leading contests," wrote Chadwick in 1868.[26] That these reports revolved around statistics reflected the temper of the times and Chadwick's reform inclinations. They also stemmed from his earlier experiences as a player and reporter of cricket. Methods for recording both individual cricket games and individual year-end statistics had long since appeared in England. Cricket box scores and other statistics appeared in American papers as early as the 1840s. In 1857 the *New York Clipper*, possibly at the urging of Chadwick, who joined the paper that year, attempted to compile its cricket data "in a systematic manner." As Chadwick himself later wrote, "I had been reporting cricket for years, and in my method of taking notes on contests, I had a peculiar plan of my own."[27] He sought to adapt these techniques to baseball.

For Chadwick, accumulating data not only provided a means of reporting on the games, but of reforming them as well. "From the time I first became an admirer of base ball," he wrote in 1868, "I have devoted myself to improving and fostering the game in every way . . . Seeing that everything connected with the game, almost, was new, its rules crude and hastily prepared . . . I began to submit amendments to the rules of the game."[28] Like his brother and other nineteenth-century reformers, Chadwick possessed a profound faith in the power of statistics to persuade. United States census official Joseph Kennedy eloquently expressed this vision in an 1859 address entitled "The Progress of Statistics." Statistics, he contended, could "ameliorat(e) . . . man's condition by the exhibition of facts whereby the administrative powers are guided and controlled by the lights of reason, and the impulses of humanity impelled to throb in the right direction." They were "the practical workings of an elevated Christianity."[29]

To Chadwick, for whom the promotion of baseball served a moral purpose, statistics were a means to this higher end. In a game that was still evolving, in his words, "step by step, little by little . . . from (an) almost simple field exercise . . . to (a) manly scientific game," the statistics gave him ammunition to support the changes he deemed indispensable to popularize the game. Disavowing "any egotistical spirit," he nonetheless confessed with the arrogance that infuriated his critics, "I have always proved . . . the correctness of my views, and, in this, I have, of course, been greatly assisted by facts and figures derived from actual observation and from a statistical analysis of each season's play."[30]

Chadwick defined his "main object" as "building up a national game."[31] The very conception of a "national game" had corollary ramifications. Baseball had to be made accessible not just to those who played the game, but to a broader audience of spectators and fans. A "national game," in order to be enjoyed and understood by those throughout the United States, must therefore have national standards: uniform rules, uniform scoring, and a means by which to measure its progress. Chadwick's first suggestion for improving baseball was thus "an innovation on the simple method of scoring then in vogue" based upon a system of shorthand reporting that he had devised. He invented a scoring system that used letters to designate each play. "The abbreviations of this system were prepared on the mnemonics plan of connecting the abbreviated words in some way or another with the movement to be described," he later recalled. Thus, "L" stood for a foul ball and "K," which Chadwick viewed as "the prominent letter of the word strike, as far as remembering the word was concerned," represented a strikeout. Over the years, numbers based on player positions replaced letters in this scheme. Only the unexpectedly lyrical "K" designation for strikeout has survived.[32]

Chadwick had created, according to Thomas Rice, "the simplest, most easily learned and most expressive of all the systems of shorthand ever invented,"[33] a form of double-entry bookkeeping in which plays on offense would balance out those on defense. To facilitate the widespread adoption of this scheme, Chadwick routinely included blank scoring forms and instructions for using his design in his annual guides. "It is requisite that all first nine contests should be recorded in a uniform manner," he insisted in *Beadle's Dime Base Ball Player* in 1861.[34]

With the practice of scoring games so thoroughly ingrained in baseball and other sports, it is easy to overlook the critical importance of Chadwick's vision and achievement. Even if one rejects Rice's effusive opinion that Chadwick's invention of baseball scoring "entitles him to a high position among the world's thinkers," the significance of Chadwick's contribution is evident. Scoring, as sportswriter Hugh Fullerton once observed, "is the process of transferring a baseball game from the field onto paper and the scorers are the recording secretaries and historians of the game." Economist Ralph Andreano adds, "Standardizing the rules of scoring was the equivalent of an industrial magnate's standardizing the weight, shape, and purity of a steel bar. If the statistics of performance were to have the meaning intended for them, it was absolutely essential that the playing situation for all teams and players be nearly comparable as possible."[35]

The end product of Chadwick's system of scoring and statistical analysis was his most artful and enduring creation, the box score. Branch Rickey has called the box score "the mortar of which baseball is held together." John Thorn and Peter Palmer have likened it to St. Peter's Book of Life. To Roger Angell it is "one of my favorite urban flowers . . . a precisely etched miniature of the sport itself."[36]

Like so many of Chadwick's innovations, the box score represented an adaptation of common cricket practice tempered by the spirit of reform. Box scores for cricket matches and, at least on one occasion an early baseball game, appeared in American newspapers as early as 1845. According to Adelman, after 1853, three years before Chadwick turned his attention to the new game, baseball box scores listing the batting order, outs made, and runs scored, the usual cricket categories, often appeared in the New York press.[37]

But the cricket box score was not readily adaptable to baseball. Cricket was a far simpler competition, despite its reputation as a more scientific game. A cricket match, although chronologically longer than baseball, lasted for only two innings. In cricket, which had only two bases, a hit and a run were synonymous. Reaching base meant running to the opposite wicket, which automatically scored a run. If the "striker" hit the ball and did not reach the opposite wicket, he was out. Thus, runs and outs were the only offensive possibilities, making the simple box score an accurate accounting of the game details.[38]

Baseball, however, had many more innings and offered many additional possibilities. Although runs remained the key to victory, a batter could reach base safely without scoring a run and he could reach base in a variety of ways: by hitting safely, by a walk (which did not exist in cricket), or through a fielder's error. In addition, hits had varying values. Some accounted for two bases, others three, and yet others four. Chadwick and others attempted to collapse this complexity into a capsule summary closely akin to the cricket box score. An 1858 *New York Tribune* box score of a Brooklyn–New York all-star game recorded a phenomenal amount of detail, including a delineation of "How Put Out," indicating whether batters were retired on a fly, bound, or foul catch or at which base they were tagged.[39]

Chadwick, who may have had a hand in the *Tribune* account, produced his first recorded baseball box score in 1859, documenting a contest in Brooklyn between the Excelsiors and the Stars. Chadwick's handiwork was strikingly similar to the modern box score. He did not list the traditional cricket categories of runs and outs, but instead runs and hits. He also listed three fielding statistics for each player: putouts, assists, and errors. Below the player information, Chadwick inserted another of his innovations, an inning-by-inning line score.[40]

For Chadwick, the reformer, however, box scores were not just game reports, but a series of mini-morality plays. Players should receive credit for their achievements and, through the category of errors, acknowledgment of their flaws. But just as reformers made distinctions between the "deserving and undeserving poor," Chadwick attempted to distinguish between positive achievements and those that befell a team or athlete as a result of opponents' misplays. In a summary section below the line score, Chadwick recorded "battery errors," which included walks as well as wild pitches or passed balls. More significantly, Chadwick introduced the concept of "earned runs," those that resulted from safe hits, "not by skillful base running and the fielding errors such running involves."[41] Chadwick apparently took this distinction, meant originally to measure batting, rather than pitching prowess, seriously. He charged the two teams with a total of sixteen errors. Out of twenty-nine runs scored in the game, he credited only five as "earned."

The issues raised in Chadwick's 1859 box score—how to adapt cricket measurements to baseball and the creation of a moral economy of baseball—would shape the evolution of baseball statistics. Ironically, Chadwick never really understood baseball and never fully appreciated the differences between baseball and cricket. He struggled (as have most serious baseball statisticians) with the significance of a hit and failed to incorporate events like the walk and the home run into his moral universe.

Despite the inclusion of hits in his 1859 box score, during the early 1860s Chadwick's box scores, which appeared with increasing frequency in the *New York Clipper*, reverted to traditional cricket categories, recording simply outs and runs. The remaining descriptive detail, including home runs, strikeouts, and "catches missed," appeared in a summary beneath the line score.[42]

Over the next decades, Chadwick expanded his reportorial and statistical horizons. The latter half of the nineteenth century was an extraordinary age of statistical innovation. In many industries and disciplines, writes historian Margo Cook, "The process of improving the data and statistical techniques was a slow and tedious one which took years of experimentation and analysis." In the 1860s insurance companies investigating mortality rates laid the foundation for gathering information on individuals, by recording details on individual cards, that could then be arranged in homogeneous groupings. The U.S. Census Bureau repeatedly revised its collection and reporting techniques, introducing both new statistics and innovative tabular reporting. Under the dynamic leadership of Francis Walker, the census bureau introduced calculating machines and revamped population reports to cross-tabulate occupational data by nation, state, and city as well as age, ethnicity, and sex. By 1870, the census reports had grown to five volumes; by 1880, twenty-two. The new social sciences of economics, anthropology, psychology, and sociology all increasingly utilized statistics.[43]

Chadwick's activities paralleled these broader developments. In the 1850s his reports had revolved primarily around providing accounts of individual games. In 1860, only four years after his baseball epiphany, Chadwick edited *Beadle's Dime Base Ball Player*, the first baseball annual. In this and subsequent volumes Chadwick's attention focused on how to present cumulative individual statistics and seasonal summaries

Historian Warren Goldstein associates the rise of individual statistics with the emergence of the professional game in the late 1860s. "Statistics were developed, employed, and promoted as measures of players' productivity on the ballfield," argues Goldstein, allowing "employers to measure the abilities of players they had never seen."[44] But it is telling how far Chadwick had advanced statistics prior to the widespread advent of professionalism. "In order to obtain an accurate estimate of a player's skill, an analysis both of his play at the bat and on the field should be made," Chadwick wrote in 1861. By 1867, at the dawn of the professional game, in addition to his annual guides and daily reports for the *Clipper* and *Eagle*, Chadwick edited a weekly *Ball Players' Chronicle*, which reported a wide array of statistics for the current year and made comparisons with past performances of preceding years as well.[45] Fans, not team owners, were Chadwick's primary audience.

Chadwick endlessly experimented with ways in which to evaluate and record player performance. In the spirit of reform, his reports stressed not just accuracy, but accountability. In the "matter-of-fact figures given at the close of the season," he argued in 1864, "we are frequently surprised to find that the modest but efficient worker, who has played earnestly and steadily through the season . . . has come in, at the close of the race, the real victor." Statistics thus had to distinguish and reward "the real victors," rather than the "dashing general player" with "a great deal of eclat in prominent matches."[46]

In 1865 Chadwick began to advance beyond simple counting of hits, runs, and outs into the realm of averages. Again borrowing from cricket, Chadwick printed runs per game figures in the *Clipper*. These figures appeared not as strict averages with decimal points, but rather as an "average and over." Dividing the number of runs scored by games played, a batter who scored twelve runs in five games had an average of two runs per game, with two left over. Two years later *The Ball Players' Chronicle* included outs per game and hits per game as well.[47]

As Chadwick expanded his statistical vistas, he became increasingly aware of the limitations of cricket statistics. In 1867 Chadwick finally reincorporated hits into his box scores. Characteristically, Chadwick now embraced hits wholeheartedly. "Outs and runs . . . is no criterion of a batsman's skill at all," he wrote in 1868. "We have known of dozens of instances in which batsmen have secured first or second base on their hits" but due to "the inferior batting of their successors, have had a large score of outs and no runs." Thus, concluded Chadwick, "There is but one true criterion of the skill at the bat, and that is the number of times bases are made on clean hits."[48] As Thorn and Palmer have demonstrated, the acceptance of hits as the key offensive statistic led inexorably to the computation of the batting average. In 1870 *Beadle's* began reporting hits per game in decimal rather than "over and under" form. In 1872 Chadwick's *Clipper* replaced games in the denominator with at bats, thus creating the modern batting average. When the National League began four years later, batting average was an official statistic and well established as the dominant measure of batting prowess.[49]

With the invention of the batting average, Chadwick, operating in his moral universe and obsessed with personal accountability, had begun to create what Thorn and Palmer have called "isolating stats . . . measure(s) of individual performance not dependent on one's own team."[50] But downgrading the significance of runs scored and elevating "clean hits" to the pinnacle of statistics nonetheless posed other problems. Not all hits were equal. *The Ball Players' Chronicle* compensated for this problem by reporting total bases and total bases per game (a forerunner of slugging percentage) as well. But, given the fielding deficiencies of the early baseball player, Chadwick felt uncomfortable placing too much credence in these statistics. "It is comparatively easy to judge whether (a player) was sure of his first base on his hit, but in running to second or third base on his hit, the errors of fielding, by which such base running is permitted, are multiplied five fold . . . and hence it is very difficult to decide impartially how often a batsmen is entitled to his second or third base on his hit," he maintained in 1868.[51]

This argument, of course, had limited applications to home runs, especially those that cleared the fence. But the home run offended Chadwick's reform sensibilities and never found favor with "Father Baseball." In the belief system of antebellum reform, science and control outweighed brute strength. Chadwick's assaults on the home run often veered into the irrational. Writing in 1868, Chadwick contrasted the "striker" who "hits a long ball and makes a clean home run" with four succeeding batters who each struck singles and later scored. "Now although the striker made four bases on his hit, he only secured one run, whereas the players who made but one base on their hits necessarily each secured a run."[52] A quarter of a century later Chadwick had not relented. The home run, he contended in 1894, was "the easiest hit . . . which the veriest novice at bat can make." Furthermore, "home run hitting . . . involves the costly expenditure of physical strength consistent upon running 120 yards at one's utmost speed, a test of strength . . . which ordinarily requires a good half-hour's rest to recuperate. . . . How much more effective is it, in the saving of strength, to earn single bases by hits." Chadwick also bemoaned that home runs deprived the opportunity "for all the attractive features of sharp in-fielding and active base running."[53]

Similarly, Chadwick, along with many of his contemporaries, experienced great difficulty locating bases on balls in the moral economy of baseball. Walks did not exist in cricket, and to Chadwick, according to later statistician Ernest Lanigan, "so long as a batter received one good pitch at which to swing, he rated no special consideration" in his personal accounting. Walks, reasoned Chadwick, were the result of poor pitching, not disciplined hitting. (Conversely, strikeouts were the product of bad hitting, and Chadwick never credited them to the pitcher in his scoring.)[54] In his earliest box scores, Chadwick recorded walks under battery errors; in his 1860s box scores he recorded them not at all. When Chadwick returned to the concept of earned runs in 1867, those runs scored as the result of bases on balls he deemed unearned by the offense.

By the mid-1870s bases on balls totals appeared in most box scores, but a debate raged as to how they should be counted in the scoring. In 1876, during the National League's inaugural season, walks counted as outs for the batter. Two years later league rules instructed scorers not to count walks as at-bats, an injunction ignored by the *New York Clipper* throughout the years that Chadwick was affiliated with its sports page.[55] In 1878, three years before Chadwick became its editor, the *Spalding Base Ball Guide* stated that a pitcher should be charged with an error for allowing a batter to reach base on called balls, "though there are times when a pitcher shows good judgment in doing so." This sanction appeared in the league rules as late as 1883. The 1885 rules restored the category of "battery errors."[56]

The debate reached its apogee in 1887. During the preseason the Joint Rules Committee of the National League and American Association, at the suggestion of star player and union leader John Montgomery Ward, decreed that bases on balls would henceforth be recorded as hits.[57] In modern parlance, on-base percentage had replaced batting average as the leading indicator of batting skill. Ward's innovation recognized that walks were as much the product of a batter's patience and skill as of a pitcher's wildness.

So entrenched had Chadwick's conception of batting averages become that the new rule met with widespread opposition, not just from Chadwick, but from others as well. Sportswriters in Boston and other cities boycotted the rule, failing to record walks as hits.[58] When the American Association's batting champion Tip O'Neill weighed in with a staggering .492 average, the die was cast. At the season's end the rules committee revoked the walk-as-hit rule. Batters who walked would again be exempted from an at bat. In addition, although walks would again be summarized as errors, runs scored as the result of walks would now be counted as earned runs.[59] Chadwick applauded the return of his original concept of batting average but dismissed the new policy on earned runs as "absurd," since it was possible to register an earned run without a single hit being made. "To estimate a pitcher's skill on such a basis is nonsense," he wrote in the 1889 *Spalding Guide*.[60]

If, however, Chadwick had lost this skirmish, he had won the broader war. Chadwick's batting average, defined as the number of hits per at bat, would henceforth prevail as the dominant, even sacred, measure of batting. The ability to reach base safely or to slug for extra bases, the two skills most essential to success in baseball, would be deemphasized in importance. Careers would be made or broken by the faithful adherence to the cult of the batting average.

As demonstrated by the great batting average debate of the late 1880s, Chadwick's role within the baseball universe had shifted. No longer the great innovator and shaper of a new national pastime, "Grandfather Chadwick," as *The Sporting News* called him in 1886,[61] had become the voice of the baseball establishment. Although clearly no less ardent or truculent than in the 1850s and 1860s, Chadwick's strident opinions now tended to be raised more on behalf of the status quo than with those seeking change. This may have represented a natural progression of age, but it also reflected his recognition that his personal livelihood and fortunes had grown dependent on those of professional baseball. In 1876, when William Hulbert and Albert Spalding of Chicago had staged the coup that created the National League, they had pointedly excluded the New York-based Chadwick from the venture. Chadwick sharply criticized the new league and for several years found himself excluded from the emerging baseball mainstream.[62] In 1881, however, Spalding, the dominant figure in the National League, welcomed Chadwick back into the fold, naming him editor of the annual *Spalding Baseball Guide*, the *ex-officio* voice of professional baseball. Chadwick, who edited the guide until his death in 1908, increasingly became the spokesperson for Spalding and the National League.

Chadwick's pronouncements on the growing rift between players and owners in the 1880s exemplified this role. In 1884 Chadwick attacked athletes for their "exorbitant" salary demands and defended the reserve clause that bound players to a single team and limited their earning power. According to David Voigt, when the players union rebelled in 1890 and formed a Players League, Chadwick was one of only a handful of major sportswriters who sided with the owners. Chadwick accused the union leaders of "a system of terrorism peculiar to revolutionary movements." Boston sportswriter Tim Murnane responded, "Anything more rabid than Chadwick's last effusion . . . would be hard to find . . . The older he gets, the worse he gets."[63]

Health problems dogged the aging Chadwick in the 1890s. He suffered from crippling inflammatory rheumatism for two years. Nonetheless, Chadwick continued to edit the *Spalding Baseball Guide*. As always, he amassed detailed statistics, and ranted against player dissipation, sloppy play, and the home run. He also received a series of honors. In 1894 the National League elected him an honorary member. In 1896 the league awarded him a $600 a year pension. In the new century President Theodore Roosevelt invited him to the White House, and he received a special medal at the 1904 St. Louis World's Fair.[64]

In 1905 a playful dispute with Spalding over whether Americans had invented baseball or it had evolved from British games like rounders resulted in the creation of the Mills Commission to "settle" the issue. Shortly thereafter, Spalding wrote to Chadwick suggesting that he write a book on "the origins and history of baseball." "Write as a baseball historian and not as a critic," Spalding advised the eighty-one-year-old Chadwick. "You are not going to live forever. Keep the book as free of statistics as possible."[65]

For the next two years Chadwick worked on his history, edited the guide, and continued to write on baseball in periodicals. In 1907 he edited the *Spalding Base Ball Record*, the first true baseball encyclopedia, which included players' statistics over four decades. The following spring, Chadwick completed work on the 1908 *Spalding Guide*, which featured the dubious report of the Mills Commission concluding that Civil War General Abner Doubleday had invented baseball.[66] On April 14, despite a "bitter east wind blow," Chadwick attended the 1908 home opener at Brooklyn's Washington Park. "Was at the game yesterday and caught a severe cold," he wrote to Jacob Morse, editor of *Baseball Magazine* on April 15. "Hurrah for Kelley and his men. No game today—rain." Typically, Chadwick added a critique of the fans. "The bleacherites behaved abominably," he noted. The following morning he rose early and at 6 A.M. wrote a poignant letter to Morse:

Please bear in mind, my old friend, that here I am, at 84 years of age, with lots of dear relatives to look after and working

harder and for less than I did forty years ago. You are probably unaware that I live in a fourth flat of a four-story apart-
ment house, and have no servant, two of my grandchildren
serving us as housekeepers alternatively . . . Fortunately my
mental powers have withstood the attacks of age and physical
incapacity . . . blessed with a treasure of a wife I have been
enabled to get along thus far on comparatively small means.
So you see how necessary it is for me to avail myself of every
chance to earn money by my pen.[67]

Chadwick's "severe cold" became pneumonia. Four days later,
on April 20, 1908, Chadwick died at the age of eighty-four. At his
funeral, Spalding, living in California, sent a floral arrangement of
white immortelles in the shape of a baseball. The National League
raised money to construct a cemetery marker decorated with
crossed bats and a granite baseball. In his will, Chadwick left his
voluminous collection of baseball writings, records, and memora-
bilia to Spalding, urging his patron to complete his unfinished
history of baseball. The result was Spalding's classic volume, *America's National Game.*[68]

Over the decades critics have frequently recognized the shortcomings of some of Chadwick's statistical innovations, particularly
the batting average. In 1919 future National League President John
Heydler, arguing that "general reforms seem to be the order of
the day almost everywhere and old established customs are falling
down all around us," suggested changing the basis for batting averages. Ten years later sportswriter F. C. Lane, in an article entitled
"The Faulty Foundations of Batting Averages," made a similar
plea.[69] In recent years commentators have savaged the statistic.
Thorn and Palmer dismiss it as "a bit of nostalgia," which will
hopefully fade way.[70] But the batting average, rooted in the artifacts of cricket and crafted by the dictates of reform, has endured
and survived its detractors.

If in this area Chadwick's handiwork has led us astray, however,
the broader imprint of his grand achievement remains. Chadwick's
incorporation of the modern passion for statistics into the core of

the game, his invention of a scoring system and insistence on uniform standards, his innovation in forms of quantitative reporting and measurement, and the moral fervor with which he pursued these activities transplanted the enjoyment of baseball from the playing field to the parlor and beyond. Henry Chadwick invented the baseball experience, which makes him, as the American ballplayer told his brother, "a great man" indeed.

Incarnations of Success
Charles Comiskey, Connie Mack, John McGraw, and Clark Griffith

Few Americans in the early 1910s were more renowned or celebrated than a quartet of former baseball players who had
come to symbolize not only the national pastime but also the contours of the American dream. Charles Comiskey, Connie Mack,
and Clark Griffith, each an owner of an American League franchise, and John McGraw, who had left the ownership ranks for
the more financially rewarding position of manager of the New
York Giants, epitomized the promise of the nation. Sons of immigrants or dirt-poor southern farm folk, they now reigned as men
of substantial prestige and wealth. Skilled baseball players who had
achieved stardom on the field and played prominent roles in player
rebellions against owner exploitation, they had risen through the
ranks and become first managers and then owners. Each had played
a key role in the ambitious creation of the American League in
1901, and each had reaped handsome rewards for his foresight. By
1913 Comiskey, Mack, and Griffith proudly bore the lofty mantle
of "magnate," the pretentious designation by which major league
owners identified themselves. McGraw reigned as the highest sal-

aried man in the game and would rejoin the ranks of the magnates at the end of the decade.

The public knew the foursome by affectionate, honorific nicknames: Comiskey, the Old Roman; Mack, the Tall Tactician; Griffith, the Old Fox; and McGraw, the Little Napoleon. Sportswriters and commentators in national periodicals acclaimed them as exemplars of American virtues. *McClure's Magazine* hailed Mack, whose Philadelphia Athletics in 1913 became the first team to win three consecutive World Championships, as a man whose habits of "clean living and quick thinking" had "more influence with the youth of America than any man." Sporting goods magnate A. J. Reach celebrated Chicago White Sox owner Comiskey as "a great national heroic figure," who had achieved this status "by his own labor and effort in the face of many discouragements." As owner of the Washington Senators, Griffith hobnobbed with President William Howard Taft and U.S. senators, congressmen, and Supreme Court justices. He had "showed himself the real goods in every detail," wrote one national journalist, "one of the men who have made baseball of such commanding influence in the sporting world," added another. The feisty, controversial McGraw, whose Giants had won five pennants in his first decade as manager, elicited fewer accolades as a role model, but nonetheless as his biographer, Charles Alexander, writes, he was an international celebrity who "epitomized what a baseball manager should be."[1]

The quartet stood, as one writer had dubbed Comiskey in 1909, as "incarnation(s) of success,"[2] before a public for whom the celebration of success had been embedded in the national psyche. Yet even as Comiskey, Mack, Griffith, and McGraw basked in public acclaim, forces had been set in motion that would illustrate the limits of their achievements and how fleeting and fickle fame and fortune could be.

The four players cum magnates had emerged from strikingly similar backgrounds. Three—Comiskey, Mack, and McGraw— were the sons of Irish immigrants. Griffith alone came from native American stock. All came from large families and all, save Comiskey, the third of eight children of Chicago alderman John Comiskey, bore the scars of childhoods marked by the grinding toil and untimely family deaths that characterized the lives of the poor in late nineteenth-century America.

Connie Mack, born Cornelius McGillicuddy, was one of seven children born to Mike and Mary McGillicuddy. Contrary to baseball folklore, which has Connie's surname shortened to fit into box scores, the family always went by Mack, except on official papers, or "when we voted," according to Connie. At the time of Connie's birth in East Brookfield, Massachusetts, in 1862, Mike Mack was serving in the Union Army. After the Civil War, Mike supported his family by working in East Brookfield's factories and mills. An epidemic in the 1870s claimed the lives of two of Connie's sisters, thirteen-year-old Nellie and one-year-old Mary Augusta, who died in Connie's arms. Mike Mack died in 1879 at the age of fifty-two, leaving sixteen-year-old Connie, the oldest son, to support his mother and surviving siblings. Early deaths continued to haunt Mack into adulthood. William Hogan, who was Mack's best friend, the brother of his childhood sweetheart, and the pitcher who had recommended Mack for his first professional contract, contracted consumption and died during their first minor league season. Mack married Hogan's sister, Margaret, three years later. She bore him three children in five years, then died at age twenty-six, leaving Connie a thirty-year-old widower.[3]

John McGraw's childhood bore an unmistakable, if even darker, resemblance to Mack's. His father, John McGraw, Sr., had migrated from Ireland, served in the Civil War, then lost his first wife in childbirth, leaving him a young widower with a baby daughter. He settled in Truxton, New York, where he labored as a railroad construction worker and remarried. Ellen McGraw bore him eight more children, including John, Jr., the oldest. In the winter of 1884–85, when John was eleven years old, a diphtheria epidemic devastated the McGraw family. Ellen McGraw died within days of giving birth to her eighth child. Four of McGraw's siblings also succumbed to the epidemic. John McGraw, Sr., unraveled, taking out his anguish and rage on his oldest son, whom he flogged regularly. In fall 1885, less than a year after his mother had died, twelve-year old John fled his home to escape his father's violent onslaught and took up residence with Mary Goddard, a neighbor who ran a hotel. Like Mack, McGraw would suffer one additional tragedy in his early life. When he was twenty-six, his wife of two years, Minnie, died at age twenty-two, after surgery for acute appendicitis.[4]

Clark Griffith, the only non-Irishman in the group, passed his childhood in the country rather than the city, but suffered poverty and hardship nonetheless. The Griffith family lived on a farm at Clear Creek, Missouri. His father supplemented the meager family income by hunting and trapping. In 1871 a local boy mistook Griffith's father for a deer and shot and killed him, leaving two-year-old Clark, his four older siblings, and his yet unborn sister fatherless. Griffith remembered his early years in post-Civil War Missouri as braced by poverty and toil. "That must have been the poorest country in the world," he later recalled. "When I was growing up there was no such thing as money. The medium of exchange was apple butter." Griffith's mother "worked . . . and slaved," to provide for her brood and, he allowed, "all the neighbors were charitable." At age thirteen Clark barely survived a bout with malaria, prompting the family to move to a small town near Bloomington, Illinois, where his mother opened a boardinghouse.[5]

Their straitened circumstances, family tragedies, and customs of the day forced all of the future ballplayers into the labor force at a relatively early age. Griffith recalled earning money as a ten-year-old trapping skunks and red foxes. McGraw worked at Goddard's hotel, distributed newspapers, and sold magazines, fruit, and candies on the local railroad line. Mack spent his summers as a stock and errand boy at the local cotton mill from the time he was nine. Upon his father's death Mack left high school to work in a local shoe factory cutting sole leather. Even Comiskey, who had a far more comfortable childhood than the others, worked while a youth, first as an apprentice to a Chicago master plumber and later as the driver of a brick wagon.[6]

Baseball cast out a lifeline that rescued each of these youths. Three of the four had secured local reputations as teenage pitchers before launching professional careers at age seventeen. Comiskey abandoned the brick wagon when future major leaguer Ted Sullivan lured him to pitch for the semiprofessional Milwaukee Alerts in 1877. The following year he pitched for the Elgin Watch factory team before joining the Dubuque Rabbits of the Northwest League.[7] Griffith signed his first contract as a hurler for the local Bloomington club of the Central International State League in 1888. John McGraw rejected the advice of both Mary Goddard and his father, who urged him to take a steady job with the railroad and forget "this baseball foolishness." Just six days shy of his seventeenth birthday in 1890, McGraw convinced a New York–Penn League franchise located near Truxton in Olean, New York, to give him a chance, offering to play any position when the manager expressed doubts about his pitching abilities.[8]

Mack took a different route to professional baseball. Still supporting his mother and siblings at age twenty-one, Mack had worked his way up to a position as foreman in the East Brookfield shoe factory. Nonetheless, in 1884, when his local batterymate William Hogan secured him an offer to catch for Meriden in the Connecticut League, Mack leaped at the opportunity to escape the drudgery of factory life.[9]

Comiskey, Griffith, McGraw, and Mack each progressed relatively rapidly to the highest levels of baseball. Comiskey spent four years with the Dubuque Rabbits, who converted him from a pitcher into a first baseman, and then joined the St. Louis Browns of the American Association in 1882 when he was twenty-two. Clark Griffith spent three years in the minors before reaching the major leagues with the Browns (where Comiskey was manager) in 1891 at age twenty-one. The precocious McGraw survived a disastrous debut at Olean, where he made eight errors in his first game, to appear as a shortstop for the American Association's Baltimore Orioles, just sixteen months later, when he was only eighteen. Mack parlayed his maturity and catching skills to reach the Washington Nationals of the National League within two seasons of signing his first professional contract. He was twenty-three years old.

Although none of the four compiled records that would have automatically qualified them for the Baseball Hall of Fame as players, each carved out substantial major league careers. McGraw was most impressive. A master at fouling off pitches until he had either slashed a base hit or secured a walk, the five-foot-five-and-one-half-inch McGraw, who weighed as little as 121 pounds in his early playing days, compiled a lifetime batting average of .334. His .466 on-base percentage ranks third of all time, behind only Babe Ruth and Ted Williams. However, the relative brevity of his playing career (he appeared in over 100 games only five times during his career) and his woeful inadequacies as a fielder (in 1893 he made 66 errors in 127 games) diminish his ranking among the game's great performers. Like McGraw, Clark Griffith rates just below the best players of all time. As one of the standout pitchers of the 1890s, Griffith won twenty or more games seven times. Over his career he won 62 percent of his decisions. Comiskey and Mack, on the other hand, were below average hitters yet first-rate fielders. Other than 1887, when he batted .335 and scored 139 runs in 125 games, Comiskey had few good offensive years. His contemporaries, however, reportedly considered him the best fielding first baseman of the era. Mack, who distributed a scant 150 pounds into his wiry six-foot-one-inch frame, compiled a paltry .251 batting average in eleven seasons while gaining recognition as a wily catcher and handler of pitchers.

What is most striking about the playing careers of McGraw, Griffith, Comiskey, and Mack, however, is not their batting, fielding, or pitching skills but the uncannily parallel reputations they acquired for iconoclasm, rebelliousness, innovation, and leadership. Although they would come to represent authority and respectability in baseball, all typified the rowdy spirit that characterized baseball in the 1880s and 1890s. During these decades immigrant (primarily Irish and German) and working-class Americans predominated in the major leagues, bringing with them a more contentious manner of play than that which had characterized the earlier years of the game. The Irish, in particular, writes Benjamin Rader, "brought with them to the playing field far more physical and emotional explosiveness" than earlier players from native Protestant backgrounds.[10]

Comiskey, an early Irish star, helped to set the pattern in the 1880s with his constant heckling of the opposition, baiting of umpires, and win-at-all-costs style. In 1886 umpire Ben Young branded Comiskey "a most aggravating player," complaining that Comiskey used sotto voce conversations with players to berate the arbiters. Sportswriter Ban Johnson, destined to conspire with Comiskey to create the American League, protested two years later that Comiskey's St. Louis Browns "employed every means to win, using foul tactics when necessary." Another reporter went even further, calling the Browns "the toughest and roughest gang that ever struck this city . . . vile of speech, insolent in bearing . . . they set at defiance all rules, grossly insulting the umpire and exciting the wrath of the spectators."[11]

In the 1890s McGraw succeeded Comiskey as the personification of the unruly Irish player. His language, said reporter John B. Sheridan, "would burn holes in nickel twelve-inches thick." He "eats gunpowder every morning and washes it down with blood," complained umpire Arlie Latham. Future National League President John Heydler decried McGraw's Orioles as "mean, vicious, ready at any time to maim a rival player or umpire," singling out McGraw as the main perpetrator, necessitating "umpires (to) bathe their feet by the hour" after being "spiked . . . through their shoes."[12]

Among the non-Irish players of the 1890s, Griffith reigned supreme as a verbally abusive competitor. The *Chicago Record Herald* predicted in 1898 that he would be the game's first designated "rowdy." He was, according to another account, the "worst umpire baiter who ever lived." His "contemptuous air . . . riled the good hitters out of their composure," and "few batters came to the plate without being singed by his scathing tongue."[13]

The intense competitiveness of the four players materialized in other ways as well. "We got away with a lot back in the days when we played with only one umpire," recalled Mack, who admitted to being "kinda tricky" as a catcher. With catchers positioned far behind the batter and any foul ball caught on the fly an out, Mack perfected the practice of slapping his mitt when a batter swung and missed to simulate the sound of a foul tip. Umpires, thinking Mack had caught a foul ball, would call the batters out. "Of course the trick was found out eventually, and the rule was changed so that a foul tip had to go ten feet in the air . . . for the batter to be called out," Mack later told a reporter. When catchers moved directly behind the batter, Mack won a reputation for surreptitiously tipping the bat as the hitter swung, deflecting its course. While managing at Pittsburgh in the 1890s, Mack would freeze baseballs prior to the game, deadening them for hitting. He would slip the frozen balls into the game when his team was fielding, replacing them with a more temperate, livelier variety when his team was at bat.[14]

Griffith and McGraw likewise bore reputations for illicit chicanery. Griffith earned his nickname "the Old Fox" while still in his early twenties as a tribute to his sly pitching tricks. He "struck them out by stalling until they were nervous wrecks, by quick pitching them when they weren't ready, by scraping the ball against his spikes," wrote Ed Fitzgerald and Shirley Povich. "Griffith scuffed, scratched, cut and spit upon every pitch without hesitation," according to another account.[15] McGraw, the quintessential member of a Baltimore Oriole team that stretched the rules to their utmost limits, specialized in grabbing the clothes of base runners, crashing into fielders after they caught the ball, and obstructing his opponents in other ingenious ways. "He adopts every low and contemptible method his erratic brain can conceive to win a play with a dirty trick," complained one reporter.[16]

Their frequently crude competitive exteriors, however, also reflected keen, analytical minds that Comiskey, Mack, Griffith, and McGraw applied to the study and transformation of the game. Appearing at a formative time in baseball history, they, like others, regularly experimented with new strategies to enhance the level of play. In later years all four would claim, or be granted credit for, some of the game's most profound developments. Charles Comiskey, reported *American Magazine* in 1911, was "the great inventive genius of his day on the diamond" who "evolved scores of plays now in constant use." Comiskey perpetuated the notion that he had pioneered the practice of first basemen playing behind and to the right of the base, rather than anchored to the bag. "For a short time, his style was ridiculed," reported umpire/writer Billy Evans in 1917, "but he soon proved that it was possible to play a deep field yet have plenty of time to return to the bag to receive throws." All infield play reportedly evolved from this breakthrough, as Comiskey taught pitchers to cover first base on ground balls hit to the first baseman and pioneered the strategy of shifting fielders' positions depending on the game situation. Other accounts credit Comiskey with suggesting that the umpire move behind the pitcher to call balls and strikes, inspiring the creation of chalk-lined coaching boxes, and inventing the headfirst slide.[17]

Similarly, Mack, by one later account, "did much to fashion (baseball) rules, pioneering in the development of the torturous art of catching." Mack, reported Bob Considine, "was one of the first catchers to move up to a position just behind the batter and catch the ball before it bounced." A more far-fetched tale has Mack telling a minor league pitcher in the days of the underhand delivery to "try throwing the ball overhand," resulting in the modern style of pitching.[18] Clark Griffith claimed to have invented the screwball and the squeeze play and maintained that a lengthy duel between him and John McGraw, in which McGraw repeatedly fouled off his pitches, led to foul balls being counted as strikes. Some historians credit McGraw with perfecting the hit-and-run play, and, as a manager, inventing platooning.[19]

Most of these claims are either exaggerated or entirely bogus, a tribute to the quartet's longevity in the game and the powers of the mythmaking process. Recent historians, for example, have largely rejected Comiskey's fielding contributions, noting that first basemen had moved off the bag as early as the 1860s.[20] Nonetheless, their reputations as innovators formed an important part of the individual and collective mystiques of all four men. When one combines their penchants for trickery and alleged predilections for innovation, the resulting composite reveals players who were considered smarter, more adventuresome, and at least one step ahead of other athletes—the type of men, in short, who demonstrated leadership qualities early in their careers that predestined inevitable success.

Not surprisingly, given these attributes and the common practice of selecting managers from the ranks of the players, all four men guided major league squads at relatively early ages. The St. Louis Browns named Comiskey team captain after his first year and tapped him as manager one year later when he was twenty-five. McGraw first managed the Orioles in 1899 at age twenty-six. Griffith and Mack were thirty-one when they began managing. All except Mack, who failed to motivate the Pittsburgh Pirates during his two-and-a-half seasons as player–manager from 1894 to 1896, quickly demonstrated exceptional leadership talents. Comiskey's Browns won the American Association championship in four of his first five years as manager. McGraw led a decimated Baltimore Oriole team to a respectable fourth-place finish in 1899 and then won five National League pennants in his first ten years as manager of the New York Giants. Griffith's Chicago White Sox won the first American League championship in 1901.

Ironically, given their futures as major league magnates, Comiskey, Mack, and Griffith all played prominent roles in late nineteenth-century player rebellions. In the late 1880s, when major league athletes formed a labor union, the Brotherhood of Professional Baseball Players, both Comiskey and Mack enlisted in its ranks. Under the leadership of New York Giant shortstop John Montgomery Ward, the players demanded a limitation on the reserve clause, which bound players to one team and curtailed their earning potential, and an end to the blacklist that arbitrarily barred teams from signing troublesome players. When the owners adopted a classification scheme that would have limited salaries to $2,500 a year, the Brotherhood responded in 1890 by creating the Players League, a cooperative venture between the athletes and an alternative group of financial backers. The vast majority of the best players in the game, including Mack and Comiskey, jumped from their National League and American Association teams to the Players League.

For Comiskey, who already received the considerable sum of $8,000 as player-manager of the St. Louis Browns, the decision to join the Players League had to be a difficult one. He would later downplay his role in the revolt, attributing his support to loyalty to his fellow players. "I couldn't do anything else and be on the level with the boys," he explained. The Brotherhood, however, saw Comiskey as a pivotal figure. It lured him away from St. Louis by promising to meet his salary and naming him manager of a team in his hometown of Chicago, where Comiskey had always hoped to return.[21] Connie Mack needed no persuasion. He had been one of the first players to join the Brotherhood in 1886. Four years later he bolted from the Washington Nationals and led most of his teammates to the Buffalo franchise, in which he invested his life savings. Mack set a major league record that would last for several decades by catching 123 of his club's 132 games. Toward the end of the season he became de facto manager of the Buffalo team that, despite his efforts, finished a distant last in the pennant race — forty-six-and-one-half games out of first place.[22]

Although its games outdrew both of the established circuits, the Players League collapsed after one season when its backers, unprepared to face additional financial losses, abandoned the Brotherhood. Mack, who lost all of his money, remained surprisingly sympathetic to its memory. "The purpose of our Brotherhood was to protect the players," he wrote a half-century later in his autobiography, with no trace of irony. "The group which vigorously opposed us was interested in protecting the magnates." He credited the Brotherhood with starting "a new era in baseball" that awakened club owners "to the realization that ballplayers are human and must be given a fair deal or rebel."[23] Comiskey, on the other hand, never romanticized his experience. Although he believed that the Players League might have prevailed with better leadership and despite remaining hostile to the triumphant National League owners, Comiskey concluded that cooperative base-

ball was not feasible. He had learned, in the words of George
Axelson, his authorized biographer, "that player and promoter
could not travel in the same harness." He nonetheless vowed to
return to Chicago with a team that would compete with the National League franchise.[24]

Neither Griffith nor McGraw had progressed to the major
leagues by 1890, but the outcome of the Brotherhood War greatly
affected their careers. Both took advantage of the chaos in baseball
to jump their contracts in 1891 and improve their lot. Griffith, who
had won twenty-seven games for Milwaukee of the Western
League, abandoned the club to pitch for Comiskey, who had re-
sumed his old post with the St. Louis Browns.[25] McGraw, just
eighteen years old, signed contracts with as many as five different
teams, precipitating at least one lawsuit, before landing with Cedar
Rapids of the Illinois–Iowa league. In August McGraw bolted Cedar Rapids to join the Baltimore Orioles.[26]

If the short-term effects of the war had benefited McGraw and
Griffith, the long-term consequences did not. The American Association collapsed after the 1891 season. The four richest clubs
joined the National League to form one expanded twelve-team
circuit. With the threat of the Brotherhood gone and no rival
league to bid up player salaries, the owners proceeded to slash
payrolls, setting a salary limit of $2,400. The nationwide depres-
sion of the 1890s also kept salaries down. Thus, although Griffith
and McGraw emerged as two of the top stars of the decade, their
earnings were limited. After an 1894 season in which he batted
.340 and scored a remarkable 156 runs in 124 games, McGraw
joined fellow Oriole standouts Hugh Jennings, Willie Keeler, and
Joe Kelley in a holdout for higher salaries. Despite the stature of
the four men (each had batted between .335 and .393, and all ultimately would be inducted into the Hall of Fame), they could not
shake the salary cap. McGraw settled for $2,100.[27]

Clark Griffith emerged as a leading voice against the new owner
tyranny. In 1897 Griffith, a star pitcher who had won ninety games
in four years, began agitating for a resurgence of a players union

and an increase in the salary ceiling from $2,400 to $3,000. One sportswriter, referring to the populist and socialist leaders of the age, labeled Griffith "the free-silver, politico pitcher . . . supporter of Bryan, Debs, and Tillman." When a new Professional Association of Baseball Players formed in 1900, Griffith became its vice president and spent the season recruiting players and urging them not to sign contracts for the 1901 season.[28]

Griffith's fortuitous appearance as a labor leader now merged with the ownership aspirations of Comiskey, Mack, and McGraw. The trio had already taken the first steps toward becoming major league magnates. On leaving the Browns after the 1891 season, Comiskey had played for and managed the Cincinnati Reds from 1892 to 1894. With his playing career at an end, he rejected what Axelson called an "attractive contract" to continue to manage the Reds and instead purchased a minor league franchise in the Western League. For the next five years Comiskey reigned as owner-manager of a team alternately called the Saints or Apostles in St. Paul, Minnesota.[29] Mack, meanwhile, after losing his initial investment in the Brotherhood League and faltering in his stint as player-manager at Pittsburgh, had become manager and part owner of the Western League's Milwaukee franchise.

McGraw also demonstrated an entrepreneurial spirit. Along with Oriole teammate Wilbert Robinson he had opened The Diamond Cafe in Baltimore. In 1900, after McGraw's first season as Oriole manager, the National League decided to eliminate four of its less profitable franchises and dropped Baltimore. McGraw and Robinson, desiring to stay in Baltimore, organized a group of investors, hoping to secure a team in a proposed new American Association. When that league died aborning, the pair reluctantly accepted assignment to St. Louis in the National League but harbored a continuing desire to return to Baltimore.[30]

Even Griffith, the union firebrand, clearly had his sights on future ownership. "When I wasn't pitching," he later related, "they used to have me serve as the club's representative at the gate, keeping track of how many admissions were paid. . . . It gave me a chance to learn something about the business end of the game, and it got me acquainted with all the executives and magnates in the league."[31]

Their personal ambitions notwithstanding, the four future owners shared a strong contempt for the men who ran the National League in the 1890s. The owners, who preferred to see themselves as "magnates" on a par with Rockefeller and Carnegie, were predominantly self-made men who, having amassed fortunes in other industries, had invested their profits into baseball clubs. A handful, most notably Albert Spalding of the Chicago White Sox, Al Reach of the Philadelphia Phillies, and Ned Hanlon of the Baltimore Orioles, had risen from the ranks of the players. For some like Spalding and Reach who had made fortunes in the sporting goods business, streetcar developers Frank and Stanley Robison who owned the Cleveland Spiders, New York real estate speculator Andrew Freedman, or brewers Harry and Herman von der Horst of Baltimore, investments in major league clubs were logical extensions of their other business interests. For other owners, like Cincinnati's John T. Brush, whose fortune came from his family's Indianapolis department store, or the Wagner brothers of the Washington Nationals, who had earned their money in meatpacking, ownership of a baseball team represented both an investment and an indulgence, an enterprise that would earn them a level of attention, if not acclaim, that their other businesses could not provide. "Convinced of their own importance . . . they even convinced themselves that they were as important to the fans as the players," writes historian David Voigt.[32]

In fall 1900 the careers and constellations of Comiskey, Mack, McGraw, and Griffith converged in a conspiracy to destroy the National League monopoly. The scheme to forge a new alliance had long gestated in the minds of Charles Comiskey and Ban Johnson, the former reporter whom Comiskey had recruited to be president of the Western League. The two men had discussed the possibility of transforming the Western League into a major circuit as early as 1893, but the depression years of the mid-1890s had not offered a promising time to launch such an ambitious venture. By the turn of the century, however, improved economic conditions and developments in baseball bode well for a bold move. After the 1899 season the National League had jettisoned its four weakest franchises in Cleveland, Washington, Louisville, and Baltimore, leaving these cities clamoring for teams and a surplus of talented players looking for jobs. In addition, during the summer of 1900 Griffith and other organizers for the Professional Association of Baseball Players had convinced many players not to sign contracts for the upcoming season until the owners made concessions on salaries, the reserve clause, and other issues.

Two weeks after the conclusion of the 1900 season Ban Johnson announced the reorganization of the Western League into a new American League.[33] The upstart association would field teams in the abandoned cities of Cleveland, Washington, and Baltimore and promote former Western League franchises in Detroit and Milwaukee to major league status. It would also challenge the National League directly in Chicago, Boston, and Philadelphia. Charles Somers, a Cleveland coal dealer, became the league's financial angel, providing initial underwriting for the Cleveland franchise and for those in Chicago, Boston, and Philadelphia as well.

Comiskey, Mack, McGraw, and Griffith constituted the core of the enterprise. Connie Mack enlisted as manager and part owner of the Philadelphia Athletics, which would compete for fans with the Phillies. Mack invested an estimated $5,000 to $10,000 for a 25 percent stake in the new club and recruited Ben Shibe of the A. J. Reach & Co. sporting goods firm as majority owner and primary financial backer. Shibe, called the "mechanical genius of baseball," had made his fortune by perfecting the machines that produced standardized baseballs.[34] In Baltimore John McGraw and Wilbert Robinson received exclusive rights to resuscitate the Orioles, with the twenty-seven-year-old McGraw serving as player and manager as well as minority owner.

The boldest initiative, however, unfolded in Chicago, where Charles Comiskey fulfilled his vow to return to his home city. Prior to the 1900 season Comiskey had secured the rights to move his St. Paul Western League franchise to the Windy City as a minor league team. He had agreed not to use Chicago in his club title, but nonetheless adopted the nickname "White Sox," hearkening back to the city's fabled first National League club. Thus, when the Western circuit metamorphosed into the American League the following year, Comiskey was already firmly ensconced in Chicago. Unlike Mack and McGraw, who became minority owners and managers of new American League teams, Comiskey assumed majority ownership of the White Sox, risking approximately $25,000 in the process. He also stepped down as field manager to run the administrative side of the organization on a full-time basis.[35]

Convincing players to bolt the established National League for the fledgling American posed the greatest challenge for the newcomers. In December 1900 a delegation from the Players' Protective Association, including Clark Griffith, presented National League owners with a uniform contract, which among other items gave players equal rights with owners to terminate any contract on ten days notice, effectively ending the reserve clause. A committee of National League owners brusquely rebuffed the athletes. Griffith, already working closely with Comiskey and Johnson and destined to become manager of Comiskey's White Sox, immediately wired the pair, "Go ahead, you can get all the players you want."[36] Johnson announced in January 1901 that his new league would honor the proposed Players' Protective Association contract. The new league also offered hefty salaries, obliterating the National League's maximum pay policy.

Griffith, Mack, McGraw, and other representatives of the American League (most notably Cleveland player-manager Jimmy McAleer, a less celebrated veteran of the Players League who would later become an owner of the Boston Braves) fanned out across the nation. They seduced National League players, most of whom, at Griffith's urging, had not yet signed contracts for the 1901 season, to abandon ship and seek shelter in the new port. "I never felt badly about going after the National League stars," commented Mack, who lured Napoleon Lajoie crosstown from the Phillies to the Athletics. "As a player I resented the $2400 rule . . . and I felt that a new major league would help the players."[37] The

American League raiders drew up a list of forty-six athletes whom they hoped to snare. Only Honus Wagner, the great Pittsburgh shortstop who remained loyal to the Pirates, eluded their net.

Thus, the American League bore many similarities to the abortive Players League of an earlier decade. It emerged, at least in part, as a result of player grievances over salaries and the reserve clause. It brought together an alliance of players, former players, and capitalists anxious to become baseball owners. Indeed, several of the key actors were veterans of the earlier venture. Most of the major stars, disgusted with the old regime, readily cast their fate with the new. Unlike the Players League, however, the American League was not a cooperative enterprise. Labor and management remained clearly distinct and separate. Financial backing for the league also seems to have been more substantial. Finally, the American League benefited from Ban Johnson's fine administrative instincts in its war against the establishment.

The American League scored an undeniable success in its inaugural season. Not surprisingly, the White Sox, carefully stocked by manager Griffith and paced by the Old Fox's own 24–7 record as pitcher, claimed the first pennant. "I signed players for the other clubs too," he later admitted, "but I managed to sign a championship club for Chicago."[38] Lajoie, playing for Mack's Athletics, batted .422 and paced the league in every major offensive category. Although the National League outdrew its new rival by over 200,000 fans, the American League attracted a healthy 1.6 million spectators, dispelling the fears that its investors, like those of the earlier Players League, would have to weather substantial losses. The new franchises in Chicago and Boston convincingly outdrew the more established teams in their cities.

Most significantly, the rivalry between the two leagues enhanced rather than detracted from interest in baseball. Unlike the catastrophic Brotherhood War that drove total baseball attendance down in 1890, overall attendance nearly doubled in 1901. Despite the competition from the new league, National League attendance actually rose. Nonetheless, the stunning inroads by the new league forced National League owners to abandon the $2,400 pay limit, touching off a bidding war that drove up team payrolls. When in 1902 each of the American League clubs in cities with teams in both leagues outdrew their National League counterparts at the gate and the American League attracted 2.2 million fans to the National's 1.7 million, the senior circuit agreed to recognize the new league. Ignoring most of the original demands of the Players' Protective Association, the two organizations negotiated the National Agreement of 1903, restoring the reserve rule without the salary cap and creating a three-man commission to rule the game.

The settlement crushed the hopes of union advocates, but the gamble to bolt organized baseball and establish a new league paid off handsomely for the four conspirators who had joined Johnson. Comiskey, Mack, and McGraw had achieved ownership status. Griffith had won recognition as a pennant-winning manager. Mack, who had experienced little previous success as a manager, guided his Athletics to the pennant in 1902. Nonetheless, the alliance among Comiskey, Mack, Griffith, and McGraw quickly unraveled. The experiences of the first two seasons had made clear to Ban Johnson that, while the nation's largest cities could easily support two major league teams, several of the original American League locales could not generate sufficient fan support.

Persistent rumors had McGraw's disappointing Orioles destined for New York to challenge the Giants. McGraw, whose investment in the Orioles had yielded no profit in 1901, hoped to lead the team into New York. However, relations between the fiery umpire-baiting Irishman and Johnson, who stressed order and discipline on the field, inevitably deteriorated. Before the inaugural season was three weeks old, Johnson had suspended McGraw for five days for mistreatment of umpires. The two men repeatedly clashed throughout the season and into the next. Convinced that Johnson would never allow him to manage in New York, McGraw staged a preemptive strike.

On June 28, 1902, McGraw provoked umpire Tom Connally and refused to leave the field when ejected from the game, resulting in an Oriole forfeit. Two days later, Johnson, proclaiming, "Rowdyism will not be tolerated in the American League," suspended

McGraw indefinitely. "No man likes to be ordered off the earth like a dog in the presence of his friends," responded McGraw right-eously. "Ballplayers are not a lot of cattle to have the whip cracked over them." Noting that he had invested his own money to help create the American League, McGraw protested, "There is an end to self-sacrifice. A man must look out for himself." On July 8 Mc-Graw negotiated the sale of his stock in the Orioles and resigned as team manager. The following day McGraw announced that he would henceforth manage Andrew Freedman's National League New York Giants.[39]

There is little doubt that McGraw orchestrated these events for his own benefit. His new contract, conceived as early as June 18, guaranteed him an annual salary of $11,000 for four years, more than any player or manager in the history of the game until that time. McGraw bitterly attacked "Czar Johnson" and the American League, which he said "is a loser and has been from the start." He called Mack's Philadelphia team a "big white elephant" and pre-dicted its demise. Not satisfied with his enhanced fortunes, Mc-Graw vindictively sought further revenge. He arranged for Andrew Freedman to covertly gain control of the Orioles. Freedman then released the Orioles' top stars. Four, including future Hall of Famers "Ironman" Joe McGinnity and Roger Bresnahan, imme-diately signed with the Giants. Johnson moved quickly to seize control of the Orioles and stock it with players from other Amer-ican teams, allowing the club to finish out the season, albeit in last place. In August Johnson announced that the team would move to New York in 1903.

Clark Griffith, although still manager of the White Sox, deter-mined that, like McGraw, he wanted to be in the potentially lu-crative limelight of the nation's metropolis. After the 1902 season, with the war between the leagues still raging, Griffith convinced six players from the National League's pennant-winning Pittsburgh Pirates to jump to the New York team. He then dispatched a telegram to Ban Johnson: SIX PIRATE PLAYERS WILL JUMP TO THE AMERICAN LEAGUE ONLY ON CONDITION THAT I AM APPOINTED TO THE NEW YORK TEAM. Although Comiskey was reported to be "boiling mad" over Griffith's proposed desertion, Johnson, anxious to have a strong team to compete with the Giants, granted the Old Fox his wish.[40]

Thus, at the dawn of baseball's new age, the quartet had maneuvered themselves into positions far advanced from their humble origins. Comiskey and Mack were now full-fledged "magnates," owners of recognized and highly successful major league clubs. McGraw had eschewed ownership for the more remunerative and celebrated position of New York Giant manager. Griffith, although not as handsomely rewarded, also reigned as a manager in the nation's largest city.

Over the next decade, as baseball achieved an unprecedented popularity, Comiskey, Mack, and McGraw came to assume near-legendary status in the emergent mass American culture. Baseball attendance doubled between 1901 and 1909, topping 7.2 million at the end of the decade. General prosperity, increased leisure time, expanded newspaper coverage, and improved urban transportation contributed to the surge. The creation of the World Series in 1903, which pitted the champions of the two leagues in a season-ending competition, fueled further interest, producing an eagerly awaited national spectacle that appealed to fans and nonfans alike.

Comiskey, Mack, and McGraw were both the apostles and beneficiaries of baseball's ascension. Mack's Athletics and McGraw's Giants each won five pennants between 1902 and 1913. Three times their clubs met in the World Series. The two dissimilar Irishmen became familiar figures to the American public, as acclaimed and celebrated as any star player. Gaunt and lanky, Mack, the "Tall Tactician," managed calmly from the bench wearing a suit with a starched white collar, tie, stickpin, and derby or boater hat no matter how hot the weather, waving his scorecard to position players and rarely showing emotion. "He is not a dominant, driving manager of the McGraw type," wrote his star second baseman Eddie Collins in 1914. "He is the persuasive kind and his men would do anything for him." Off the field, Mack compelled the Athletics to wear business suits on road trips to present a better image.[41] McGraw, the "Little Napoleon," stood a half-foot shorter than Mack, and as the years passed his stocky frame filled out his Giants' uniform with added poundage. He remained ever the fiery baiter of umpires and intense motivator of players. Mack, a tee-totaler, "clean as a hound's tooth," according to *American Magazine* in 1910, symbolized the "lace-curtain" Irishman, who had risen from rags to respectability.[42] McGraw, a hard drinker and near-compulsive gambler, epitomized the rougher side of Irish working-class America.

Although his team did not fare as well on the field, Charles Comiskey had achieved far greater material success and an equal measure of acclaim. His White Sox, regardless of where they stood in the standings, usually led the American League in attendance. Numerous articles written in national periodicals between 1909 and 1917 portrayed Comiskey as an exemplar of the American success story, "the Prince of Magnates," "the self-made man of base-ball." "Just as the Comiskey of the early 80's was different from other players, so Comiskey the millionaire baseball magnate is different from the other magnates of his time," wrote Hugh C. Weir in 1914. Comiskey, explained Weir, was the only owner who had risen from the ranks to sole ownership of a major league team devoid of entangling partnerships. In Chicago, he reigned as a beloved folk hero. "If the question were asked in the Windy City today, 'Who is the most popular man in town?' there would be a tremendous chorus of voices . . . shouting Comiskey," claimed sportswriter George C. Rice. Rumors constantly floated that the Old Roman would follow his father into politics and run for mayor.[43]

The construction of Comiskey Park in 1910, a few hundred feet from the site of the Old Brotherhood Park where Comiskey had managed in 1890, marked the crowning achievement of Comiskey's rise. Comiskey Park was the third of thirteen modern stadiums built or reconstructed by major league baseball teams between 1909 and 1915. These new ballparks, as several historians have noted, symbolized the maturity and permanency of baseball as a feature in American life. In addition, according to Benjamin Rader, "They were akin to the great public buildings, skyscrapers and railroad terminals of the day . . . edifices that local residents proudly pointed to as evidence of their city's size and achievements."[44]

Reflecting the philosophies of the City Beautiful Movement of the Progressive Era, Comiskey, like most of his fellow stadium builders, adopted a classical motif, designing Comiskey Park to reflect Rome's colosseum. If the appearance of these stadia harkened back to an earlier age, however, their planning and construction evoked the technology and style of the new century. The dramatic growth in attendance had rendered the older, primarily wooden ballparks seating no more than 10,000 to 20,000 people obsolete. The introduction of concrete reinforced by steel rods offered the possibility of building permanent stadiums with upper decks. Shibe Park in Philadelphia, built to house Mack's Athletics in 1909, became the first major league ballpark to capitalize on the new technology. Its double-decked stands allowed it to seat 23,000 people. An additional 7,000 crammed in as standees to celebrate its opening. Pittsburgh's Forbes Field, unveiled shortly thereafter, boasted three decks.[45]

Comiskey's Chicago edifice, which initially seated 28,500 people, was the largest ballpark yet built. Like Forbes Field and Shibe Park, its construction reflected elements of American modernity. The new arenas were fireproof, eliminating the danger of fires that had plagued the old wooden arenas. They featured elevators and telephones. Although Shibe Park had stairs to move the crowds from one deck to another, Forbes Field and Comiskey Park featured wide ramps that were safer and facilitated fan movement. Comiskey envisioned his ballpark as a "monument to the game."[46] Privately built at a cost of $700,000 and proudly bearing Comiskey's name, it was also clearly a monument to the Old Roman's personal achievements.

To this point Clark Griffith's accomplishments had been far less substantial. Since leaving Comiskey's employ in 1903, he had spent nine relatively undistinguished seasons managing the American League New York Highlanders and National League Cincinnati Reds. After the 1911 season he seized the opportunity to purchase a 10-percent interest in the Washington Senators of the American

League. As the manager and largest single shareholder, Griffith became the controlling figure on the club. When the old wooden National Park burned down during spring training in 1912, Griffith hastily constructed his own concrete and steel stadium. More modest than those built by Mack and Comiskey, the new arena eventually came to be known as Clark Griffith Park. The combination of the new ballpark, Griffith's opening day coup of handing President William Howard Taft a ball to throw out the first pitch, the emergence of Walter Johnson as the league's dominant pitcher, and the Senators surprising second-place finishes in 1912 and 1913 elevated Griffith to the heights of public acclaim enjoyed by Comiskey, Mack, and McGraw. Over the next decade Griffith would steadily increase his ownership share in the Senators. Griffith, wrote Frank C. Lane in 1912, "is one of those men whose unswerving faith in baseball has made possible some of its most pronounced successes. . . . There is no more shrewd, able and successful manager than he." "Everybody is strong for the Little Fox," added William A. Phelon in 1913.[47]

Everybody was even stronger for Mack and McGraw. In 1912 McGraw signed a five-year, $30,000-a-year contract with the Giants, securing his place atop baseball's salary structure. In 1913, after Mack's Athletics claimed their third World Championship in four years, defeating McGraw's Giants in the World Series, the New York Highlanders attempted to lure Mack away from the Athletics. Mack, still a minority owner of the Athletics, used the lucrative Highlander overture to leverage greater control over his club. Faced with the prospect of losing his celebrated manager, majority owner Ben Shibe lent Mack $113,000 to buy out the other minority interests and become an equal partner in the Athletics.[48]

The relationship between Shibe and Mack illustrated a critical point. Despite their pretensions, the fortunes of baseball's self-made magnates rested on fragile foundations. Comiskey, who favored recruiting former players as owners, might protest that "one more millionaire will break the American League" and Americans could extol baseball's "incarnations of success" as living symbols of the American dream. But, as umpire/writer Billy Evans noted, most major league owners who "boast(ed) of fat bankrolls" had "amassed their fortunes in other lines of endeavor."[49] Comiskey, Mack, and Griffith, who depended solely on team profits for their incomes, found themselves increasingly at a disadvantage.

The obvious way to overcome this obstacle was to drive down player salaries. Once they had donned the garb of management, the former players rapidly grasped the need for payroll constraints. Connie Mack's teams, which regularly finished high in the standings, usually ranked near the bottom of the salary scale. Both Mack's second-place 1903 club and his pennant-winning 1914 team reportedly had the lowest payrolls in the league. Some of Mack's players received less money playing for the Athletics than they had in the minor leagues.[50] Laudatory articles about Comiskey praised his fairness and generosity in dealing with players. Yet the gestures they described were often more of a charitable nature, keeping players as coaches after they retired or paying for children's education, rather than making wage concessions. Reports circulated that Comiskey was "free with his friends, but 'close' with his ballplayers." As early as 1902 White Sox manager Clark Griffith, just one year removed from the vice presidency of the Players' Protective Association, rationalized Comiskey's financial practices by arguing that reductions in salary during a player's reserve year did not constitute a pay cut. Ring Lardner, whose classic *You Know Me Al* stories first appeared in 1914, repeatedly depicted Comiskey fleecing naïve pitcher Jack Keefe in salary negotiations.[51]

As in 1890 and 1901 pecunious owner practices precipitated the creation of a new players' association and the formation of yet another new league. In 1913 lawyer David Fultz, a former major league outfielder who had played for Connie Mack's A's (for whom he led the American League in scoring in 1902) and Clark Griffith's Highlanders, organized the Fraternity of Professional Baseball Players. The following year a group of investors led by oil baron Harry Sinclair, ice magnate Phil Ball, and Brooklyn baking mogul Robert B. Ward launched the Federal League and began raiding National and American League rosters. As in the past, the end of major league baseball's monopoly triggered dramatic salary increases. Although few top stars jumped to the new league, most were able to negotiate more generous contracts with their old employers.[52]

For Griffith, just two years an owner and deeply in debt, the Federal League challenge drove home the realities of baseball economics. When Walter Johnson, his star pitcher, succumbed to the lures of the Chicago Whales, Griffith, the former contract jumper, union official, and league promoter lectured the "Big Train" on the virtues of loyalty. When this failed to sway Johnson, Griffith matched Chicago's salary offer. A chastened Johnson nonetheless lamented "That's all very fine, Griff, but we've already spent the $10,000 bonus they gave me." Griffith, his resources depleted, secured the money to pay back the bonus from Comiskey, who feared having Johnson pitching in Chicago for a rival team. Johnson remained with the Senators.[53]

The Federal League war proved far more devastating for Mack. His Athletics had won three World Series in four years and they opened a big lead in the American League race at the start of the 1914 campaign. But as the season progressed, the atmosphere around the team changed. "We had to write a lot of new contracts in the middle of the season," he later explained. "But the Feds kept raising their offers and a good many of our players became more and more dissatisfied." According to Mack, the team divided into two factions, one loyal to the Athletics and the other ready to jump to the new league.[54] The Athletics held on to win the American League pennant, but the Boston Braves embarrassed them, winning four straight games in the World Series.

"The Federal League wrecked my club by completely changing the spirit of my players," complained Mack. Before they had thought only of winning, he protested, now they were obsessed with money. But Mack had already begun to suspect the shortcomings of success. "When you win," he would later explain, "you have a general rise in all expenses. When a club is behind, salaries are low, so are expenses." As half-owner of the team, and personally burdened by his substantial indebtedness to Shibe, Mack decided to dismantle his championship squad. "If the players were going to 'cash in' and leave me to hold the bag, there was nothing for me to do but cash in too," he rationalized.[55]

Within weeks of the 1914 World Series Mack waived future Hall of Fame pitchers Eddie Plank and Chief Bender despite their combined 32–10 record. The team's best player, second baseman Eddie Collins, who in a recent *American Magazine* article had expressed the desire to play out his career under Mack (who "treated folks in a decent, white way"),[56] became the next to go. Mack shocked the baseball world by selling Collins to Comiskey's White Sox for $50,000. Over the next year selling shortstop Jack Barry, pitcher Bob Shawkey, third baseman Frank "Home Run" Baker, and others netted Mack an additional $130,000.[57] By the end of the 1915 season Mack had succeeded in slashing the already low Athletics payroll to an unprecedented level. He also transformed a pennant-winning squad that had won 65 percent of its games into a last-place club with an abysmal .283 winning percentage. Seven years would pass before the Athletics would climb out of the cellar.

Unlike Mack and Griffith, whose quest for ownership had left them deeply in debt at the outbreak of the Federal League challenge, Comiskey, who had "run a shoestring into better than a cool million,"[58] seemed to be one of the prime beneficiaries of the hostilities. His substantial resources enabled him to purchase Eddie Collins from the Athletics and "Shoeless Joe" Jackson from the Cleveland Indians. None of his White Sox players jumped to the Federal League as Comiskey met their escalated salary demands. His reconstituted White Sox would finish second in 1916 and win pennants in 1917 and 1919. Yet, in many ways, Comiskey would become the most profound victim of the Federal League war.

The Federal League collapsed after only two years, but the damage to major league baseball was considerable. National and American League attendance, which had peaked at 7.2 million in 1909, dropped to 4.4 million in 1914 and 4.8 million in 1915. At the same time player salaries rose dramatically. Major league owners sought to recoup their losses by freezing or cutting salaries. The 1916 season saw a substantial resurgence at the box office, but American entry into World War I in April 1917 erased most of the recovery.

In 1918 the two leagues played a 130-game schedule and total attendance barely topped 3 million. Planning another short season and fearing continued losses in 1919, many owners lowered salaries further and slashed expenses.

Although the aura surrounding Mack and Griffith, and to a lesser extent McGraw, had declined during these years, Comiskey's continued to shine. After his club won the 1917 World Series an article attempted to demonstrate how the "Old Roman" had "Won a Fortune and Whole Army of Personal Followers Through Enlightened Business Methods." Prior to the 1919 season Chicago sportswriter George Axelson authored *Commy*, a loving paean to the White Sox owner. Axelson portrayed Comiskey as a man of energy, daring, honesty, foresight, fairness, and generosity. Comiskey, in an afterword, cheered baseball as "the most honest pastime in the world," asserting, "Crookedness and baseball do not mix." His current Chicago White Sox team, declared Comiskey, "is the best bunch of fighters I ever saw. No game is lost until the last man is out." He predicted that 1919 would be "the greatest season of them all."[59]

Rarely does a book bristle so thoroughly with retrospective irony as does Axelson's *Commy*. In 1919 the sins of the reserve clause, shortsighted major league salary practices, and the consequences of the Federal League era came home to roost in Comiskey's White Sox. After winning the American League pennant several of the White Sox players conspired with gamblers to fix the World Series. Others with knowledge of the plot became complicit with their silence. Over the years, particularly since the 1963 publication of Eliot Asinof's *Eight Men Out*, the definitive history of the scandal, Comiskey has emerged as the arch-villain of these events. "What were the pressures of the baseball world, of America in 1919 itself, that would turn decent, normal, talented men to engage in such a betrayal?" asked Asinof. The answer he found rested largely with Comiskey, whose "ballplayers were the best and were paid as poorly as the worst."[60] Comiskey allotted the lowest subsidy in the league for meal money and alone among the owners deducted the costs of laundering uniforms from player wages. "He had no reason in the world not to deal fairly with his players," argues historian Bill James. "The White Sox drew the largest crowds in baseball in this period . . . yet the White Sox were one of the lowest-paying teams."[61]

Others have judged Comiskey more generously. "The idea that the White Sox were grossly underpaid doesn't really stand close scrutiny," writes Charles Alexander. Some players, like Eddie Collins and Ray Schalk, ranked among the best paid in the game and, although Joe Jackson was grossly undercompensated, other White Sox players had incomes commensurate with those on other teams. Nonetheless, as Robert F. Burk has pointed out, baseball salaries had largely stagnated since the collapse of the Federal League in 1915. Wartime and postwar inflation "severely eroded the real earnings of players."[62] In 1919, with the war over and Babe Ruth in ascendance, baseball attendance had mushroomed to record levels, generating dramatic profits for the owners without comparable rewards for the players. Comiskey's White Sox, as participants in the World Series, found themselves in a position to capitalize on their accumulated resentments.

In the end Comiskey's primary sin rested not so much with his employment practices, as abysmal as they may have been, but with his subsequent efforts to protect his team and investment by covering up the scandal and undermining the prosecution of the participants. Neither Comiskey nor the White Sox, at least during his lifetime, ever recovered from the devastation of 1919. Forty years would pass before the White Sox would win another pennant. Comiskey was, by all accounts, broken by the scandal. Although he died a wealthy man in 1931, his estate totaled far less than it might have had the Black Sox tragedy not occurred. The priest who delivered his funeral sermon attributed his death to "a broken heart."[63]

McGraw, Griffith, and Mack would all experience bright moments in the 1920s and early 1930s. McGraw rejoined the ownership ranks in 1919 when he joined the syndicate headed by Charles Stoneham that purchased the New York Giants. His Giants won four straight pennants and two World Series from 1921 to 1924.

For the next seven years his clubs always played winning baseball, but never again finished first. He stepped down as Giants' manager in 1932 and died in 1934. McGraw's opponents in his final World Series in 1924 were Griffith's Washington Senators, who had surprised the Babe Ruth Yankees to win their first American League pennant. The Senators topped the Giants in seven games. The Senators repeated as American League champs in 1925 and again in 1933. Mack's Athletics returned to championship form in 1929, 1930, and 1931, but, when the Great Depression threatened his profits, Mack again divested his roster of its high-priced stars and plunged his team into the second division.

Both Mack and Griffith continued as baseball owners into the 1950s. They became revered and honored grand old men of baseball, reminders of an age in which a player might become an owner and join the magnates of American industry. Their time, however, had clearly passed. Neither the Athletics nor the Senators ever again contended for pennants during their lifetimes. Attendance for the two clubs always languished near the bottom of the major leagues. Of greater significance, few former players ever again secured a significant ownership share of a major league club. In modern America success would assume different incarnations.

New Ways of Knowing
Baseball in the 1920s

The world broke in two in 1922 or thereabouts," wrote novelist Willa Cather.[1] Cather apparently had little interest in baseball—none of her numerous writings mention the game. Yet the 1922 World Series pitting John McGraw's New York Giants against Babe Ruth's New York Yankees, and particularly the manner in which Americans followed its progress, endorsed Cather's vision of a world suddenly divided between a more traditional culture and a modern technological sensibility.

Throughout the United States tens of millions of people gathered, as they had for decades, in town squares, city intersections, and indoor urban arenas to witness a pitch-by-pitch recreation of World Series games on large electrical and mechanical scoreboards. A "mammoth web" of 45,000 miles of telegraph wires brought the World Series to most corners of the nation, where it was transcribed into a public display.[2] Wilmer Thomson, a Chester, Pennsylvania, resident, described the modest scoreboard erected outside the local newspaper office when he was a boy. "When a ball was pitched they would show a yellow light," he reminisced almost three-quarters of a century later. "For a strike red lights would be turned on. Blue lights would show the number of outs. The bases would have lights to show the positions of runners. Whenever there was a hit they would ring a bell." About 150 men would gather each World Series day in Chester to share this communal experience, at once local and national in nature.[3]

In the New York metropolitan area, however, several million people enjoyed the 1922 World Series in a novel manner. In a promotion to encourage the sale of its new product, radio manufacturer RCA-Westinghouse arranged for WJZ, its pioneer radio affiliate, to broadcast the first two games of the series live from the Polo Grounds. Sportswriter Grantland Rice, sitting in a box seat near the Yankee dugout, described the action to what the *New York Tribune* called "the greatest audience ever assembled to listen to one man."[4] The *New York Times* marveled at the new technology. "Not only the voice of the official radio observer could be heard, but the voice of the umpire on the field announcing the batteries of the day mingled with the voice of the boy selling ice cream cones," reported the *Times* the next day. "The clamor of the forty thousand fans inside the Polo Grounds made the fans feel as if they were inside the grandstand. The cheers which greeted Babe Ruth when he stepped to the plate could be heard throughout the land."[5]

The rival transmissions of the 1922 World Series—one via telegraph, the other via radio—capture baseball at a crucial cultural turning point in American history. In the years following World War I, Americans underwent a dramatic transformation in the ways in which they assimilated information. There emerged what historian Warren Susman has called "new ways of knowing that stood in sharp contrast with the old ways of knowing available in the book and the printed word." Radio represented just one of these "new ways of knowing."[6] Media devoted to pictorial and visual display—movies, newsreels, tabloid newspapers, magazines, and advertising—revolutionized people's ability to vicariously participate in the world around them. "Photographs have the kind of authority over imagination today, which the printed word had yesterday, and the spoken word before that. They seem utterly real . . . and they are the most effortless food for the mind conceivable," observed Walter Lippmann in 1922. "In the whole experience of the race there has been no aid to visualization comparable to the cinema."[7] The addition of radio (and later talking pictures) added yet another dimension to this phenomenon.

Baseball became one of the foremost agents and beneficiaries of these changes. Fans who only a few years earlier could never have hoped to attend a major league game, yet who followed its progress assiduously through newspaper reports and scoreboard recreations, suddenly could see their heroes in motion picture theaters and dramatic photo displays. They could hear live radio broadcasts that placed them at the games. As these opportunities dramatically expanded the popularity of the national pastime, they also revolutionized people's perceptions and reshaped the baseball experience for millions of Americans.

The scoreboards themselves, of course, had already represented a grand advance into the modern era. Instantaneous telegraph transmissions allowed baseball fans to experience games as they transpired. What sportswriter H. G. Salsinger called an "invisible host of fandom"[8] thus shared in the exhilarating local communal experience of gathering for the games, while simultaneously participating in a national rite of autumn. As early as the 1890s communities began to translate these telegraphic reports of baseball games into visual recreations.[9] At the Atlanta opera house, young boys bearing the names of real players would run the bases on a baseball diamond laid out on the stage. In 1894 the "Compton Electrical System," a ten-by-ten foot board that featured lineups listed on either side of a diamond and lights to indicate which player was batting, the current baserunners, an up-to-the-minute ball/strike count, and other information appeared in many cities. After 1905, when the World Series became a permanent fixture on the national scene, scoreboard-watching became an equally entrenched annual ritual. Newspapers erected large displays in front of their offices, attracting crowds numbering in the thousands in large cities, often snarling traffic for many blocks.

In 1906 the *Chicago Tribune* began the practice of renting armories and theaters to hold the crowds. The indoor setting allowed scoreboards in the major cities to become increasingly more elaborate. In 1912 Madison Square Garden and other venues in New York City presented the Series on a display that moved the balls and players with magnets. Another model, "The Playograph," used a ball affixed to an invisible cord that emulated the course of the ball while white footprints illuminated the path of the baserunners. A Jackson Manikin Board employed for the 1915 World Series showed mechanical athletes that moved in and out of dugouts, swung the bat left- and right-handed, and even argued with the umpire.

For millions of baseball fans, these recreations seemed truly miraculous, enabling them to "attend" games played hundreds and thousands of miles away. "Before many of the thirty-six thousand spectators at the Polo Grounds were aware that the umpire had called a strike on the batter, fans in Denver, Colorado, and San Antonio, Texas, knew that the umpire had called a strike," asserted F. C. Lane. The fan, explained Salsinger, "visualized each man as he comes to bat. [He] 'sees' every pitched ball, closely follows the course of every batted ball." To Irving Sanborn, the crowds in the ballparks were no "more enthusiastically alive to every critical situation or more loudly appreciative of every fine play than those millions jammed into the various halls or thronging the streets in front of newspaper audiences." Some argued that the man in the street saw the game more clearly than fans at the stadium. The ballpark, after all, offered many distractions. Those watching the scoreboard, however, saw only the raw essentials of the game affording them, according to Lane, "a clearer view of what was happening at the Polo Grounds than was possible to a fraction of the fans who were actually present."[10]

This hyperbole notwithstanding, few Americans would actually have traded a seat at the ballpark for a space in front of a recreated display. Nor could the vicarious experience of scoreboard-watching compare to the new excitement offered by the radio in the 1920s. Commercialized radio began in 1920 when WWJ in Detroit broadcast local election returns. Three months later KDKA debuted in Pittsburgh, disseminating the results of the presidential election.

Since in its infancy radio emphasized news and information reporting, baseball proved a logical focus. In 1921, its first summer on the air, KDKA began offering baseball scores. On August 5, 1921, Harold Arlin, the station's innovative engineer/announcer, broadcast a Pirates' game live from Forbes Field.[11] That fall, WJZ in Newark, New Jersey, offered a primitive recreation of the World Series. A reporter for the *Newark Call* telephoned the play-by-play to an announcer in Newark, who dictated the action over the air to a limited host of listeners.[12]

The following year Grantland Rice's World Series broadcast attracted a broader audience. Local radio stations agreed to remain silent to allow WJZ's transmission to be heard over as broad a range as possible. Two additional stations—WGY in Schenectady and WBZ in Springfield, Massachusetts—also picked up the signal. Most listeners, in an audience generously estimated as high as five million people, heard the games in a communal venue not dissimilar to the scoreboard-watchers in other parts of the country. They gathered outside radio stores in groups large and small to listen to the games over loudspeakers erected for the occasion. Those lucky enough to own a radio, including many who had recently succumbed to Westinghouse newspaper advertisements heralding Rice's broadcast, listened in the privacy of their homes.

The broadcast that they heard was quite primitive. WJZ, unable to secure rights to use telephone lines for the transmission, dispatched the game over telegraph wires that diluted the voice quality and added a background hum. Rice had no idea what the role of a radio announcer should be. He simply described what happened in a voice "a little flat, atonal, somewhat awkwardly modulated and unmistakably Southern." He contributed no additional commentary, leaving dead space between the plays. "The broadcast officials wanted me to keep talking. But I didn't know what to say," he later revealed.[13]

The World Series returned to the air in 1923 with a greatly improved product. WEAF, owned by American Telephone and Telegraph, transmitted the game over telephone lines that enhanced the reception. Seeking baseball expertise, the station once again turned to a reporter, W. O. McGeehan of the *New York Tribune*, to call the game. To assist him the station assigned Graham McNamee, a broadcasting veteran of all of four months, not to speak but, as McNamee explained, to coach McGeehan, "so that he would not crowd the instrument, sit too far away, or unduly raise or lower his voice." McGeehan apparently felt no more comfortable behind a microphone than had Rice. In the fourth inning of the third game McGeehan abruptly left and McNamee relieved him, broadcasting the balance of the six-game series.[14]

Graham McNamee was not a baseball expert, but, as a former concert singer, he understood the rudiments of pace, style, and performing for an audience, even one he could not see. Earlier reproductions of baseball action had focused on eliciting the facts. The Western Union operator who telegraphed World Series information was expected to remain, as F. C. Lane wrote in 1922, "perfectly cool and collected, no matter what happens. . . . He cannot yield to any enthusiasm of the moment . . . He must be above personal prejudice. . . . he is stationed at his responsible post to see facts and to narrate them without any mistakes and without any personal sentimental coloring."[15] Newsmen Rice and McGeehan had approached radio in the same way. McNamee, however, intuitively recognized that the new medium required a different approach. As he later explained,

> The broadcaster must see to it that in his announcement that there are very few . . . "breaks on the air." For, with the breaks, the listener immediately imagines that something has gone wrong with his set. Besides, he did not buy it just to listen to dead silence. . . . I found myself more than ever falling back on general description. And that is where the imagination comes in. . . . You must make each of your listeners, though miles from the spot, feel that he or she, too, is there with you in that press stand, watching the movements of the game, the color, and flags; the pop-bottles thrown in the air;

the straw hats demolished; Gloria Swanson arriving in her new ermine coat; McGraw in his dugout, apparently motionless, but giving signals all the time."[16]

In the eighth inning of the sixth game of the Series, with the Yankees leading the series three games to two, but trailing in the game 4–1, Babe Ruth strode to the plate with the bases loaded. McNamee fully engaged his listeners into the action of the moment. "Here was the most advertised athlete in the game, one whose name appears in headlines more often than the President's," McNamee later wrote, capturing the drama that he had conveyed over the air. "Only one little crack—just a solid connection between ash and leather, and the series would be over. The chance that was the immortal Casey's was now the Babe's." Ruth "squared his shoulders and set himself menacingly enough," but like Mighty Casey, the Babe struck out, "making an ignominious exit . . . his face almost green now where before it had been white."[17]

"People who weren't around in the twenties when radio exploded can't know what it meant, this milestone for mankind," observed Red Barber, whose own career helped define the craft of sportscasting. "Suddenly with radio, there was instant human communication. . . . The world came into our homes for the first time. . . . We heard drama that we ourselves played a part in." McNamee, who reigned as voice of the World Series and many other events for the remainder of the decade, initiated millions of Americans into this experience. "When the nation heard him say, 'Good evening, ladies and gentleman of the radio audience, this is Graham McNamee speaking,' the nation hugged itself happily . . . waiting for something vital to come into the living room," recalled Barber. McNamee, according to Heywood Broun, "individualized and particularized every emotion. He made me feel the temperature and tension. The wind hit him and it deflected off to me . . . No mere ticker report could be comparable, because McNamee allowed you to follow the ball on the wing."[18]

Not everyone was as enamored of McNamee and the new technology. Several sportswriters expressed disdain for his "general description." "I don't know which game to write about," wrote Ring Lardner after one World Series contest, "the one I saw today, or the one I heard Graham McNamee announce as I sat next to him at the Polo Grounds." Unlike the telegraph operator who strove for accuracy, McNamee could and did make mistakes. "He mixed players and innings and teams," complained one reporter in 1927. "He made right handed batters left handed. . . . He put players on base where they weren't and left them off bases where they were."[19]

For the average listener, however, the medium, not the miscalls, provided the message. Raymond Francis Yates described Mc-Namee's broadcast of the 1924 World Series as "one of the greatest heartbumping events of American sport. It made the game bigger" and gave the fans "almost as much of a thrill as though they were at the Polo Grounds." McNamee, wrote Yates, made every listener a spectator. He allowed them "to use their eyes—he painted word pictures that other minds could feast upon. . . . Very little imagi-nation was required . . . especially when the announcer turned his microphone on the roaring, booing and cheering crowd. These little inserts of realism transplanted the atmosphere of the diamond to every nook and corner of the United States."[20] These nooks included a New York hospital where 800 patients, "a majority of whom are playing their last game and waiting for the exit gates to open," had listened to a McNamee broadcast. "Your colorful de-scription made a hit here; and it was no ordinary bunt, but a powerful wallop that has had us talking ever since," wrote a hos-pital worker to McNamee. "Their little Main Street is quite nar-row, and the radio is bringing the world to their feet."[21]

The popularity of McNamee's World Series extravaganzas en-couraged several teams to experiment with regular season broad-casts. In 1924 WMAQ in Chicago transmitted all Cub and White Sox home games to local fans. Cubs' owner, William Wrigley, who believed that radio games increased interest in his team, allowed any station to broadcast Cubs games free of charge. In the late 1920s five stations carried the Cubs. In 1925 the two Boston clubs also began offering their games on the air. In general, however, teams in the eastern cities shied away from the radio, while those in the West embraced the new technology. By the end of the decade, St. Louis, Cleveland, Detroit, Cincinnati, Boston, and Chicago all featured regular broadcasts of home games, but none of the New York, Washington, D.C., or Pennsylvania teams followed suit.[22]

The opponents of baseball on the radio were numerous and adamant. Many feared that games delivered over the air would crimp attendance. Why, asked one owner, "should anyone pay between fifty cents and a dollar and a half for the entertainment that one could receive comfortably seated in an easy chair at home?" *The Sporting News*, in particular, waged sustained warfare against the medium. "Mr. Radio is going to butt into the business of telling the world all about the ball game without the world having to come to the ballpark to find out," warned the baseball weekly in 1922. Three years later it protested that "Baseball is more an inspiration to the brain through the eye than it is by the ear. . . . A nation that begins to take its sport by the ears will shortly adapt the white flag as its national emblem, and the dove as its national bird."[23]

The experiences in those communities that regularly broadcast games, however, confounded these predictions. In almost all these cities attendance rose in the 1920s. The radio stimulated interest not only within the urban confines, but, as reporter John Sheridan predicted in 1922, in surrounding areas as well. Sheridan noted that in towns of the Midwest crowds would gather around loudspeakers awaiting baseball scores. This prompted them to organize excursions to nearby cities to attend games. The combination of "radio communication, good roads, and the automobile" had expanded the radius of a team's fan territory from five miles at the turn of the century to 200 miles in the 1920s, argued Sheridan.[24]

The radio also encouraged the creation of a new type of baseball community that revolved around the local baseball announcer. "The announcers are stealing the glory which was once attached to the baseball writer," observed Frank Wallace of the *New York Post* after a swing through the Midwest.[25] In city after city the men who re-created the games developed devoted followings. In

Boston, Fred Hoey became, in the eyes of future announcer Ken Coleman, "a regional giant. The guy was loved. . . . On the air, Fred was Boston baseball." In Detroit Ty Tyson reigned supreme. "Ty was so vivid, he made games come alive," recalled one listener. "It was new, naturally, but it was his voice too—it was graphic . . . he had an urgency inside him and transmitted that to us . . . he made you feel like Gehringer, Cochrane and Goslin were right next door."[26]

The new community that emerged from radio, however, was profoundly different from that which had existed before 1922. For most fans major league baseball still entailed an act of imagination. But the process of fantasy had changed, transformed from belated newspaper coverage, to instant telegraphic recreations, to detailed broadcast descriptions. By 1929 one-third of all American families, and a majority of those who had electricity, owned radios. Increasingly they listened to the games in the privacy of their homes, rather than in the public spaces that had hosted the elevated scoreboards and loudspeakers of an earlier age. The arrival of radio, recalled Wilmer Thomson, marked "the end of the need for the scoreboard" in Chester.[27] The radio had, in a very important sense, democratized major league baseball, transmitting a more intimate sense of being at the game to millions who could never attend. Yet the process had become more familial or individualistic, replacing the communal experience with a more isolated one. Radio made baseball, more than ever, a national sport, but in a context far removed from earlier meanings of that term.

In whichever manner people in the 1920s experienced major league baseball—attending games, watching community scoreboards, listening to radio broadcasts, or perusing news stories, photographs, and newsreels—when they attempted to capture the essence of that experience, they invariably invoked the same image: that of Babe Ruth at the plate. Sportswriter F. C. Lane, wishing to convey the passion of scoreboard watchers during the 1921 World Series, described "the ninth and final" inning of the fourth game with Babe Ruth at bat. Young Wilmer Thomson, ringing the scoreboard bell that designated World Series hits, "felt like Babe Ruth." Graham McNamee, searching for "the most exciting experience I have ever had in broadcasting," selected Ruth striking out with the bases loaded in the 1923 World Series.[28] For Lane, Thomson, and McNamee, as for millions of others, Babe Ruth epitomized the national pastime.

"The Ruth is mighty and shall prevail," punned Heywood Broun.[29] The colossus that was Ruth prevailed not just in baseball, but throughout the national culture. He was arguably the most photographed of all Americans during the decade. A 1927 survey of the faces most likely to appear in the press concluded that Ruth's "phlegmatic, slightly puzzled expression peer[ed] out of the Sunday supplements" regardless of the season or setting. As early as October 1920 *Current Opinion* dubbed him "The Most Talked of American." The *Literary Digest* in 1922 captioned a photo of Ruth, "Everybody knows him," explaining that "backwoods citizens" and "darkies way out there in the wilderness and swamps" who might not know President Warren G. Harding would recognize Ruth.[30]

Richard Vidmer of the *New York Times* captured the essence of Ruth's passage through the South during spring training in 1927. On a rainy morning the Yankee train was scheduled to stop in a small Tennessee town.

> All morning long the rain beat down in silver sheets. The little hamlet of Etowah, Tennessee was drenched and dripping . . . Etowah wasn't going to overlook the opportunity of seeing Ruth. The citizens searched the attic and closets, clothed themselves in garments best suited for the weather, and flocked to the station.
>
> The train was an hour late, but when it finally arrived and passed, the platform contained all but four of the hamlet's inhabitants. Three were still looking for their rubbers, and the other had pneumonia already. Through the Babe's sweet, charitable nature they weren't disappointed. . . . The township of Etowah came to worship at the shrine of the king and

left with a feeling of friendship. When the Babe grins, awe vanishes and he makes a pal.[31]

To many commentators, both contemporary and historical, the American fascination with Ruth represented the peculiar hungers of the Roaring Twenties. Westbrook Pegler, according to his biographer, saw Ruth as "an unequaled exhibition whose strength and accuracy with baseball were of a pace with the madness for crazy pleasure, unheard of speed, and aimless bigness convulsing the nation." John Sheridan equated the excitement of Ruth's home runs with "flapper thrills over her cigarette and still shorter skirt." Historian Benjamin Rader has labeled Ruth a "compensatory hero," who "assisted the public in compensating for the passing of the traditional dream of success . . . and feelings of individual powerlessness," while Warren Susman viewed him an ideal hero for the world of consumption emerging in the 1920s.[32]

Yet, to see Ruth as a particular product of the twenties, or even the modern age, seems to over-intellectualize a simple subject. It is hard to imagine any people, in any era, who would not have been enthralled by Babe Ruth. Ruth fascinated because he was fascinating. His life, as many have noted, had a mythical, almost godlike quality. He is, wrote biographer Marshall Smelser, "our Hercules, our Samson, Beowulf, Siegfried." Born in the slums of Baltimore, raised in the wilderness of reform school, he grew to become, in the eyes of Roger Kahn, "a real-life John Henry."[33] At the age of twenty-one he had already established himself as one of the game's greatest pitchers. Three years later he forsook the mound to revolutionize the art of hitting. He hit more home runs than anyone in history, and he hit them harder and farther and with an unparalleled majesty. He performed miracles on the baseball field, healed the sick, and was laid low by his own human frailties and hubris, only to achieve redemption and new heights of acclaim and worship.

Ruth dominated baseball as no other man ever had before or ever would again, and he did so with an infectious ebullience that characterized his personal life as well. Many contemporary observers understood this. People "will always idolize the man that can do something that no other man on Earth can equal," noted *Baseball Magazine*. "Other baseball champions excel competition by a slight margin," wrote F. C. Lane in 1921. "Babe Ruth excels all competition by a margin so wide that there is simply no comparison." For Lane and other sportswriters, Ruth was "a theme which never grows threadbare. . . . Familiar from every angle, there is yet something about him which is always new. . . . He is still forever doing something unexpected and novel."[34]

Remarkably, Ruth's off-the-field exploits matched his oversized athletic persona. In this arena he also elicited divine comparisons, evoking images of Bacchus and Dionysus, the gods of wine and sensual pleasure.[35] Although sportswriters of the 1920s rarely reported on Ruth's prodigious sexual appetites or his unattractive qualities, his profligate lifestyle and repeated conflicts with baseball officialdom were well known. Ruth might well have possessed, as American League President Ban Johnson protested, "the mind of a fifteen-year old," and he may have been "crude, uncultured, ill-educated, unrefined" and prone to "wild license . . . utter disregard of regulations . . . and coarse escapades," as the increasingly disillusioned Lane complained in 1925. This excess of humanity, however, endeared him to people all the more. "With Ruth they often loved him for his naughtiness," explained Fred Lieb in 1927. "He would go off the reservation and then try to regain favor by knocking a few more over fences which had never been cleared. And the regaining was never difficult."[36] Ruth's ability to rebound from self-imposed adversity, after suspensions, fines, and physical dissipation had led many to believe that he had squandered his talents, added to his appeal.

"Fortunately, the Bambino does not have to step out of character to be what he is—an appealing swashbuckling, roistering, boisterous figure who is as natural a showman as the late Phineas T. Barnum," explained New York *Times* sportswriter John Kieran in 1927.[37] These extraordinary aspects of the Ruthian character would doubtless have captivated Americans in the 1890s or 1950s

as much as they did in the 1920s. Yet, while Ruth's appeal transcended chronological boundaries, it is impossible to imagine the
Ruthian phenomenon reaching full flower in any previous generation. In the 1920s people across the nation could see Babe Ruth
in pictures and newsreels, they could hear Babe Ruth (or at least
descriptions of him) on radio, and they could experience the drama
of Babe Ruth at the moment that it unfolded. In an age in which
the modern ideal of celebrity was virtually invented, Ruth, along
with a handful of Hollywood stars, personified that concept. Others might briefly eclipse his fame—Jack Dempsey on the eve of
one of his infrequent heavyweight championship fights or Charles
Lindbergh after his transatlantic flight in 1927—but from 1919 until
his retirement in 1935 the omnipresent Ruth alone appealed to the
popular imagination on a day-in, day-out basis.

Ruth emerged as a national figure simultaneously with the new
technologies and media forms transforming American communications. Nineteen-nineteen, the year that Ruth first captured the
public fancy, witnessed the appearance of the *New York Daily News*,
the nation's first successful tabloid newspaper; *True Story Magazine*, which would revolutionize popular periodical publishing; and
the *Fox Movietone News*, which helped to bring newsreels into the
modern age. Traded to the New York Yankees for the 1920 season,
Ruth arrived in the nation's media center in the same year that the
first radio stations took to the air. The advertising industry stood
poised on the brink of an expansion that would more than double
its revenues in less than a decade. Hollywood would also achieve
its maturity in the succeeding years. Ruth thus stood at the hub
of an unprecedented media crossroads. He could fully exploit the
traditional opportunities open to players to increase their income
and notoriety, but he also had a wide range of alternative vehicles
to enhance his celebrity.

In an age in which most Americans lacked the opportunity to
see major league baseball, players could earn considerable sums
exhibiting themselves once the season had ended. Many formed
teams that traveled across the nation playing games against local
or other all-star competition. Ruth's presence elevated these time-

honored tours to a new level. His 1927 barnstorming junket covered 8,000 miles and attracted 200,000 people, earning Ruth $30,000. Vaudeville also beckoned Ruth. In 1921 he signed a record $3,000-per-week, twenty-week contract to appear on the stage with song-and-dance man Wellington Cross, performing hokey magic tricks and delivering bad one-liners. Five years later his weekly fee for a vaudeville tour soared to more than $8,000.[38]

The new media, however, afforded Ruth his greatest exposure. Newspapers had dramatically expanded their sports coverage since the turn of the century, increasing the space afforded athletics by 50 percent. The fledgling tabloid newspapers, with their emphasis on what critic Silas Bent described as "bigger and bigger headlines . . . more and more pictures," the kind of pictures "a multitude of morons . . . like to see, and the kind of stuff they like to read," carried this trend further.[39] *Daily News* publisher Joe Patterson, wanting "very biff, bang, boom stuff," made Marshall Hunt the tabloid's year-round Babe Ruth correspondent. Wherever Ruth appeared, whether at ball games, nightclubs, or orphanages, Hunt was never far behind. When things slowed down, Hunt would create news opportunities and file exclusive coverage to the *Daily News*.[40]

The tabloids, Sunday rotogravure sections, and weekly magazines of the 1920s stimulated the demand for pictorial images. The sports photograph, long a staple of the press, became even more prevalent. Modern cameras "geared to take a picture in a thousandth of a second or less recorded breathless base slidings and fierce lunges at the ball by energetic batters" observed Lane.[41] Few subjects appeared as often as Babe Ruth. His distinctive physiognomy and insatiable hunger for attention rendered him a natural target for photographers both on and off the field. Ruth's face appeared on the covers not just of major periodicals, but on such arcane journals as *American Boy, Strength*, and *Hardware Age*. Photos of Ruth posing with children, chimpanzees, and celebrities and garbed in an astounding variety of outfits permeated the press. Silas Bent suspected that Ruth was striving for a "pictorial frequency record" to complement his baseball marks.[42]

The Babe had also alighted into an age of motion pictures. The first newsreel for American audiences had surfaced in 1911. By 1919, when *Fox Movietone News* made its debut, four major companies produced news films for exhibition in the nation's theaters. With new features appearing twice each week, the newsreels reached an audience in excess of 30 million people. For major stories the film-makers rushed footage to the theaters almost as quickly as news-paper coverage. Sports coverage accounted for the largest single category of film, arising at its peak to as much as 25 percent of the program.[43] As with radio, the availability of filmed images invited speculation as to their impact on baseball. Walter Lippmann, an-ticipating the onset of instant replay, predicted that "the last vestige of dispute could be taken out of the game . . . if somebody thought it worth while to photograph every play." Ruth naturally appeared frequently in these film clips. In 1920 Educational Pictures of New York, an enterprising movie company, collated available newsreel footage into a series of *Babe Ruth Instructional Films*, including "How Babe Ruth Hits a Home Run" and "Play Ball With Babe Ruth."[44] He was a familiar figure in Fox Movietone, Pathe, Hearst, and Paramount newsreels. Americans could thus see the Babe in action almost as often as they went to a movie theater.

Inevitably, given the public's unflagging desire to see Ruth, of-fers to star in feature films also came his way. Even before he arrived in New York City, Ruth was reported under contract to make several movie shorts. The proposed titles included both the predictable (*Home Sweet Home* and *Touch All Bases)* and the im-probable (*Oliver Twist.)* The films were mercifully never made. During the 1920 season, Ruth's first with the Yankees, Ruth skipped batting practice for a week and arrived at the Polo Grounds each day wearing makeup to star in *Heading Home*, a silent feature that bombed at the box office.[45] This failure tempo-rarily stalled Ruth's acting career as plans to shoot a film with director Raoul Walsh were cancelled. In 1926 Ruth traveled to Hollywood where he filmed *The Babe Comes Home*. Reviews of the movie proved less than flattering. "There is no reason for John Barrymore or any other thespian to become agitated about the matter," commented one reviewer. Ruth, observed another, "was never built for romance under the kliegs." The assessment by Ruth's teammate Mark Koenig was even more blunt. "He couldn't act worth crap," said Koenig. Like its predecessor, *The Babe Comes Home* flopped.[46]

The failure of Ruth's movies to attract an audience spoke less to a lack of interest in the Yankee star than to the inability of a scripted venue to capture his natural exuberance. He came across as stiff rather than animated, shy rather than rambunctious. This often proved true of his adventures in radio as well. In 1921 Harold Arlin at KDKA, pioneering the practice of interviewing famous personalities, naturally sought out Ruth for a broadcast. Taking precautions, Arlin wrote out a speech for Ruth to deliver. The Babe, confronted by a brand-new medium and unfamiliar script, froze in front of the microphone. Arlin quickly grabbed the speech and pretended to be Ruth. Since few people knew the sound of Babe's voice, the ruse worked. Letters to KDKA praised Ruth's surprisingly rich tones.[47]

In later years, Ruth grew more comfortable on the radio but was never at his best with a prepared text. On one occasion he appeared with Graham McNamee on a national broadcast. He had rehearsed his role until he had his timing down perfectly, but when the show began, according to Grantland Rice, Ruth abandoned the script and "was off and running." A line designed to refer to the Duke of Wellington's adage that the Battle of Waterloo had been won on the playing fields of Eton, came out, "As Duke Ellington once said, the Battle of Waterloo was won on the playing fields of Elkton." The listeners and the network, wrote Rice, "got a load of Ruth at his purest that night."[48] Only an unstructured, spontaneous setting could bring out the unalloyed Babe.

The vast dimensions of Ruth's celebrity propelled him into yet another emergent field of the modern era, public relations. The profession had emerged in the first decade of the twentieth century, when business leaders, hoping to offset the adverse images propagated in the muckraking press, began to hire specialists to plant news items portraying them in a more favorable light. In the

1910s John D. Rockefeller employed Ivy Lee to transform the millionaire's negative reputation. Numerous individuals, businesses, and enterprises followed suit. On the eve of American entry into World War I, the Newspaper Publishers Association listed 1,200 people working as publicity agents in New York City. By the mid-1920s an estimated 5,000 agents practiced in New York, 2,000 in Washington, D.C., and presumably similar numbers in other great cities. In Hollywood, studio press agents had grown legion.[49] "The great corporations have them, the banks have them, the railroads have them, all of the organizations of business and social and political activity have them," wrote Frank Cobb in 1919.[50] Two years later Babe Ruth had one as well.

The demands of Ruth's fame and his own natural naivete in business matters made it inevitable that Ruth would need someone to manage his affairs. Promoters approached Ruth with a wide variety of endorsement opportunities and business propositions. In his early years in Boston Ruth employed a friend, Johnny Igoe, to attempt to coordinate his affairs. Igoe, however, could neither rein in Ruth's impulsive instincts and spendthrift ways nor secure or collect adequate compensation for the slugger's efforts. Ruth was never fully paid for his starring role in *Heading Home* (the check from the producers bounced) and at the peak of his home run prowess accepted a paltry five dollars per homer for a syndicated account of each clout.[51] Fortunately for Ruth, in 1921 he fell into the enterprising and benevolent clutches of Christy Walsh.

Walsh was, by his own description, one of "thousands of young dreamers anxious to escape the smaller hometown and hie for the city." He had worked as a sports cartoonist for the *Los Angeles Herald* and in 1919 served as a ghostwriter for World War I hero Eddie Rickenbacker describing the running of the Indianapolis 500. He moved to New York City and worked at an advertising agency until the recession of 1921 led to his dismissal. "I was out of a job in the biggest city in the world and didn't have money for rent," he wrote in his autobiography, *Farewell to Ghosts*. "I was blocking traffic on this great highway to fame." Recalling his experience with Rickenbacker, Walsh decided to form a ghostwriting syndicate, which would offer articles written by professional writers under the byline of celebrities, whose names and thought would attract readers, but who had neither the time, talent, nor inclination to write.[52] Walsh did not invent this concept. Ghostwriters had invaded baseball as early as the 1911 World Series. What Walsh did, according to sportswriter Joe Williams, was "to put the proposition on a sound systematic basis."[53]

In early 1921 Walsh lined up a few clients, including Rickenbacker, but he felt that he needed the biggest celebrity in New York to establish his credibility. Walsh found it amazing that "such a gift from the gods (as Ruth) should be on the loose." The Babe, wrote Walsh, "was pursued by every glib talker in town." Walsh established an outpost outside the Ansonia Hotel, where Ruth made his home, but could never corner the Yankee star. Walsh wisely cultivated an acquaintance with the corner bootlegger, who, in the face of Prohibition, illicitly supplied Ruth with his beer. One evening, Ruth called while the regular delivery boy was on another errand. Walsh volunteered to transport Ruth's order. Ruth, never a man to notice details, did not realize that the gentleman in coat and tie was not the usual emissary. When Walsh informed him of his identity, Ruth laughed appreciatively about the ruse and listened to Walsh's pitch. Walsh promised that, if Ruth would sign an exclusive contract with him, he would increase his earnings from writing from $5 a home run to thousands of dollars a year. He pledged to pay Ruth the first installment of $1,000 within ninety days.[54]

Ruth was no stranger to ghosted stories. In addition to his home run sagas, he had already "written" several articles (including "Why I Hate to Walk" ghosted by Westbrook Pegler) and one book, *The Home Run King—Or How Pep Pindar Won His Title*. He might have just wanted to get rid of the pesky Walsh. For whatever reason, Ruth impulsively agreed to sign a contract naming Walsh as his exclusive representative. On opening day Walsh approached the Babe at the Polo Grounds and handed him a check for $1,000, more than a month ahead of schedule. "I shall never forget the expression on Babe Ruth's face when I handed him a check," recalled Walsh. "Here was a fellow who had been skinned so many times by strangers that I felt the way to win his confidence was to pay in advance."[55]

With Ruth in the fold, Walsh was able to sign up dozens of other top athletes. Although he had originally conceived of a syndicate representing all types of celebrities, Walsh now began to specialize in sports. He became, according to Joe Williams, "the literary godfather of the athletes . . . who harnessed this literary Niagara of writing genius and turned it into artistically useful channels." Thus, "the reading public was assured the best thoughts of the best athletic minds in the best manner."[56]

Walsh's syndicate expanded and prospered, but he retained a special relationship with Ruth. He consolidated Ruth's literary enterprises, raising his writing income from $500 in 1920 to $15,000 in 1921. Walsh also took command of all of Ruth's moneymaking activities, emerging, in Dan Parker's words, as "the man behind the Bam, the man who relieves Babe of his burden of thinking." Before his relationship with Walsh, wrote Parker, "Babe didn't know how to make use of his by-products. But what Armour did for the cow, Christy did for Babe."[57] Walsh lined up Ruth's 1921 vaudeville tour and negotiated Ruth's contract with the Yankees that called for Ruth to receive, on top of his record salary, 10 percent of the gate for all exhibition games. He took charge of Ruth's public appearances, booking him to materialize at various functions, like banquets and county fairs, and arranging for photo opportunities and publicity for Ruth's charitable activities. He hired Ruth out to "guest edit" newspaper sports pages.[58]

Most significantly, Walsh capitalized on the growing market for advertising that surfaced in the 1920s. Newspaper, magazine, and billboard advertising quadrupled between 1917 and 1929. Although copywriters had discovered the power of testimonials long ago, endorsements "gained a new popularity during the 1920s as advertisers searched for a personal approach," according to Roland Marchand.[59] Few figures were as sought after or as willing to endorse products as Babe Ruth. Ruth appeared in advertisements for cigarettes, men's clothing, sporting goods, milk, appliances, kennels, pajamas, underwear, and innumerable other items. He endorsed Cadillacs in New York, Packards in Boston, and Reos in St. Louis. Ruth also became one of the first celebrities to lend his name to an extraordinary variety of products, including Babe Ruth sweaters, Babe Ruth caps, Babe Ruth Gum, Babe Ruth Home Run Shoes, and Bambino Smoking Tobacco.[60]

As Ruth's business manager/publicity agent, Walsh found that he had inadvertently "detoured right smack into the main stem, a grand adventurous thoroughfare of imagination, invention, and high pressure competition." And Ruth, in danger of drowning in a sea of con artists and swindlers, had luckily latched onto a sound life preserver. Walsh combined the proper blend of honesty and chicanery that characterizes the best publicity men. In operating his ghostwriting syndicate, Walsh espoused a flexible code of ethics. "There is a wide difference between illusion and deceit," he averred. Walsh "never knowingly released copy that was 'fake',", although he admitted that emergency circumstances sometimes forced him "to distribute a signed article that had neither been discussed with, nor approved by the author." Walsh never claimed that the athletes wrote their own copy, simply that the article "was written by a man who enjoyed the author's confidence and understood his views on the subject." To cover Ruth, Walsh employed four different ghostwriters, most frequently Bill Slocum, whom Ruth allowed innocently, "writes more like me than anyone I know."[61]

Walsh's early dealings with Ruth embraced the same benign ethical code. Unbeknownst to Ruth, the $1,000 that Walsh paid Ruth on opening day 1921 came not from writing income but rather from a bank loan borrowed at 6 percent interest. Walsh, who undoubtedly collected more than the standard 10 percent agent's fee, earned enough to retire in 1937 at age forty-six. "He had grown rich showing Babe how to get rich," noted Dan Parker. But, avowed Parker, the Ruth/Walsh axis "is the most equitable partnership ever established in athletics." Walsh "steers him away from the phony investments that formerly lured Babe and his lucre. He has taught him that there is a rainy day ahead and it behooves even a demigod to lay aside an odd penny for that evil day."[62]

Walsh battled desperately and usually in vain to get Ruth to curb his spending. Despite Ruth's dogged resistance ("You never have any fun outta life," Ruth would complain), Walsh managed to channel a small fraction of the slugger's immense earnings into an irrevocable trust fund. He placed the money in annuities, rather than stocks, thus cushioning Ruth from the impact of the stock market crash. "They will not have to hold benefit games for the Babe, though he has been the most profligate athlete since John L. Sullivan," predicted Parker in 1927. When Ruth retired, the trust, amounting to a quarter of a million dollars, allowed him to live comfortably for the remainder of his life.[63]

Walsh also helped to steer Ruth's popular image away from a Rabelaisian bad boy of the early 1920s to the beloved benefactor of charities and children celebrated in countless photographs. Although Ruth appeared at hospitals and orphanages willingly and often without fanfare, Walsh guaranteed that these visits would not be forgotten, cementing the saintly side of Ruth's persona.[64] Assisted by Walsh's keen instincts, Ruth became the first true celebrity of the modern era, recognized as much for his fame as for his audacious feats. He symbolized not only the exuberance and excesses of the 1920s, but the emergent triumph of personality and image in a modern America suddenly positioned to glorify these attributes. Lavishly chronicled on radio and in print, memorialized in photos and film, elevated to a new form of adoration in testimonial advertising, and molded by shrewd public relations, Ruth fulfilled people's fantasies and embodied their new reality.

Baseball itself rode the coattails of the public's fascination with Ruth and the new media that brought him to their doorsteps. Baseball fans relished their expanding universe, and so the national pastime prospered in the 1920s as never before. Yet baseball's brain trust, never the most farsighted of thinkers, saw potential gloom on the distant horizon. The ever-vigilant, ever-pessimistic, but nonetheless prescient *Sporting News* posited a dark vision of the technological future: "When Ruth hits a homer . . . a film will catch him in the act, wireless will carry it a thousand miles broadcast and the family sitting in the darkened living room at home will see the scene reproduced simultaneously on the wall. Then what will become of baseball?"[65]

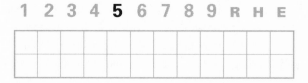

Adjusting to the New Order
Branch Rickey, Larry MacPhail, and the Great Depression

The Great Depression ensnared baseball slowly, but inexorably. In 1930, as the nation slid into a deep recession, baseball flourished. Major league hitters, led by Chicago Cub Hack Wilson, who hit a National League record 56 home runs and drove in an astonishing 190 runs, and Babe Ruth, who again led the American League in home runs, treated fans to an unprecedented offensive outburst. A heart-stopping four-team pennant race in the National League further stimulated attendance. Thus, despite the economic downturn, attendance in 1930 topped ten million for the first time and major league profits soared to almost $2 million, more than triple the 1929 surplus. The season seemed to uphold the conventional wisdom that "poor business years are good baseball years." In past recessions, baseball had found that unemployed workers, many with savings to tide them over, had ample time and adequate funds to attend games. The latest economic slump, reasoned baseball owners, would be no different.[1]

The year 1931, however, hinted at a disturbing reality. Attendance fell by more than 15 percent and income plummeted. Although the major leagues as a whole showed a $217,000 profit, most teams lost money, and several others barely edged into the black. In 1932, as the Depression dragged into its third year with no end in sight, baseball finally felt its full brunt. Attendance dropped below 7 million for the first time since 1919. All but four clubs ran deficits. Total losses exceeded $1.2 million. The *Literary Digest*, in an article entitled "Hard Times Hit the Majors," observed, "Whereas in July 1930 it was a case of scaring up four bits for a bleacher seat at the Stadium, [now] it [was] a matter of getting enough for a cheap meal." The hemorrhaging escalated in 1933 as the major league deficit grew to $1.65 million.[2]

Thus, in the early 1930s the baseball industry confronted the dilemma shared by a multitude of American businesses during the Great Depression. Faced by declining revenues and a reduced demand for their product, what was the appropriate strategy for survival? Commissioner Kennesaw Mountain Landis, echoing the classic conservative reaction to the Depression, preached patience. "The American people love baseball," commented Landis. "They will return as paying customers as soon as they have money." Washington Senator owner Clark Griffith agreed. "Our business has held up at least as well as any other. We're just going on the way we are," he cautioned those calling for change. Others, however, argued that the response to the Depression necessitated, in President Franklin D. Roosevelt's words, "bold, persistent, experimentation." The Great Depression, warned *The Sporting News*, required baseball officials to "adjust themselves to the new order, or make way for others not so shackled by precedent."[3] Rather than passively endure the storm, baseball might seize the opportunities offered by economic stringency to restructure and rationalize its operations or develop new ways to stimulate interest in the game.

As was true for most businesses, the solutions to baseball's problems lay in the realm of supply and demand. Alone among baseball officials, Branch Rickey and Larry MacPhail, two very disparate men, stepped forward to accept these challenges. Rickey, the veteran baseball man, attacked the supply side of the equation, creating the farm system to streamline the player development process. MacPhail, a newcomer more attuned to the dictates of twentieth-century consumer culture, addressed the question of demand. Rickey and MacPhail were, according to Gerald Holland, "as far apart as their favorite drinks," martinis for MacPhail and root beer and milk for Rickey. They began as allies and ended as bitter personal enemies. Yet, asserts Holland, they did "more to change the face of baseball than any other two men or two hundred men ever connected with the game."[4]

The prosperity of the 1920s had obscured several fundamental weaknesses in baseball's economic foundation. The industry had, in effect, achieved horizontal integration, defeating or absorbing all of its rivals in the decades before World War I. Yet its haphazard relationship with the minor leagues, its primary source of players, precluded any true vertical integration, preventing teams from controlling the process and cost of player development. Furthermore, as G. Edward White has observed, baseball leaders maintained a limited vision of the potential audience for major league games. Attendance had boomed in 1920 but then remained relatively static throughout the remainder of the decade. As an industry, baseball had been slow to recognize the emerging consumer society and reluctant to incorporate new technology into its domain. It had never fully embraced radio as an ally, and it had totally ignored the possibility of night baseball.[5]

In the face of the Depression most baseball men demonstrated minimal imagination. They refused to lower ticket prices, reasoning, probably correctly, that the impoverished masses could not afford games at any price. Instead, faced by plummeting revenues and staggering financial losses, the baseball industry followed the path of most American businesses, "adjusting to the new order" by driving down labor costs. At the December 1931 winter meetings, owners agreed to pare down the active rosters from twenty-five to twenty-three players. Teams hired fewer coaches and front-office employees. A growing number of clubs turned to player-managers, eliminating one more slot from the payroll. The greatest savings came from slashing player salaries. The 1932 winter meetings produced a formal resolution to roll back these expenses.[6] "The problem of the top-heavy payroll is the true cause of much of the financial difficulty that now embarrasses Major League Baseball," explained *Baseball Magazine* editor Frank C. Lane. "Salaries and wages elsewhere have been drastically reduced. Boom time salaries are no longer defensible in baseball."[7]

The new policy spared few. Commissioner Landis voluntarily accepted a reduction in pay from $65,000 to $40,000. Babe Ruth, despite again "having a better year than the President," saw his salary drop $28,000 below his $80,000 peak. The cuts trickled down throughout the major leagues as owners reduced their payrolls by an estimated $800,000. Philadelphia Athletics owner Connie Mack replicated his 1914 purge. In that year, faced by higher salaries inspired by the upstart Federal League, Mack had broken up his championship team and sold off his stars. After more than a decade in debasement Mack rebuilt another dynasty, winning three consecutive pennants from 1929 to 1931. In 1932, however, the Athletics dropped to second place and attendance fell to less than half its 1929 levels. Faced by a high payroll and declining income, Mack again divested his team. Between October 1932 and December 1935, Mack sold the contracts of Al Simmons, Lefty Grove, Mickey Cochrane, Jimmy Foxx, and others, garnering $590,000 while returning his club to the bottom of the standings in the process.[8]

Not all members of the baseball establishment advocated inaction and retrenchment. Chicago Cubs president Bill Veeck, Sr., suggested scheduling interleague play during July and August to stimulate attendance. Some clubs sought to attract more fans by scheduling doubleheaders on Sundays, a variation on the increasingly common business practice of offering premiums. The two leagues adopted a livelier ball to inflate offensive production for the 1934 season, hoping, in the words of sportswriter John E. Wray, that "The new deal baseball will act like the New Deal dollar is supposed to—it would stimulate business."[9] It is probably also not coincidental, as historian Bill James has noted, that baseball's three greatest honors—the Most Valuable Player Award, the All-Star Game, and election to the Hall of Fame—emerged from the maelstrom of depression as a psychological and financial boost for the troubled game. "Baseball needed to show that it was not in a state of decadence," argued *Chicago Tribune* writer Arch Ward in proposing the annual all-star exhibition, the proceeds of which would provide a charity fund for indigent former ballplayers. National League President Ford Frick also recognized the broad economic value of a baseball Valhalla, when he threw his support behind promoters from Cooperstown, New York, who wished to establish a Hall of Fame in baseball's alleged birthplace.[10]

St. Louis Cardinal General Manager Branch Rickey adopted a broader view of the opportunities offered by the Great Depression. Raised in the late nineteenth century on a midwestern farm, Rickey instinctively saw the challenge in terms of production. As general manager of the St. Louis Cardinals, the products that Rickey planted, harvested, and ultimately sold to the public were the men who played the game. From the beginning of his career in baseball management Rickey had focused his energies on the recruitment, development, and training of these athletes. He maintained close contacts with college baseball programs to identify top prospects at an early stage. He hired and encouraged the efforts of scouts, most notably his brother Frank, who scoured the nation for talented youngsters. As a field manager with the St. Louis Browns, Rickey stressed the importance of drills and fundamentals to perfect his output. "He is a Professor of Baseball," wrote a sportswriter in 1914. "His efficiency courses in sliding, baserunning, and batting mark a new departure in the game."[11] Throughout his career Rickey focused on devising new training techniques and technology to further refine his product.

When Rickey became the general manager of the St. Louis Cardinals in 1916, he felt the problem of player development even more acutely. Operating in one of the smallest markets in the major leagues and competing against the crosstown Browns, Rickey lacked the financial resources to compete with more prosperous teams for players. In the early decades of the twentieth century minor league teams tended to be independent operations with the right to sell their players to the highest bidder. Knowledge of Rickey's interest in a prospect often allowed these club owners to drive up the price or to sell the player to another club. In 1919 the cash-poor Cardinals paid $10,000 to purchase the contract of pitcher Jesse Haines. Unable to sustain this level of expenditure, Rickey needed an alternative method to produce his players more cheaply and efficiently. He knew that he could "find them young . . . develop them . . . and keep them until they were ready for the Cardinals." But he "needed . . . the place to train them," beyond the reach of other clubs.[12]

"Good farmer that he was," observed Harold Seymour, "Rickey decided to grow his own crop on his own land." The invention of the farm system, Rickey contended, was "the result of stark necessity," a desperate solution to meeting "a question of supply and demand for young players."[13] In the past some major league clubs had owned minor league affiliates or had entered into working agreements with them. Rickey, however, was the first to envision a vertically integrated network of teams owned by the parent club, ranging from the lowest to the highest levels of Organized Baseball through which players might be trained, sifted, and selected en route to the major leagues. In 1919, around the time of the Haines purchase, the Cardinals bought a half-interest in the Fort Smith, Arkansas, franchise. Over the next decade, the Cardinals secured control of four other teams as well.

The system, although still modest, worked exceptionally well. Although the Cardinals had ranked among the laggards in league attendance during the first half of the 1920s, by 1926 the team had built a squad that would win four pennants in six years. Attendance doubled and Rickey supplemented the team's profits by selling off his surplus—players who did not make the Cardinals—to other teams. Despite the limited size of its market, the Cardinals became the most profitable franchise in the major leagues. Because Rickey collected 10 percent of all profits on top of his $40,000 a year salary, he shared handsomely in the rewards of the farm system.[14]

The onset of the Depression enabled Rickey to dramatically expand and perfect his organizational pyramid. Minor league operators, struggling to make ends meet, welcomed affiliation with a major league club that would underwrite payroll costs and other expenses. With salaries dropping as low as $300 a month, the burden on the Cardinals of assuming these obligations also declined. Between 1929 and 1936 the Cardinals added twenty-three clubs to their empire. By 1940 they owned thirty-two teams and had working agreements with eight more. The majority of these clubs were at the lowest, or D level, of the minors. To fill out their rosters, Rickey expanded his scouting system and established three-day try-out camps that attracted thousands of young men anxious for a chance to play professional baseball. The Cardinals selected the most promising of these athletes and signed them to contracts. Baseball's reserve clause guaranteed that these "green peas," as one sportswriter dubbed them, would be bound to the Cardinals as long as that club had a use for them. They could remain on the farm, as Rickey would say, until they "ripened into money."[15]

"Out of quantity comes quality," preached Rickey, expounding his own version of Darwinian selection.[16] The Cardinals finished in first or second place fifteen times in twenty seasons between 1930 and 1949. Players developed in the Cardinal farm system appeared on rosters throughout the major leagues. Other teams attempted to emulate the Rickey model in the 1930s, but only the Yankees approached his level of success.

Commissioner Landis watched the expansion of Rickey's empire with growing horror. Landis feared that a relationship in which major league teams moved players at will, without regard to the fortunes of their minor league affiliates, would make a mockery of competition at the lower levels and destroy the independence and fabric of minor league baseball.[17] Revealingly, Landis and other critics likened Rickey's system not to a farm, which still possessed a certain sanctity in American folklore, but to the modern chain store movement, a bête noire of twentieth-century populism. The chains, which replaced local businesses with affiliates of national corporations, had attracted a growing opposition from small businessmen in the 1920s and 1930s. Yet, as Rickey understood, they also reflected the incorporation of small-town America into a national culture. Radio, newsreels, and advertising had blurred the boundaries between national and local. The problems of minor league baseball stemmed more from a lack of fan support than a lack of independence.[18]

During the early 1920s veteran owners Barney Dreyfuss of the Pittsburgh Pirates and Frank Navin of the Detroit Tigers had convinced Landis that Rickey's scheme was impractical and that his pyramid would ultimately implode. Thus, Landis, although ruling that a major league club could not own stock in more than one team in a league, initially did nothing to block Rickey's broader design. By 1930, however, Landis had seen enough. He openly accused Rickey, whom he privately referred to as "that sanctimonious so-and-so," of "raping the minors."[19] Rickey defended himself in a speech to the national 1930 Minor League Convention. Rickey noted that thirteen minor leagues had failed in the preceding years. None of those leagues had major league affiliations. Those teams aligned with the Cardinals, he pointed out, "had not suffered at all in comparison with those who are unable to continue." Taking aim at Landis, seated nearby, Rickey assailed the do-nothing approach to the Great Depression. "I deplore the philosophy of indifference that is going on," he asserted. In 1933, the owners, defying Landis, unanimously approved a rule allowing the establishment of farm systems. In later years Rickey argued that dependence had brought stability to the minor leagues. "The farm system," he maintained, "was the savior of (minor league) baseball."[20]

In addition to raising fundamental issues about the growing incursions of the national economy into the local marketplace, Rickey's strategies also revealed an often callous exploitation of labor during the hard times of the Depression. Rickey was notorious for his parsimony in salary negotiations with major and minor league players alike. "It was easy to figure out Mr. Rickey's thinking about contracts," said Chuck Connors, who played for Rickey before moving on to an acting career. "He had both players and money—and just didn't like to see the two of them mix." Enos Slaughter, who played his way up through Rickey's Cardinal system, commented, "When you talked money to him you could get none of it. He was always going to the vault to give you a nickel's change." That Rickey received a percentage of team profits made these one-sided negotiations all the more galling. "He knocked down everyone's salary," recalled minor league catcher Lou Kahn, "and he put the difference between what they got and what they should've got, in his own pocket."[21]

Rickey justified his treatment of ballplayers in the time-honored tradition of the nineteenth-century capitalist entrepreneur. Work agreements were contracts entered into by individuals as equals, extending opportunity, rewarding the worthy, and uplifting all participants. "I offered millhands, plowboys, high school kids a better way of life," he stated. "They rose on sandlots to big city diamonds. And no young man who signed a contract with me has ever suffered educationally or morally. . . . When he quit the Cardinal chain, he had learned the lesson 'clean living' and 'moral stamina.' "[22] But in light of the youth of the players, the desperate economic times, and the one-sided ironclad guarantees provided by the reserve clause, Rickey's practices could hardly be called equitable. Many viewed Rickey's labor policies in a less flattering light. Lou Kahn complained, "I was just a number to Branch Rickey. He ran baseball factories and he screwed his players every way but right side up." Jim McLaughlin, later a major league scouting director, described Rickey and "the way he manipulated people and then made those pious speeches" as an "ethical fraud."[23]

Although not a baseball player, Larry MacPhail first entered Branch Rickey's orbit via the Cardinal farm system. Unlike Rickey, who had settled on a career in baseball at an early age, the peripatetic MacPhail had, at age 40, already tried his hand in a variety of businesses. The son of a Michigan banker, MacPhail practiced law with a Chicago firm and ran a department store in Nashville, Tennessee, before enlisting in the army in World War I at age twenty-seven. A combat veteran of two major campaigns, MacPhail barely escaped court-martial for his participation in a quixotic attempt to kidnap the Kaiser at the war's end. He mustered out to a life in Columbus, Ohio, in which he owned first a glass company, then an auto dealership, and finally a construction firm. He also refereed college football games and was active in the Ohio Golf Association. Although many of his business ventures were successful, the failure of a building project left him broke at the dawn of the Depression.[24]

In search of a new enterprise, MacPhail acquired an option to purchase the Columbus Senators of the American Association. Knowing that the Cardinals were looking for minor league affiliates, MacPhail telephoned Rickey, who expressed an interest in acquiring the team. According to MacPhail's biographer, Don Warfield, when MacPhail asked Rickey for an appointment, Rickey, assuming a day's train travel between Columbus and St. Louis, told MacPhail to be there at three o'clock, expecting to see him on the morrow. MacPhail dashed to the airport, caught a plane to St. Louis, and appeared at Rickey's office that afternoon. Duly impressed by MacPhail's industriousness, Rickey agreed to purchase the Columbus franchise and installed MacPhail as the club president.[25]

The circumstances of their first meeting demonstrate a critical difference between the two men. Although they were only nine years apart in age—Rickey born in 1881 and MacPhail in 1890—the two men reflected the generational divide of the centuries. Rickey represented the world of the impoverished nineteenth-century agricultural producer, MacPhail the affluent twentieth-century modern. Both men were known for their verbosity, but reporters depicted Rickey as a traditionalist preacher, MacPhail as an expansive blusterer. Rickey, who also became an avid flyer, was not averse to innovation, but he was rarely as quick as MacPhail to understand the potential of new technology. Whereas Rickey viewed the baseball business from a perspective of containing costs, MacPhail embodied the consumer component of modern capitalism. Revealingly, while MacPhail frequently spoke of "what the customers want" and the "fellow who sits out there in the bleachers," Rickey, the most quoted man in baseball history, left no remembered adages about fans.

MacPhail's stint with the Columbus team (renamed the Red Birds on its affiliation with the Cardinals) proved a dress rehearsal for his future baseball enterprises. He took over a floundering operation at the worst possible moment. Columbus had not won a pennant in twenty-three years and had landed in the second division for fifteen straight years, including a sixth-place finish in 1930. The club had lost $500,000 during the prosperous 1920s and now faced the Great Depression with dim prospects. MacPhail, however, believed that he could convince local fans to come out to the games. With Rickey and the Cardinals providing the players and in essence handling the supply side, MacPhail focused on stimulating demand. Refashioning ramshackle Neil Park into a more attractive place became his first priority. MacPhail surrounded his Columbus Red Birds in a sea of bright red, with large red birds painted on the outfield fence, a bright red flagpole in centerfield, and ushers, vendors, and ticket sellers bedecked in red fedoras and neckties. He added distance markers down the foul lines and piped in music over the loudspeaker system. Boys under sixteen could attend games for free five days a week, while women could buy a season ticket for three dollars.[26]

The 1931 season wreaked devastation across the minor leagues, but in Columbus attendance increased by 50 percent. The Red Birds were the only team in the American Association to turn a profit. MacPhail's success convinced Rickey and Cardinal owner Sam Breadon to build a new ballpark in Columbus. On opening day 1932, 18,000 fans turned out to celebrate MacPhail's new showcase. For those who could not attend, MacPhail had the game broadcast over the radio—a Columbus first.

On June 17 MacPhail unveiled yet another twist: night baseball. The technology for night games had longed existed, but Oganized Baseball, displaying its usual wisdom, had been slow to adopt it. Although night games promised an opportunity for working people to attend games and a relief from the heat of the summer, baseball officials dismissed it as "unnatural." Clark Griffith called it " "bush league stuff . . . just a step above dog racing."[27] As early as 1929 the Kansas City Monarchs of the Negro National League had equipped themselves with a traveling lighting unit enabling them to play night games. In 1930 several minor league teams introduced night baseball. On April 18 Independence, Kansas, hosted the first night game in the minor leagues, using a portable lighting system. In Des Moines, Iowa, the hometown Demons installed permanent floodlights and on May 2 drew national attention and a live NBC radio broadcast to its first night game. Other minor league teams followed suit.[28]

Columbus's 1932 entry into the ranks of teams offering night baseball secured the club's success. With a new stadium, night games, and radio broadcasts, the Red Birds drew a record 310,000 fans, outdrawing the parent Cardinals. Yet if MacPhail's ability to draw crowds pleased Rickey, their divergent personalities and inclinations inevitably led to discord. Rickey, the archetype of nineteenth-century Protestant morality, believed in a world of frugality, moderation, and temperance. MacPhail dressed in bold, garish clothes (a "municipal eyesore," according to one Columbus colleague) and swaggered boldly through life, employing a voice likened by one sportswriter to "the call of an adult male moose" and another as "a living loudspeaker in human form."[29] His physical appearance with bright red hair and a face freckled to a similar shade enhanced his impact. MacPhail spent lavishly, entertained frequently, and, Prohibition notwithstanding, drank to excess. Rickey blamed MacPhail for cost overruns at the new stadium and particularly bristled at his lavish office appointed with walnut paneling and Oriental rugs. On one occasion MacPhail became embroiled in a drunken dispute with a hotel manager and uprooted his team in the middle of the night. In May 1933, after a controversy arose over the handling of players sent by Rickey to the Red Birds, Rickey forced a reluctant MacPhail from the club presidency.[30]

Yet the apparent rift between the two men was misleading. MacPhail possessed the irrepressible, uninhibited type of persona that alternately exasperated and captivated Rickey. Despite his prohibitionist leanings, Rickey often surrounded himself with talented but intemperate employees. He once described his famed Cardinal "Gas House Gang" as "a high class team with nine heavy drinkers," among them the tempestuous Leo Durocher who later managed

Rickey's Brooklyn Dodger teams. MacPhail likewise felt a kinship to Rickey. "He thinks the world of you," wrote MacPhail's brother Herman to Rickey after the 1933 dispute. "And he never tackled anything as wholeheartedly as he did baseball in Columbus. If there is any way possible for you to sponsor him . . . I wish you would because nobody had the influence over him you seem to have." Later that year, the Cincinnati Reds approached Rickey about taking over the club. Rickey declined, but recommended MacPhail for the job. "He has great imagination and is completely fearless," Rickey reportedly told the team's directors. "He has ideas enough to revive baseball enthusiasm in your city. He's a wild man at times, but you've got to stay with him."[31]

The Reds had finished in last place for three consecutive seasons. Only 218,000 fans had paid their way into the ballpark in 1933. But MacPhail had what Roger Kahn would call a "passion [for] salvaging wrecks." He officially took control of the club in December 1933 and within a month was hailed as "a revelation" in the baseball world. "He thinks baseball needs promotion and he is ready to promote," commented the *New York Evening Post*.[32] Recognizing the need for more substantial financial backing, MacPhail approached Powel Crosley, Jr., one of Cincinnati's wealthiest citizens. Crosley manufactured radios and refrigerators. More significantly, he owned and operated several radio stations. Major league owners were still leery of radio, many of them blaming it for their attendance woes during the Depression. The Cardinals prohibited broadcasts of all games in 1934, and the three New York teams agreed to a five-year radio blackout. MacPhail, on the other hand, convinced Crosley that radio and baseball offered a perfect marriage of interests. Not only would game broadcasts stimulate interest in the Reds, they would also enhance the popularity of his radio station. In February 1934 Crosley purchased a controlling share of the Reds. Among the assets he brought with him was a young radio announcer already in his employ named Walter "Red" Barber, whom Crosley assigned to announce the Reds' games in 1934.[33]

Crosley promised MacPhail ample capital to spruce up the local stadium, create a farm system, and purchase players for the Reds. As at Columbus, MacPhail immediately painted the ballpark, now renamed Crosley Field, outfitted the ushers in sprightlier uniforms, and brought in young women to peddle cigarettes in the stands. Always interested in setting precedents and garnering publicity, MacPhail chartered two airplanes to fly the Reds to Chicago, a major league first. Although several players opted for a train, MacPhail generated excitement by placing a shortwave transmitter on board and having Barber send live reports back to Cincinnati.[34] Yet no amount of hoopla could have rescued the Reds in 1934. The team lost twenty-three of its first twenty-eight home games, sank quickly into last place, and actually drew fewer fans than the preceding year.

MacPhail sought salvation in lights. At the winter meetings in December he asked the National League to lift its ban on night baseball. "Young man, you can write this down. Not in my life-time or yours will you ever see a baseball game played at night in the majors," Commissioner Landis warned him before the meeting. Opposition by any single club could doom his proposal, and Giants owner Charles Stoneham vowed, "I'll never vote for night baseball." MacPhail, who had prepared a forty-page brief on the virtues of night games, spoke for three hours to convince his National League rivals. In the end seven teams voted approval and Stoneham abstained, thus allowing the plan to go forward.[35]

MacPhail enlisted General Electric to design the best possible illumination system and recruited President Franklin D. Roosevelt to switch on the lights via telegraph from Washington, D.C. On May 24, 1935, more than 20,000 fans, perhaps ten times the usual weekday crowd, descended on Crosley Field to attend the Reds' first night contest. Drum and bugle corps, high school bands, and fireworks enlivened the occasion. The new Mutual Broadcasting System featured the game as its first national sports event. Red Barber, announcing for both Cincinnati and Mutual, later described the evening:

A silence fell over the crowd as the magic moment of 8:30 approached. Precisely on time, President Franklin D. Roosevelt pressed a telegraph key in the White House. . . . A mighty roar went up from the crowd. . . . There was light—tremendous, almost blinding light.[36]

Other major league officials remained unimpressed. Yankee General Manager Ed Barrow dismissed it as a fad that "will never last once the novelty wears off." Detroit Tigers owner Frank Navin foresaw "the ruination of baseball." Night games, he protested, "change the players from athletes to actors."[37] MacPhail, always more attuned to fan desires, recognized the sport's inherent theatricality. "Sure, night baseball is a spectacle with a lot of hoopla," MacPhail countered his critics, "but that's what the customers want. Baseball under the lights looks more glamorous, colorful . . . the uniforms look better, the players look faster and bigger, and the fans react accordingly." They "loved the brilliantly lit park set against a background of darkness," recalled Barber.[38]

The Reds played seven night games in 1935, attracting almost 124,000 people to these contests. Special excursion trains brought people from cities and towns throughout the Ohio Valley to witness the spectacle.[39] Total Cincinnati attendance more than doubled, and the club turned a profit for the first time in years. The Reds even climbed out of the cellar, attaining sixth place, the club's highest finish since 1928.

The team continued to improve in the standings and at the gate in 1936. But MacPhail's alcoholic self-destructiveness again began to surface. "It seemed he couldn't live without success," as Harold Parrott observed. "Worse yet, he couldn't live with it." MacPhail seemed increasingly unable to control his temper or moderate his booming voice. "We were slightly afraid of our father. When he was angry he was formidable," remembered his son Lee. The senior MacPhail often humiliated his employees, who bore the brunt of his volatility. During the 1936 season he punched and broke the jaw of a policeman during an altercation at a downtown Cincinnati hotel. "Boy, isn't that great publicity," he allegedly commented when confronted by Crosley. As the season drew to a close in mid-September, MacPhail left the Reds, voluntarily by some reports, fired according to others.[40]

"There is a thin line between genius and insanity," Leo Durocher would later say of MacPhail, "and in Larry's case it was sometimes so thin you could see him drifting back and forth." In 1936 MacPhail himself clearly recognized that he was treading perilously close to a psychological brink. He had developed a nervous facial tic and allowed his drinking to get out of hand. According to Rickey's friend and biographer Arthur Mann, after leaving Cincinnati MacPhail stopped in St. Louis to see Rickey. He told Rickey that he was heading back to rest with his family in his native Michigan and wouldn't "drink another drop for a year." Rickey responded, "Why a year? Why put a time limit on it at all?"[41]

MacPhail remained out of baseball for the 1937 season, but another wreck in need of salvage soon beckoned. The Brooklyn Dodgers had lost over a half-million dollars in three years. The Ebbets and McKeever families, who shared club ownership, were at constant loggerheads. The Brooklyn Trust Company, the bank that had underwritten the team's losses, now declined further financial support for the feuding regime. As at Cincinnati in 1934 the Dodgers' Board of Directors unsuccessfully attempted to woo Rickey away from the Cardinals. At this point, depending on which tale one believes, either Rickey or National League President Ford Frick or both suggested MacPhail as the Dodger savior. MacPhail requested and received absolute control over all operations and a virtually unlimited credit line from Brooklyn Trust.[42]

MacPhail attacked the Dodger debacle with his usual energy. As always, he made the ballpark his first priority. Neglect had plunged Ebbets Field into a severe state of disrepair. MacPhail resurfaced the infield, replaced broken seats, renovated the dugouts, clubhouses, and restrooms, and repainted the entire facility an eye-catching turquoise blue. To create a more hospitable atmosphere, MacPhail imported ushers from Chicago to instruct the infamously surly Brooklyn employees in courtesy. He introduced the Knothole

Club, which offered free admission to thousands of children. He also hatched plans to install lights for night baseball.[43]

MacPhail recognized, however, that no amount of renovation could overcome a bad team. "People won't come to see us play day or night if we are lousy," he barked. Without the luxury of an established farm system and instinctively inclined to purchase what he needed, MacPhail bolstered the Dodgers' lineup by buying players from other teams. He paid the Phillies $50,000 for first baseman Dolph Camilli and made innumerable lesser acquisitions. He also began building a farm system and bolstered the Dodgers' scouting staff, laying the groundwork for the future. "I don't know how to make money without spending plenty of it," he explained.[44]

Despite MacPhail's best efforts, the Dodgers started poorly on the field and at the gate. As in the past, MacPhail responded with night baseball. Remarkably, despite the success of his Cincinnati experiment three years earlier and the extensive use of lights in the minors, no other major league team had dared brave the darkness. The American League had unconditionally banned night baseball. Over the protests of the Yankees and Giants, MacPhail installed a $72,000 six-tower lighting system and scheduled the first game on June 15 against his former squad, the Cincinnati Reds. He supplemented the festivities with fireworks, marching bands, and a race featuring Olympic legend Jesse Owens. Cincinnati hurler Johnny Vander Meer rose to the occasion by hurling his second consecutive no-hitter, a feat unmatched in baseball history.[45]

Three days later, with people still buzzing about the historic evening, MacPhail staged another coup, signing Babe Ruth, who had been out of baseball since his retirement in 1935, to coach at first base. Twenty-nine thousand fans turned out for Ruth's debut, and 50,000 more attended a series of exhibition games designed specifically to showcase the Babe. "Keep the customers awake and you'll keep 'em coming," MacPhail explained his philosophy.[46]

When the dust had settled on the 1938 season, although the Dodgers finished in seventh place, they had drawn almost 200,000 more fans than in 1937. MacPhail, reported *The Sporting News* in

August, used these "profits of his successful debut as Brooklyn's baseball boss to strengthen the Dodgers for the future," buying five players from other clubs.[47] Although MacPhail had laid out hundreds of thousands of dollars for ballpark improvements, lights, and players, the Dodgers posted an operating deficit of only $11,000, a vast improvement over earlier years.

MacPhail stepped up the pace in 1939. He released Babe Ruth and hired shortstop Leo Durocher as player-manager. When the five-year New York City blackout on radio broadcasts expired, MacPhail and the Dodgers refused to participate in an extension. He contracted with 50,000-watt station WOR to carry the games, signed an agreement with General Mills as a sponsor, and brought in Red Barber from Cincinnati to handle the games. "I'll have the most powerful station and the best sponsor and the world's greatest announcer at the mike," boasted MacPhail.[48] The Dodgers broadcast both home and away games to their growing mass of devotees.

"There was little he wouldn't try," recalled Barber. "The dead hand of tradition never gripped him. . . . One of the things he dearly loved was to be first . . . particularly . . . in something new and constructive." Thus, when NBC, flush with the success of live television demonstrations at the New York World's Fair, suggested televising a Dodger game, MacPhail jumped at the chance. MacPhail, the team board of directors, and a handful of writers watched in the press box as Barber, working without a monitor and unaware of where the cameras were pointed, announced the game from an upper deck seat behind third base. "The players were clearly distinguishable, but it was not possible to pick out the ball," reported Harold Parrott in *The Sporting News*. Nonetheless, recognizing the potential of the new technology, MacPhail initiated weekly telecasts of Dodger games in 1940.[49] That year MacPhail also reintroduced air travel to baseball, flying the Dodgers home to Brooklyn after a western road trip. Thirty thousand fans flocked to Floyd Bennett Field to greet the team.[50]

The 1939 version of the Brooklyn Dodgers finished in third place, trailing only the pennant-winning Cincinnati Reds, a team that MacPhail had resuscitated and largely assembled, and Rickey's St. Louis Cardinals. Attendance approached the million mark and club profits exceeded $140,000. The Dodger improvement continued in 1940, when the team finished second to Cincinnati.

By the start of the 1941 season MacPhail had become an institution in Brooklyn. His wardrobe, nearly scandalous in Columbus and Cincinnati, grew even more garish in Brooklyn. "He wears loud check suits and ties with stripes two inches broad," wrote Robert L. Taylor in a *New Yorker* article entitled "Borough Defender." "He likes color contrasts, when wearing a pair of pale green trousers with a jacket of yellow plaid. Most of his shirts are custom made and silk." Although he had his critics among the press (Dan Parker translated his initials L. S. to stand for "Lucifer Sulphurous"), he had won over most of the sportswriters by building a new press box with an adjoining club room equipped with a bar, affectionately dubbed "Larry's Saloon."[51] When the Dodgers edged past Rickey's Cardinals to win the pennant in 1941, drawing 1.2 million fans and ushering in the golden age of Brooklyn baseball, MacPhail became a local hero.

The Dodger triumph in 1941, following so closely on the heels of two Cincinnati pennants, elevated MacPhail alongside Branch Rickey to the pinnacle of the baseball world. Their approaches still differed dramatically. Rickey's Cardinals, who depended on player sales for the bulk of their income, had not bought anyone since Jesse Haines in 1919. By contrast, MacPhail's favorite activity, as Taylor noted, was buying ballplayers. "His main belief in building up the Brooklyn club," observed Taylor, "has been that in order to make a dollar you have to spend as much as fifty cents." By the start of the 1941 season he had purchased three catchers, twelve pitchers, six infielders, and eight outfielders at a cost of a million dollars.[52] MacPhail, despite his relative inexperience in baseball, proved a shrewd judge of talent. His spending spree brought standouts Pee Wee Reese, Dixie Walker, Billy Herman, and Whitlow Wyatt to the Dodgers.

Throughout the early years in Brooklyn MacPhail retained a strong relationship with Branch Rickey. In 1939 MacPhail hired

Branch Rickey, Jr., who had been laboring in his father's shadow at St. Louis, to direct and build the Dodger farm system. Rickey returned the favor, promising MacPhail's son Lee a job in the Cardinal organization when he graduated from college and later offering him a position as a general manger with Toronto in the high-level International League.[53] In 1938, after Commissioner Landis, in his strongest attack on Rickey's farm pyramid, ordered seventy-four Cardinal farmhands released from their contracts, Rickey had entrusted Pete Reiser, the best of those players, into MacPhail's safekeeping. MacPhail promised that the Dodgers would hide Reiser in the low minor leagues until the Cardinals could legally buy back his contract after the 1940 season.[54]

By the early 1940s, however, relations between the two men had begun to sour. Their first conflict stemmed from the Reiser deal. MacPhail, despite the best of intentions, could not keep the talented twenty-year-old hidden. Leo Durocher, unaware of MacPhail's promises, had spotted the player at spring training in 1939 and inserted him into the Dodger lineup in three games, coincidentally against the Cardinals. Reiser hit four home runs and reached base eleven consecutive times. Durocher bragged about his "find" to sportswriters, who nicknamed Reiser "Pistol Pete" in their dispatches. MacPhail ordered Durocher not to play Reiser again and sent the young player to the Eastern League. The damage, however, had been done. When Reiser tore up the Eastern League in 1939 and again in the early months of 1940, MacPhail informed Rickey that any attempt to return him to St. Louis would bring down the wrath of the Brooklyn fans and press. "Branch, they'd lynch me," MacPhail reportedly cried. Knowing that his archenemy Commissioner Landis was closely monitoring the situation, Rickey acquiesced.[55]

In June 1940, perhaps as partial compensation for Reiser, MacPhail sent four fringe players and, more significantly, $125,000 to the Cardinals for all-star outfielder Joe Medwick and pitcher Curt Davis. MacPhail justified the high price in the belief that the acquisition of Medwick would secure a Dodger pennant. On June

19, however, just one week after Medwick had joined the club, Cardinal pitcher Bob Bowman beaned him with a fastball. As Medwick lay unconscious on the ground, MacPhail, doubtless under the influence of alcohol, exploded onto the field. "Waving his arms and roaring in his vibrant moose voice, he galloped across the diamond to the pitcher's box," according to one account, challenging Bowman and other Cardinals to a fight. Some, including Red Barber, believe that MacPhail had convinced himself that Rickey had ordered the beaning.[56]

MacPhail's inebriated excursion onto the field was one of several signs that he had once again begun to unravel. As his son Lee recalled, "After a couple of martinis," his father would grow "insulting and pugnacious." In 1939 he punched *Brooklyn Eagle* reporter Harold Parrott in the nose for leaking a potentially damaging story. He repeatedly fired and instantly rehired manager Leo Durocher. According to Rickey biographer Murray Polner, reports reached Rickey of the oppressive and unpredictable atmosphere that permeated the Dodger offices. As Harold Parrott later wrote, "There was no doubt that when [MacPhail] roared in the Dodger office, everybody jumped." Another reporter called MacPhail's tenure the "reign of terror." Dodger farm director Branch Rickey, Jr., told a friend that he "hated to enter the office every morning." Another friend informed the senior Rickey that his son "is really getting himself worked up more and more about the thought of quitting the Brooklyn organization immediately." Office politics grew more difficult when MacPhail left his wife of three decades to take up with a much younger Dodger switchboard operator.[57]

In 1942 MacPhail added yet another innovation to his repertoire. At his daughter's urging he had installed an organ in the park and hired Gladys Goodding to serenade the fans and play rally music.[58] Meanwhile, the Dodgers won a club record 104 games, but lost the pennant to the Cardinals on the last day of the season. After the final game MacPhail called a press conference. "The five years I have spent in Brooklyn," he announced tearfully, "have been the happiest years of my life." His reign, he proclaimed, had ended. With war raging in Europe and Asia, MacPhail, now fifty-two years old, had reenlisted in the army as a lieutenant colonel.[59]

MacPhail departed with a flourish of patriotism, but other factors were also at work. He had grown characteristically restive, the five years in Brooklyn exceeding his tenure in any previous position that he had held. The challenge of rebuilding had ended. Nor were the Dodger directors and shareholders necessarily disappointed to see him go. MacPhail had worked miracles with the team, converting a perennial second division finisher into a pennant winner and paying off almost a million dollars in debts while generating a surplus of $300,000. In the process, as Gerald Eskenazi has noted, he had "made America Brooklyn Dodger conscious," making the team synonymous with the nation during the war years. Yet MacPhail's behavior and endless spending had alienated some of his employers. Most of the Dodger revenues had been funneled back into operations, leaving little in the way of realized profits. Some have speculated that the Dodgers did not plan to renew his contract. When MacPhail asked the team to establish an interim management in his absence, the Board of Directors declined this offer and instead accepted his resignation.[60]

Nor did the Dodgers hesitate in naming MacPhail's replacement. On November 1 they announced that they had lured Branch Rickey away from the Cardinals. Rickey, whose relationship with Cardinal owner Sam Breadon had frayed badly, welcomed the opportunity to be reunited with his son and to assume leadership of a pennant-contending club.

The transition from MacPhail to Rickey did not go smoothly. MacPhail no doubt resented being replaced by his old mentor and rival, especially after Rickey acquired an ownership interest in the team, a goal that had eluded MacPhail. According to Harold Parrott, when Jack MacDonald, MacPhail's former secretary, transferred his allegiance to Rickey and authored a mildly critical article in the *Saturday Evening Post*, provocatively entitled "The Fall of the House of MacPhail," the former general manager responded angrily with a message quoting a biblical verse. Rickey immediately recognized the passage as a reference to Judas. "Our egomaniacal friend is appointing himself as Christ Almighty in that telegram," commented Rickey. The exchange, wrote Parrott, now a Rickey assistant, "was the first inkling I had of a real falling out between these two giants."[61]

Rickey also apparently still bore ill feelings toward MacPhail over the abortive Reiser transaction. Reiser had more than fulfilled his promise, leading the National League in hitting in 1941. The next season he had injured himself crashing into a fence, only to be allowed by MacPhail to continue playing against doctors' orders, compounding his maladies. "That character should have never been entrusted with anything so fine," a bitter Rickey reportedly told Parrott.[62]

MacPhail's drinking buddies among the press dreaded Rickey's ascension. At the annual New York writers show, Louis Effrat sang "Will the lights go on again . . . in Larry's Saloon?"

> Will Branch serve Ruppert's beer
> Or Seven-Up on draft?
> It seems a shame to waste the gin,
> And serve us Rickey Finn.

Many mercilessly attacked Rickey for both his handling of players and his pontificating style, labeling him "El Cheapo" and dubbing his office "The Cave of the Winds." They began to call his son Branch, Jr., the "Twig."[63]

Rickey's approach to building a team remained diametrically opposed to MacPhail's. Rickey vowed to end the practice of buying players and moved to dispose of some of the older high-salaried players whom MacPhail had accumulated. He traded fan favorites Joe Medwick and Dolph Camilli. Since the club also lost Pee Wee Reese, Pete Reiser, and Hugh Casey to the military, the Dodgers won twenty-three fewer games during Rickey's first year at the helm than they had in 1942 and slipped to third place. Nineteen forty-four proved even worse. The Dodgers finished in seventh place, forty-two games behind the Cardinals. Reporters and fans blamed Rickey for the club's decline. Rickey, however, had already shifted Dodger priorities. With his eye firmly focused, as always, on player development, Rickey expanded the farm system that MacPhail and Rickey, Jr., had started. He also launched two behind-the-scenes initiatives that delivered little immediate assistance to the Brooklyn club but would yield significant long-term results. Unlike other teams who curtailed their scouting efforts during the war years fearing to lose players to the war, Rickey, gambling on a relatively short conflict, stepped up his recruitment efforts and signed players too young for the draft. In addition, Rickey secretly began scouting the Negro Leagues and the Caribbean for African-American players. These strategies would make the Dodgers a dynasty in the postwar years.[64]

MacPhail, meanwhile, plotted his return to baseball. Even as he worked at the Pentagon, MacPhail nonetheless found time to peruse the baseball horizon for postwar opportunities. He found one literally in Rickey's backyard where ownership of the New York Yankees had become available. While still in the military, MacPhail lined up Dan Topping, an heir to Anaconda Copper, and construction magnate Del Webb to underwrite his purchase of the Yankees. In February 1945 MacPhail left the army to become a co-owner and general manager of baseball's most fabled franchise.[65]

With the two now hostile rivals competing in the same city, conflict was inevitable. The controversial issue of racial integration became their first battleground. Pressures were building on all three New York clubs to add African-American players to their rosters. In April 1945 *Amsterdam News* reporter Joe Bostic brought two Negro League players to the Dodger training camp demanding a tryout. A second confrontation occurred ten days later in Boston when Wendell Smith of the *Pittsburgh Courier* coerced the Red Sox into staging a workout for future major leaguers Jackie Robinson and Sam Jethroe. On April 24 major league baseball created a Committee on Baseball Integration. Rickey, MacPhail, and *Baltimore Afro-American* reporter Sam Lacy were named to the panel. The group never met because "MacPhail always had some excuse," remembered Lacy. Later that summer, New York Mayor

Fiorello La Guardia formed his own Committee on Baseball, with Rickey and MacPhail again represented.[66]

In October 1945 MacPhail publicly expressed his views on the race issue. He condemned "political and social minded drumbeaters" for their efforts on behalf of integration and called for a strengthening of the Negro Leagues. This might allow a few African Americans of "ability and character" to move into Organized Baseball. A few weeks later MacPhail's opinion became moot.[67] On October 23 Branch Rickey announced that Jackie Robinson had been signed to play for the Dodgers' top farm club at Montreal, marking the beginning of the end of baseball's color line.

MacPhail believed that in acquiring Robinson, Rickey had "double-crossed his associates for his own personal advantage." He made no public criticism, but almost a year later he found the opportunity to vent his rage at the man who had succeeded him in Brooklyn. In July 1946 the major leagues created a steering committee to define the challenges facing Organized Baseball. MacPhail headed the committee and wrote its report, including a lengthy section on the "Race Question." As before, he attacked advocates of integration "who know little about baseball and nothing about the business end of its operation." Tellingly, MacPhail questioned the ultimate consequences of increased black attendance at the ballparks. Noting that Robinson's presence in the International League had attracted thousands of black fans, MacPhail worried that "a situation might be presented . . . in which the preponderance of Negro attendance . . . could conceivably threaten the value of Major League franchises." MacPhail concluded his report with a coldly calculated attack on Rickey. "Your committee does not desire to question the motives of any organization or individual who is sincerely opposed to segregation," wrote MacPhail. However, "The individual action of any one club may exert tremendous pressures on the whole structure of Professional Baseball," threatening the stability of several clubs.[68]

The differences between Rickey and MacPhail on this matter reflect the growing personal animus between the two men and a number of more substantive issues as well. MacPhail, unlike

Rickey, clearly had little sympathy for integration. Furthermore, MacPhail's Yankees drew a considerable income from the rental of Yankee Stadium and their minor league ballparks in Newark and Kansas City to Negro League teams. Most significantly, their attitude toward desegregation sprang naturally from their approach to baseball. Although religion and morality played critical roles in Rickey's historic undertaking, labor considerations were never far from his thinking. "The greatest untapped reservoir of raw material in the history of the game is the black race!" he told his family. Furthermore, since Rickey, with his distaste for buying players, had no intention of paying the Negro League teams for this "raw material," he had uncovered a remarkably cheap source of talent. MacPhail, on the other hand, had his eye on the box office. "I've always believed that the ball club belongs to the fellow who goes out there and pays his way in," he told a reporter when he purchased the Yankees. "I've always tried to keep faith with the fans and I believe I've been fairly close to the fellow who sits out there in the bleachers."[69] These fellows, he believed, would not want to sit next to Negroes. The resulting decline in attendance, MacPhail feared, would be devastating.

As the Jackie Robinson drama played itself out in 1946 and 1947, both the Dodgers and the Yankees and Rickey and MacPhail headed on a collision course. The New York club acquired by MacPhail was not in any sense a wreck, but by Yankee standards the team had fallen on hard times. After winning seven pennants in eight years, the Yankees finished third in 1944 and fourth in MacPhail's first season at the helm. Wartime attendance had remained modest. MacPhail arrived too late to institute significant changes in 1945, but for the 1946 campaign he inaugurated his trademark makeover. He ordered lights installed at Yankee Stadium and undertook a major renovation of the ballpark itself. He created baseball's first Stadium Club, a members-only restaurant for season ticket holders. He also expanded the general catering facilities. Amid the postwar euphoria attendance shot upward throughout the major leagues in 1946, but nowhere more so than in the Bronx. Despite a third-place finish, the introduction of night games and other MacPhailian promotions brought a major league record 2,265,512 fans to Yankee Stadium, almost doubling the previous club best.[70] In 1947 the Yankees returned to form, running away with the American League pennant, while again drawing over 2 million fans. MacPhail also sold the television rights to Yankee home games, allowing millions more to enjoy the club's resurgence.

Rickey's Dodgers had also experienced a rebirth. With the war over, the return of Reese and other stars and the harvest of Rickey's well-stocked Dodger farm system returned Brooklyn to pennant contention. In 1946 the team finished two games behind the Cardinals and attracted almost 1.8 million fans to Ebbets Field. The addition of Jackie Robinson would drive the team to the National League Championship and new attendance highs in 1947.

Robinson's debut, however, was almost overshadowed by a bizarre offshoot of the growing Rickey–MacPhail feud. During spring training in 1947 Rickey and Leo Durocher had protested the presence of gamblers in MacPhail's box seats in a game in Havana. MacPhail, complaining that he had been slandered and libeled, filed charges against the Dodgers with Baseball Commissioner Happy Chandler. Chandler held hearings to investigate the allegations. In a baffling decision, handed down just days before Robinson's scheduled debut, Chandler fined both the Yankees and Dodgers for irregularities and, most significantly, suspended Dodger manager Leo Durocher for the 1947 season.[71]

Many believed that Chandler and MacPhail had conspired to punish Rickey for signing Robinson. Others dismissed the Robinson angle, but nonetheless saw Chandler, whom MacPhail had handpicked for the commissioner's job in 1945, as a tool of the Yankee owner. When MacPhail charged that Rickey himself had orchestrated Durocher's dismissal, Rickey exploded with rage. "I've taken all I can stand. I'm suing MacPhail for a million dollars," he raged.[72] Rickey never followed through on this threat, but tensions continued to simmer as the Yankees and Dodgers headed for a showdown in the 1947 World Series.

Few World Series in baseball history match the drama and excitement of that 1947 classic. Five of the seven games were settled by two runs or less. In the fourth game Yankee pitcher Bill Bevens carried a no-hitter into the ninth inning only to lose when Cookie Lavagetto doubled with two outs and two on. In the sixth game, Dodger outfielder Al Gionfriddo robbed Joe DiMaggio of a game-tying three run home run with one of the most memorable catches in baseball history, allowing the Dodgers to tie the Series at three games apiece. The Dodgers grabbed an early lead in the seventh game, but the Yankees prevailed to win the World Championship.

The victory should have marked MacPhail's ultimate achievement. He had restored the Yankees to dominance, breaking attendance records in the process. The four World Series games at Yankee Stadium had attracted an average of over 70,000 fans. He had triumphed over his former team and his archrival. MacPhail embraced the moment with an orgy of alcoholic self-destruction. "That's it! It's all over! I'm through. No more pressure! I'm retiring from baseball and resigning as president of the Yankees," he screamed into the microphone at the postgame celebration, tears running down his inflamed cheeks. He berated his former secretary John MacDonald, then punched him in the eye and knocked him down. He unceremoniously fired George Weiss, who had built the Yankee farm system. Seeing Rickey in the crowd, he put one arm around the old man's shoulder and extended the other for a handshake. Speaking in a voice so low as to be almost inaudible, Rickey told him, "I am taking your hand only because there are so many people watching. But don't you ever speak to me again!" By the next day Topping and Webb had purchased MacPhail's interest in the Yankees, and he had severed all relations with the club.[73]

MacPhail's fourth, final, and most ferocious exit from baseball largely brought his tempestuous relationship with Rickey to an end. The two men would clash again briefly in February 1948 when Rickey charged that other baseball owners had unanimously voted against his decision to bring Robinson to the majors. MacPhail denounced Rickey's statements as "false and inflammatory," adding, "Churchill must have had Rickey in mind when he said, 'There but for the grace of God goes God.' " Ten years later a still bitter

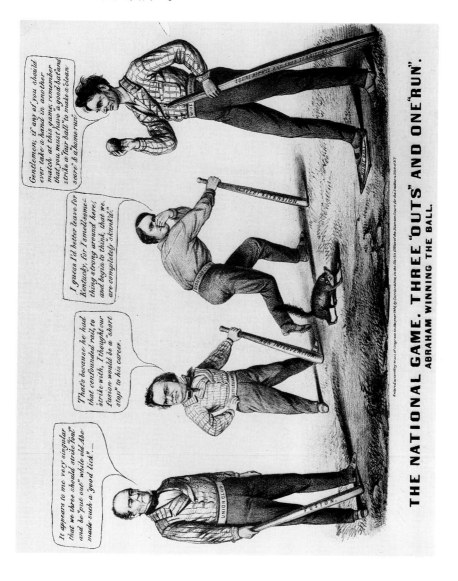

This 1860 Currier & Ives lithograph using baseball as a metaphor for politics in the aftermath of Abraham Lincoln's election to the presidency demonstrates how rapidly baseball had grown in popularity and familiarity in the pre–Civil War years. (LIBRARY OF CONGRESS)

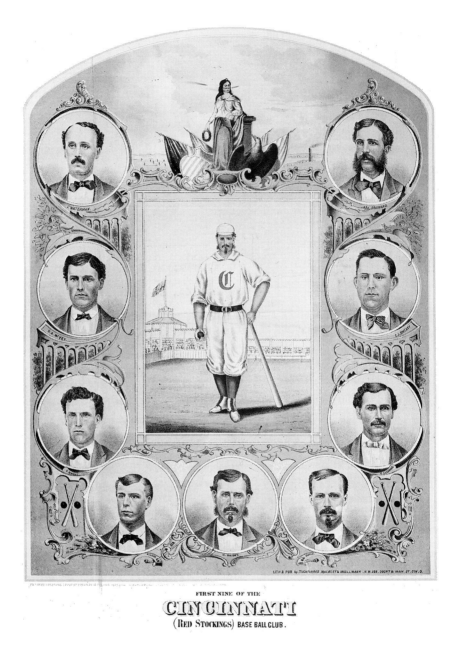

FIRST NINE OF THE

CINCINNATI

(RED STOCKINGS) BASE BALL CLUB.

The 1869 Cincinnati Red Stockings, baseball's first all-professional team, toured the nation, attracting a reported 179,000 fans and ushering in a new age for the sport. (LIBRARY OF CONGRESS)

Henry Chadwick, "The Father of Baseball,"
invented baseball scoring, the box score, and
many of the statistics still in use today. (NATIONAL
BASEBALL HALL OF FAME)

Albert Spalding, star pitcher, manager,
owner, founder of the National League,
and sporting goods magnate, played a
critical role in the development of the
national pastime in the nineteenth century. (TRANSCENDENTAL GRAPHICS)

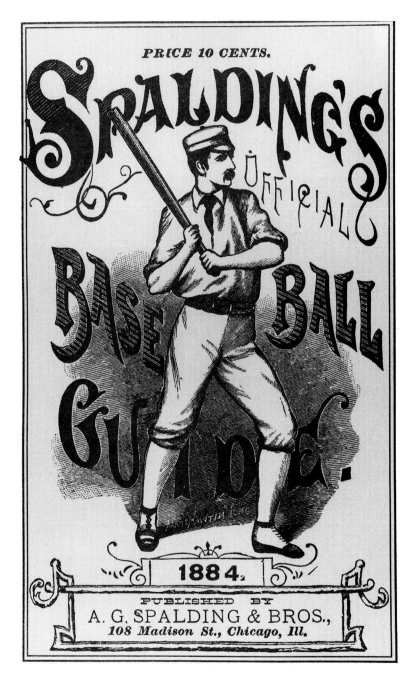

Spalding Baseball Guide, 1884, edited by Henry Chadwick. (TRANSCENDENTAL GRAPHICS)

Four future owners as young baseball players: Charles Comiskey as player-manager of the St. Louis
Browns in 1886; Connie Mack, a catcher with Meriden in the Connecticut League in 1884; Clark Griffith as pitcher for Milwaukee in the Western League in 1889; and a slender John McGraw, third baseman for Olean in the New York Penn League, 1890. (LIBRARY OF CONGRESS; NATIONAL BASEBALL HALL OF FAME;
LIBRARY OF CONGRESS; NATIONAL BASEBALL HALL OF FAME)

The 1913 World Series pitted Connie Mack's Philadelphia Athletics against John McGraw's New York Giants, who were in the series for the fifth time in ten years. (TRANSCENDENTAL GRAPHICS)

Connie Mack and John McGraw as grand old men of the game in the 1930s. (NATIONAL BASEBALL HALL OF FAME)

Above: Crowds gather in front of a Play-O-Graph Scoreboard to follow World Series action. (NATIONAL BASE-BALL HALL OF FAME)

Left: Graham McNamee broadcasting the World Series in the early 1920s. "He painted word pictures that other minds could feast upon." (NATIONAL BASEBALL HALL OF FAME)

Above: A scene from the 1926 movie *The Babe Comes Home* starring Babe Ruth and Anna Q. Wilson. "He couldn't act worth crap," said New York Yankee teammate Mark Koenig. (NATIONAL BASEBALL HALL OF FAME)

Left: "The most equitable partnership ever established in athletics," Babe Ruth and his agent/manager Christy Walsh. (NATIONAL BASEBALL HALL OF FAME)

Branch Rickey confers with Larry MacPhail, whom he replaced as Brooklyn Dodger general manager, at the 1943 all-star game. MacPhail is wearing his army uniform. (NATIONAL BASEBALL HALL OF FAME)

Branch Rickey, in a familiar pose, signs a young prospect to a contract. The prospect, Duke University all-American basketball and baseball star Dick Groat, will become an All-Star shortstop for the Pittsburgh Pirates. (CORBIS-BETTMAN/NATIONAL BASEBALL HALL OF FAME)

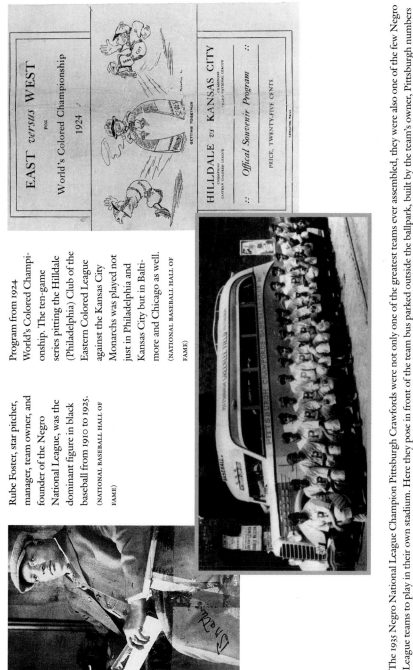

Rube Foster, star pitcher, manager, team owner, and founder of the Negro National League, was the dominant figure in black baseball from 1910 to 1925. (NATIONAL BASEBALL HALL OF FAME)

Program from 1924 World's Colored Championship. The ten-game series pitting the Hilldale (Philadelphia) Club of the Eastern Colored League against the Kansas City Monarchs was played not just in Philadelphia and Kansas City but in Baltimore and Chicago as well. (NATIONAL BASEBALL HALL OF FAME)

The 1935 Negro National League Champion Pittsburgh Crawfords were not only one of the greatest teams ever assembled, they were also one of the few Negro League teams to play in their own stadium. Here they pose in front of the team bus parked outside the ballpark, built by the team's owner, Pittsburgh numbers king Gus Greenlee. (NATIONAL BASEBALL LIBRARY/TRANSCENDENTAL GRAPHICS)

Baseball's Shot Heard 'Round the World. Bobby Thomson drives
Ralph Branca's pitch into the left field stands at the Polo Grounds
to end the 1951 playoffs. (NATIONAL BASEBALL HALL OF FAME)

Below, Bobby Thomson surrounded by the jubilant New York
Giants as he steps on home plate following his game-winning
home run. (CORBIS-BETTMAN/NATIONAL BASEBALL HALL OF FAME)

On the opposite page, New York Giants' announcer Russ Hodges
in the press box in 1951, the year he made his unforgettable call of
Thomson's home run. (THE SPORTING NEWS)

Milwaukee celebrates the Braves' National League pennant in 1957 in a ticker-tape parade complete with Indian braves. (AP/NATIONAL BASEBALL HALL OF FAME)

Throngs of excited San Franciscans welcome the Giants and their star center fielder, Willie Mays, on the day before the 1958 season opener pitting the Giants against the Los Angeles Dodgers in the first major league game played on the Pacific Coast. (AP/NATIONAL BASEBALL HALL OF FAME)

A major league record 78,672 fans attended the Dodgers' first home game at the Los Angeles Coliseum on April 18, 1958, but most sat far from the action in the cavernous, misshapen arena. (AP/NATIONAL BASEBALL HALL OF FAME)

In 1998 Sammy Sosa and Mark McGwire rejuvenated interest in baseball with their pursuit of Roger Maris's single season home run record. Fans followed this historic chase via Internet, cable television, and satellite transmissions, symbolizing a new age in baseball communications. (ED NESSEN/THE SPORTING NEWS)

MacPhail told reporter Gerald Holland, "Branch Rickey never did a damn thing for me except to fire me at Columbus."[74]

In the end, their personal differences had overwhelmed their common love for the national pastime. Yet together, Rickey and MacPhail had prepared baseball for the economic realities of post–World War II America. Rickey, in his ceaseless attempts to find better ways to "put the dollar sign on the muscle," had perfected the farm system and rationalized player development. All teams would emulate this model in the 1940s and 1950s. In signing Jackie Robinson, Rickey had positioned baseball in the forefront of American social progress and identified new sources of players to sustain and expand baseball's talent pool. MacPhail, focusing his efforts on "the fellow who digs down in his jeans and clicks the turnstiles," had ushered baseball into the consumer age. National League President Warren Giles once dismissed MacPhail as a "sensationalist . . . whose only contribution to baseball consisted of painting the seats at Cincinnati, Brooklyn and New York red or yellow instead of green."[75] But MacPhail, in his startlingly brief thirteen-year period as a baseball executive, had dramatically enhanced the vistas for baseball attendance and profitability. His profound faith in the ability of radio to simultaneously generate interest and revenue streams, his unswerving commitment to night baseball, and his experiments with television had restored baseball's popularity and redefined the ways in which millions of fans experienced the game. His interest in air travel paved the way for expansion beyond the eastern and midwestern states.

These lessons of supply and demand derived by MacPhail and Rickey from the scarcity of the Great Depression would prove even more valuable in the affluent society of the postwar years. Their visible hands had reshaped the baseball marketplace, establishing a new order for a modern age.

Unreconciled Strivings
Baseball in Jim Crow America

A ndrew "Rube" Foster epitomized African-American pride. A tall, imposing, right-handed pitcher, he had migrated from his native Texas to Chicago in 1902 to play for the Chicago Union Giants. When warned that he might face "the best clubs in the land, white clubs," he announced, "I fear nobody." Over the next decade he established himself as perhaps the outstanding pitcher in all of baseball. In 1911 he formed his own team, the Chicago American Giants, and won a reputation as a managerial genius equal to his friend, John McGraw. Nine years later Foster, seeking to "keep colored baseball from control of the whites" and "to do something concrete for the loyalty of the Race," created the Negro National League. Foster criticized white owners for not letting African Americans "count a ticket [or] learn anything about the business," and called for a league dominated by black men. "There can be no such thing as [a black baseball league] with four or five of the directors white any more than you can call a streetcar a steamship," he asserted. Foster urged black fans: "It is your league. Nurse it! Help it! Keep it!" Yet Foster's intense racial pride notwithstanding, he also made his ultimate goal clear. "We have to be ready," he proclaimed, "when the time comes for integration."[1]

Rube Foster—and indeed, the entire experience of blacks in baseball in early twentieth-century America[2]—exemplifies elements of Booker T. Washington's call for the development of separate economic spheres so that his race might prepare itself for ultimate inclusion in American life. Yet black baseball also captured what Washington's rival, W.E.B. Du Bois, labeled the "twoness" of the African-American experience. "One ever feels his twoness—an American, a Negro," wrote Du Bois, "two souls, two thoughts, two unreconciled strivings; two warring ideals in one dark body, whose dogged strength alone keeps it from being torn asunder." The architects of black baseball embodied this dualism. They strove to create viable enterprises that served their communities and simultaneously might win a measure of respectability in the broader society. These ventures would prepare them for the day on which, according to Du Bois's vision, it would be "possible for a man to be both a Negro and American, without being cursed and spit upon by his fellows, without having the doors of Opportunity closed roughly in his face."[3]

The essence of black professional baseball is far more elusive than that of its white counterpart. The major leagues always constituted the epitome and cultural core of mainstream baseball, but the formal Negro Leagues represented no more than a segment of the black baseball experience. No leagues existed until 1920, and even during their halcyon days official contests never constituted more than perhaps a third of the games played. Some of the strongest black teams and best players performed outside the league structure. Top teams often boasted names like the Homestead Grays, Bachrach Giants, or the Hilldale Club, reflecting affiliations not to major cities but to people and smaller communities. The most popular attractions often involved exhibitions against white semiprofessional and professional teams. In all of these many guises and varieties, black baseball constituted a vital element of African-American culture, while also dramatizing the contradictions and challenges of survival in a world dominated by whites.

Within the African-American community, the officials, players, and teams of black baseball symbolized pride and achievement while creating a sphere of style and excitement that overlapped with the worlds of black business, politics, religion, and entertainment. During the baseball season Negro League teams constituted a constant presence in the black community. Placards announcing the games appeared in the windows of local businesses, along with advertisements featuring player endorsements and commands to "get those pretty clothes" for the "opening day . . . Fashion Parade."[4] In Kansas City fans could purchase tickets in a number of locales where African Americans congregated, including the Monarch Billiard Parlor, Stark's Newspaper Stand, the Panama Taxi Stand, and McCampbell's and Hueston's Drug Store. The Elbon and Lincoln movie theaters would show pictures of the players, advertisements for the games, and newsreel footage of the lavish opening day ceremonies.[5]

Local businesses rallied around the teams. Some, like Herman Stark's clothing store in Detroit, offered prizes to the first player to hit a home run or get a hit in a Sunday or opening day contest.[6] Several cities featured booster clubs, like the Hilldale Royal Rooters and Baltimore's Frontiers Club, that supported their teams. The Kansas City Booster Club, the most lavish of these organizations, included both black and white merchants whose stores served the black community. Formed in 1926, the Kansas City Boosters organized the opening day parade, sponsored banquets for the players, and staged beauty contests at the ball game.[7] These businesses profited, in turn, from black baseball. "The cafes, beer joints, and rooming houses of the Negro neighborhoods all benefited as black baseball monies sometimes trickled, sometimes rippled through the black community," writes Donn Rogosin. After the 1944 East-West all-star game in Chicago, reported Wendell Smith, "Hot spots were all loaded, and so were most of the patrons."[8]

African-American baseball also provided one of the most popular features of black newspapers. As early as the turn of the century the *Indianapolis Freeman* had discovered that baseball coverage attracted readers. Sportswriter David Wyatt, who had played for the Cuban Giants and Chicago Union Giants from 1896 to 1902, reported on news of black baseball from all over the country. The Indianapolis ABCs and other teams would arrange matches by placing ads in the *Freeman*.[9] Other black weeklies began covering the game more seriously after 1910. The *Philadelphia Tribune* forged a close alliance with Ed Bolden's Hilldale Club. Bolden advertised games in the *Tribune* and provided press releases and game results. Beginning in 1914 the *Tribune* began to print box scores and in 1915 published Bolden's weekly column, "Hilldale Pickups."[10] Black newspapermen, led by Wyatt, played key roles in the creation and promotion of the Negro National League in 1920. "Behind this opening should be the concentrated support of every race man in Detroit," asserted the *Detroit Contender*. "If the league succeeds your race succeeds; if the league fails, the race fails. . . . Our ability to put over large projects will be measured largely by the way we handle this one."[11]

Nonetheless, reporting in the African-American journals was frequently sketchy. Black newspapers could not afford to send writers to accompany clubs on the road and depended heavily on reports submitted by the teams. This source proved highly unreliable, as the traveling squads often failed to call in or refused to reveal losses. In addition, since many of the black weeklies appeared on Saturday, they tended to focus on previews of the following day's contests, rather than results of the previous week, making it difficult for fans to follow a team with any consistency. Nonetheless, by the 1920s and 1930s all the major black weeklies had substantial sports sections with regular coverage and standout columnists like Frank A. (Fay) Young of the *Chicago Defender*, Wendell Smith of the *Pittsburgh Courier*, and Sam Lacy of the *Baltimore Afro-American*. The black press played a critical role in promoting the East-West all-star game, the showcase event of Negro League baseball. The newspapers printed ballots and lists of eligible players and by 1939 top performers received as many as 500,000 votes. "The success of the game was made by Negro newspapers," commented Fay Young. "It was the Negro press that carried the percentages, the feats of the various stars all through the year, and it was the readers of the Negro newspapers who had knowledge of what they were going to see."[12]

Owners and officials of black clubs often ranked among the most prominent figures in the African-American community. Club officials participated actively in local business, fraternal, and civil rights organizations. Ed Bolden, owner of the Philadelphia-based Hilldale Club in the 1920s, belonged to local black fraternal groups and the Citizen's Republican Club. Kansas City Monarchs' secretary Quincy J. Gilmore was the guiding force behind the local Elks Club and the Negro Twilight League that brought together industrial, youth, and semiprofessional teams in the Kansas City area. Homestead Grays owner Cum Posey served on the Homestead school board.[13] Bolden, Posey, Rube Foster, and others wrote regular columns for local black newspapers.

Several team owners figured prominently in civil rights activities. Olivia Taylor, who inherited the Indianapolis ABCs from her husband, became president of the Indianapolis NAACP chapter in 1925.[14] Newark Eagle owner Effa Manley was an indefatigable campaigner against discrimination. In the years before she and her husband Abe purchased the ball club, Manley had achieved prominence in New York City as the secretary of the Citizen's League for Fair Play, which waged successful campaigns against Harlem businesses that refused to employ African Americans. In Newark Manley served as the treasurer of the New Jersey chapter of the NAACP and on several occasions held ballpark benefits for the organization. At one event the Eagles sold NAACP "Stop Lynching" buttons to fans. Manley also joined the "Citizen's Committee to End Jim Crow in Baseball Committee" created by the Congress of Industrial Organizations in 1942.[15]

Black teams hosted numerous benefit games for African-American charities and causes, raising funds for churches, hospitals, youth groups, and civil rights bodies. The Kansas City Monarchs staged benefits for the Negro National Business League and

the Red Cross. The Newark Eagles regularly raised money to pur-
chase medical equipment for the Booker T. Washington Com-
munity Hospital. During World War I the Indianapolis ABCs and
Chicago American Giants played games on behalf of the Red
Cross, and in the 1920s Hilldale played fund-raisers for war vet-
erans. The first black baseball game at Yankee Stadium pitted the
Lincoln Giants and Baltimore Black Sox in a 1930 benefit for the
Brotherhood of Sleeping Car Porters. The outbreak of World War
II prompted additional efforts.[16]

The players themselves often had close ties to the cities in which
they performed. Many teams recruited from the local sandlots and
discovered some of their best players literally perched on their
doorsteps. Hall of Fame outfielder Oscar Charleston, who grew
up on Indianapolis's East Side, served as a batboy for the ABCs
before joining the squad as a player. He performed alongside Frank
Warfield, "the pride of Indianapolis's West Side." The Homestead
Grays discovered Josh Gibson playing semiprofessional baseball in
Pittsburgh's Hill district. Memphis Blues pitching ace Verdell
Mathis grew up within a short walk of Martin Field. Effa Manley's
Eagles frequently found their best players—including Monte Irvin,
Larry Doby, and Don Newcombe—in the Newark area.[17] The Bir-
mingham Black Barons snatched the fifteen-year-old Willie Mays
from a local high school.

The players often made the Negro League cities their year-round
homes and became fixtures in their communities. In Detroit in the
1920s players found winter jobs in the local automobile plants.
Turkey Stearnes and other Detroit Stars worked in factories owned
by Detroit Tigers co-owner Walter O. Briggs, glad to hire them
in his legendarily grimy and unsafe paint shops, but not on his
baseball team. In Pittsburgh many of the Crawfords found work
as lookouts for owner Gus Greenlee's gambling operations.[18] Some
athletes stayed on in the cities where they had won their fame,
opening up bars or other small businesses. John Henry "Pop"
Lloyd, who had played for, among other teams, the Bachrach Giants of Atlantic City, settled there on retirement and reigned as "a

sort of foster father" to the city's children. Lloyd became the commissioner of the local little league and had a neighborhood ball field named in his honor.[19]

Those who did not have homes in the city often resided during the season at the finest black hotels. In an age when most mainstream hotels even in northern cities barred African Americans, each major city featured a showplace hotel where traveling athletes, entertainers, and members of the black elite lodged and congregated. These were the places, as poet Amiri Baraka describes Newark's Grand Hotel, where "the ballplayers and the slick people could meet."[20] In Detroit the players stayed at the Norwood, which also housed the Plantation nightclub. In Baltimore the Black Sox lived at the Smith Hotel, owned by the city's black Democratic political boss. Street's Hotel in Kansas City, located at Eighteenth and Vine Streets, was the place, according to its manager, that "everybody that came to KC stopped at."[21]

As a teenager in Newark, Baraka reveled in mixing with the postgame throngs at the Grand Hotel, where "Everybody's super clean and high-falutin'." Monte Irvin recalls, "To the fans, the hotel presented an opportunity to join the ballplayers' special circle."[22] This circle often included not just ballplayers, but the entertainment royalty of black America—jazz musicians, dancers, actors and actresses, theater and movie stars, and boxers like Jack Johnson and Joe Louis. Indeed, a close bond formed between the itinerant athletes and performers. Entertainers often could be found at the ballparks, rooting for their favorite clubs and clowning around with their favorite players. The Mills Brothers loved to don Pittsburgh Crawford uniforms and work out with the club. When they appeared at team owner Gus Greenlee's Crawford Grille, Satchel Paige, a talented singer, would return the favor, joining them on stage for impromptu jazz sessions. In Memphis, where Martin Park bordered the Beale Street music district, bluesman B. B. King would set up near first base and sing as the fans filed in. Lena Horne, whose father was Gus Greenlee's right-hand man, appeared frequently at Negro League games. The New York Black Yankees, co-owned by dancer Bill "Bojangles" Robinson, attracted a parade of celebrities to games at Dyckman's Oval in Harlem. When Count Basie was in Kansas City on a Sunday, he headed out to see the Monarchs, "because that's where everyone else was going on a Sunday afternoon."[23]

The games themselves, particularly season openers and Sunday games, were festive occasions in the black community. As the *Chicago Defender* reported in 1923, fans would turn out for the first home game "like a lot of bees hidden away all winter . . . getting active when the sun shines."[24] The contests often marked the culmination of daylong celebrations. David Wyatt, a former player turned sports reporter, described the scene in Indianapolis in 1917:

> The big noise, the mammoth street parade, swung into motion promptly at 10 o'clock upon Saturday. There were something like one hundred conveyances of the gasoline, electric or other propelling types in the line . . . occupied by persons of both races, some internationally known to fame. . . . [We] jammed the downtown district and went on our way rejoicing.[25]

In Kansas City the Monarchs' Booster Club organized an annual parade that snaked through the city's black district and arrived at the park in time for the opening ceremonies.[26] These ceremonies in most cities featured high school bands, color guards, prominent black celebrities, or black and white politicians to throw out the first pitch.

Indeed, as the African-American citizenry in northern cities expanded in numbers and influence, baseball stadiums became a prime location for politicians courting the black vote. In Atlantic City in the 1920s the Bachrach Giants were named for Mayor Henry Bachrach, who had brought an African-American team up from Florida to entertain the resort town's growing population of black hotel workers. Playing at a converted dog track near the Boardwalk, the Bachrach Giants became a popular fixture and an advertisement for the mayor for the remainder of the decade. Indiana Governor Harry Leslie, hoping to rebuild black support for the Republicans in the wake of the party's flirtation with the Ku Klux Klan, threw out the first pitch at the ABCs home opener in 1930.[27] Although attendance by governors proved rare, in the 1930s and 1940s big-city mayors routinely kicked off the local black season. When Pittsburgh Crawfords' owner Gus Greenlee unveiled his new stadium in 1932, the mayor, city council, and county commissioner all attended. In 1935 Mayor Fiorello La Guardia performed the first-pitch honors at a Brooklyn Eagles–Homestead Grays game, and Cleveland Mayor Harry L. Davis joined 8,000 fans at a match between the Crawfords and American Giants honoring Ohio State track star Jesse Owens. The mayors of Baltimore, Kansas City, and Newark all frequently appeared at opening games. The mayor of Newark, recalls Jerry Izenberg, could avoid the Eagles' home opener only "if he chose not to be re-elected."[28]

Opening day and Sunday contests attracted a wide cross section of the African-American community, dressed in their finest clothes. A white writer who attended a Sunday game in Detroit in 1922 reported, "All the youth, beauty, and chivalry of local African aristocracy is there to see and be seen. The latest 'modes and the most advanced fashions in "nobby suitings for young men" are on view'. . . . Gallons of perfumery and tons of powder are expended on this great social event." The tradition continued into the 1940s. Memphis blues/soul singer Rufus Thomas recalls: "They put on their best frocks, the best suits, the best everything they had and went to the ballgame and when they would sit up there watching the game, it looked like a fashion parade." For a rookie pitcher, like Newark's James Walker, the intimidating scene "looked like a big cloud of flowers of different colors."[29]

The Sunday spectacle, according to Newark resident Connie Woodruff, represented "a combination of two things, an opportunity for all women to show off their Sunday finery" and "a once a week family affair." People would arrive, according to Woodruff, "with big baskets of chicken, potato salad, all the things you would have on a picnic . . . it was the thrill of being there, being seen, seeing who they could see."[30] For recent arrivals from the South, Sunday games often served as reunions. Lena Cox, the sister of

Homestead Grays' star Buck Leonard, had migrated from Rocky Mount, North Carolina, to Washington, D.C. "You would see everyone from home when you went to the ball game," she recalled. Many people went directly from church to the ballpark. Clubs often played benefit games for churches and gave free passes to ministers, who, in return, urged their flocks to accompany them to the games. In Washington, D.C., where Elder Michaux operated a popular church across the street from Griffith Stadium, his parishioners would cross Georgia Avenue to catch the Homestead Grays in action during the 1940s after the service.[31]

The Sunday games, asserted Black Yankees outfielder Charlie Biot, "were THE event of the week." Teams capitalized on the popularity of these contests by throwing their star pitchers and scheduling four-team doubleheaders. According to an intimate of Rube Foster, Foster commanded Negro National League affiliates in the 1920s that "no star twirler was used to the limit before a small Saturday crowd with the prospects of a good Sunday attendance." In Memphis in the 1940s ace Verdell Mathis became known as the "Sunday Feature," because he almost always hurled the first game of the scheduled doubleheader.[32]

This emphasis on Sunday games, however, also revealed the limitations of black baseball. The black professional game depended, as Janet Bruce has written, "on an impoverished people who had too little discretionary money and too little leisure time."[33] As most blacks who could afford to attend games worked or searched for casual work six days a week, Sunday was often the only day they could attend games. Sunday matchups usually attracted between 4,000 and 8,000 fans; weekday contests drew a few hundred. As Foster noted, "There are only twenty-seven Sundays and holidays in the playing season. It is a proven fact that on Sundays only have clubs been able to play at a profit. The weekdays have on many occasions been a complete loss."[34] Since several states, most notably Pennsylvania, had "blue laws" prohibiting Sunday games, teams like the Hilldale Club lost these lucrative home dates. Teams that shared facilities with white major and minor league squads could only schedule home Sunday dates when the host club was on the road. A few Sunday rainouts could devastate a team's narrow profit margin.

Attempts to stage a World Series between the champions of the Negro National League and the Eastern Colored League in 1924 illustrated the problem. Since black fans in any city could not be expected to afford tickets for more than a few consecutive games, the ten-game series pitting the Hilldale Club against the Monarchs was played not just in Philadelphia and Kansas City, but in Baltimore and Chicago as well. Three Sunday dates attracted an average of almost 7,000 fans a game. Two Monday games, including the finale to a tightly contested series, attracted crowds of 534 and 1,549. This pattern continued into the 1930s and 1940s. The Newark Eagles, for example, averaged 4,293 Sunday admissions in 1940, but only 870 on other days.[35]

These realities of black baseball exposed a great deal about the complex racial dynamics of America. As early as 1911 David Wyatt pointed out that "baseball can not live or thrive upon the attendance of colored only," and noted the necessity of scheduling weekday games against white teams. As Neil Lanctot demonstrates, the success of the Hilldale Club in the early 1920s stemmed from the availability of white opponents. Hilldale played almost two-thirds of its games against white semiprofessional and industrial teams.[36]

White baseball fans across the nation attended games that pitted black teams against white semiprofessional and professional squads, but most whites had minimal exposure to top-level competition between black athletes. The daily press in most cities rarely covered constructive black activities of any kind. When several white papers deigned to mention the 1924 Negro World Series, the *Kansas City Call* observed, "Negro sport has done what Negro Churches, Negro lodges, Negro business could not do . . . shown that a Negro can get attention for a good deed well done, and that publicity is no longer the exclusive mark of our criminals." In the 1930s and 1940s Effa Manley discovered that "it was next to impossible to get much space in the white metropolitan dailies."[37] Reports of games that found their way into the white press often lampooned the fans and festivities or referred to the players as "duskies" and other racist terms.

White fans appear to have been more likely to attend all-black games in the early years of the century. In 1907 a three-game series in Chicago between the Indianapolis ABCs and Lincoln Giants attracted 30,000 fans of both races. "There was no color line anywhere; our white brethren outnumbered us by a few hundred, and bumped elbows in the grandstands . . . the box seats and bleachers," reported Wyatt. The ABCs, Monarchs, Hilldales, and Lincoln Giants (who played in Harlem) all reported substantial white attendance during these years.[38] During the 1920s, however, perhaps due to the more rigid segregation arising in response to the Great Migration and 1919 race riots, white attendance dropped to 10 percent or less. Efforts to bolster profits by attracting more whites inevitably proved unsuccessful. In 1939 Effa Manley made a strong effort to lure whites to Newark Eagles' games, but the *Philadelphia Tribune* reported in 1940 that "Up in Newark . . . [one] would have seen 95 colored faces for every five white ones." Chicago reporter Fay Young frequently criticized attempts to get more whites to the games. Although the leagues had employed white promoters to bolster attendance at all-star games in Chicago and New York in 1939, observed Young, the 32,000 fans in Chicago included only 1,500 whites, and "the white people in New York didn't give a tinker's damn about Negro baseball." Two years later, Young noted, the crowd of 50,000 people who attended the East–West game "didn't have 5,000 white people out."[39]

Although whites rarely attended Negro League games, blacks in many cities frequented major and minor league ballparks. Many African Americans, particularly those who read only mainstream newspapers, were more aware of white baseball than the black alternative. "Scores of people in Harlem . . . do not know there is a colored baseball club in the city," alleged the *Amsterdam News* in 1929. The *Philadelphia Tribune* reported that black children attending a Hilldale game in the 1920s "had heard of Cobb, Speaker, Hornsby and Babe Ruth and other pale-faced stars, but knew not that they had players of their own group who could hold their own with any stars of any league." Buck O'Neil recalled that as children in Florida he and his friends, unfamiliar with black baseball, emulated the intensely racist Ty Cobb and other major league players in their imaginary games.[40]

African-American newspapermen repeatedly chided blacks for supporting organized baseball. "It is bad enough to ride on Jim Crow cars, but to go into ecstasies over a Jim Crow sport is unforgivable," admonished the *Chicago Whip* in 1921. Two years later a sportswriter in Washington, D.C., where African Americans avidly rooted for the Senators, asked, "Why then should we continue to support, foster and fill the coffers of a national enterprise that has no place or future for men of color, although they have the ability to make the grade?"[41] Wendell Smith offered a scathing critique of black fans in 1938:

> Why we continue to flock to major league ball parks, spending our hard earned dough, screaming and hollering, stamping our feet and clapping our hands, begging and pleading for some white batter to knock some white pitcher's ears off, almost having fits if the home team loses and crying for joy when they win, is a question that will probably never be settled satisfactorily. What in the world are we thinking about anyway?
>
> The fact that major league baseball refuses to admit Negro players within its folds makes the question just that much more perplexing. Surely, it's sufficient reason for us to quit spending our money and time in their ball parks. Major league baseball does not want us. It never has. Still we continue to help support this institution that places a bold "Not Welcome" sign over its thriving portal and refuse to patronize the very place that has shown that it is more than welcome to have us. We black folks are a strange tribe![42]

The presence of black fans at white games grated for many reasons. As a Kansas City minister commented about the patronage of white-owned businesses, "All of that money goes into the white man's pocket and then out of our neighborhood." The prevalence of segregated seating provoked additional irritation. In St. Louis, where fans had to sit in a separate area behind a screen, a black newspaper condemned fans who ignored the St. Louis Stars, but chose to "fork over six bits to see a game at Sportsman's Park . . . and get Jim Crowed in the bargain." In Kansas City blacks faced segregated seating at minor league Blues games throughout the 1920s. When former major league catcher Johnny Kling bought the team in the 1930s, he ended this policy, but when the Yankees purchased the club in 1938, the organization reinstituted Jim Crow. Other ballparks, like Griffith Stadium in Washington, had no formal policy dividing the races, but African Americans always sat in specific areas of the outfield. "There were no signs," remembered one black Senators fan. "You just knew that was where you would sit."[43]

Many of these same ballparks regularly hosted Negro League and other black contests. After 50,000 fans attended the all-star extravaganza at Comiskey Park in 1941, Fay Young protested, "The East versus West game ought to make Chicago folk get busy and have a ballyard of their own. Why is it we have to 'rent' the other fellows belongings?" But the cost of constructing a stadium fell beyond the limited resources of most team owners. Only a handful of teams—the Memphis Red Sox, the Pittsburgh Crawfords in the 1930s, and the Nashville Elite Giants—owned the stadiums they played in.[44] Most leased or rented facilities usually controlled by whites, often in white neighborhoods, and governed by the unpredictable racial mores of the era.

The thorny issue of acquiring a place for black teams to play further illustrated the complex American racial dynamics. For the independent clubs of the early twentieth century, the ability to secure reliable access to a playing field often elevated the team from sandlot to professional level. After 1907 the Indianapolis ABCs held a lease to play at Northwestern Park, a small black-owned stadium in the city's African-American district. The club advertised itself as one of the few black teams to "own their own park" and its ability to guarantee playing dates attracted a steady stream of frontline opponents. In the 1910s Ed Bolden obtained the use of Hilldale Park in Darby, Pennsylvania, just outside Philadelphia. Connected by trolley to Philadelphia's African-American area, Hilldale Park seated 8,000 fans, providing Bolden's Hilldale Club with a steady following.[45]

Hilldale Park was a curious affair, with several trees and tree stumps scattered through the outfield and a hazardous depression that ran across center field. Indeed, many of the ballparks left much to be desired as playing fields. Early teams in Newark performed at Sprague Stadium, hemmed in on one side by a laundry building so close to the infield that balls hit on its roof became ground-rule doubles. The Baltimore Black Sox played in what the *Afro-American* called "a sewer known as Maryland Park, which featured broken seats, holes in the roof, nonworking toilets and weeds on the field."[46]

As the popularity of black baseball increased, however, teams began renting larger and better white-owned facilities from recreation entrepreneurs or major and minor league teams. Some parks were located in black neighborhoods, but others brought players and fans across town into white districts. When the White Sox abandoned 18,000-seat South Side Park in Chicago's Black Belt for the new Comiskey Stadium, Charles Comiskey's brother-in-law, John Schorling, refurbished the arena and offered it to Rube Foster's American Giants. After 1923 the Kansas City Monarchs leased Muehlebach Stadium, home of the Kansas City Blues of the American Association, another ballpark located in a black section. The Detroit Stars, on the other hand, played at Mack Park, situated amid a German working-class neighborhood. After Mack Park burned down in 1929 the Stars moved to a field in Hamtramck, a Polish community.[47]

Playing in a white-owned facility raised numerous problems for black teams and players. Many stadiums refused to allow African-American players to use the locker rooms. When the Pittsburgh Crawfords or Homestead Grays played at Ammons Field or Forbes Field, the players had to dress and shower at the local YMCA. Some ballparks, like American Association Park in Kansas

City, where the Monarchs played from 1920 to 1922, insisted on segregated seating, even for Negro League games.[48] The shift from a small black-owned arena to a larger white-owned one also raised the specter of racial betrayal. The 1916 move by the ABCs from Northwestern Park to Federal League Park posed a familiar dilemma. Switching to the new park placed the ABCs in a modern facility, comparable to many major league fields. However, as the *Indianapolis Freeman* complained, the relocation would transfer rent and concession money as well as jobs from blacks to whites.[49] When the Lincoln Giants moved their games from Olympic Stadium in Harlem to the more distant, but attractive Protectory Oval, the *New York Amsterdam News* protested, "To see a good baseball game in which colored men engage you now have to travel miles out of the district."[50]

By the late 1930s and early 1940s several major and minor league teams had discovered that renting their stadiums for Sunday Negro League doubleheaders could be a lucrative proposition. In 1932 the New York Yankees began scheduling four-team doubleheaders at Yankee Stadium when the Yankees were on the road. In 1939 the Yankees even donated a "Jacob Ruppert Memorial Cup," named after the team's late owner, to the black club that won the most games at the stadium that year. By the end of the decade the Yankees also rented out the ballparks of their Kansas City and Newark affiliates to the Monarchs and Eagles.[51] In 1939 the Baltimore Orioles, who had previously refused to allow the Elite Giants to use Oriole Park, accepted several Sunday dates. The Homestead Grays played regular Sunday dates at Griffith Stadium starting in 1940, averaging better than 10,000 fans a game. Even Shibe Park in Philadelphia, where blacks had rarely played previously, began scheduling Negro League games in the 1940s.[52]

These bookings marked important breakthroughs. They demonstrated the economic potential of black baseball fans and their respectability as well. As the *Kansas City Call* commented in a 1949 editorial, "From a sociological point of view, the Monarchs have done more than any other single agent to break the damnable outrage of prejudice that exists in this city. White fans, the thinking class at least, can not have watched the orderly crowds at Association Park . . . and not concede that we are humans at least, and worthy of consideration as such."[53]

Perhaps the most significant area of racial controversy revolved around the white owners and booking agents who profited from black baseball. In 1917 David Wyatt derided "the white man who has now and in the past secured grounds and induced some one in the role of the 'good old Nigger' to gather a lot of athletes and then used circus methods to drag a bunch of our best citizens out, only to undergo humiliation, with all kinds of indignities flaunted in their faces, while he sits back and grows rich off a percentage of the proceeds."[54] Yet, as Wyatt well knew, few African Americans in the early twentieth century had the resources to underwrite a baseball enterprise. As *Pittsburgh Courier* columnist Rollo Wilson observed in 1933: "Mighty few teams have been entirely financed by Negro capital. . . . There have been many instances of so-called Negro 'owners' being nothing but a 'front' for the white interest behind him."[55] Before the 1930s, when the urban "numbers kings" began bankrolling Negro League franchises, economic survival almost always required either partial or complete white ownership or an alliance with white booking agents who controlled access to playing fields.

Both contemporaries and historians have frequently portrayed white booking agents as the Shylockian villains of black baseball. Operating in a universe in which few African-American teams owned playing fields, these baseball entrepreneurs controlled access to the best ballparks and many of the most popular opponents. Nat Strong personified these individuals. A former sporting goods salesman, Strong, like the men who founded vaudeville, had glimpsed an opportunity to profit along the fringes of American entertainment. Recognizing the broad interest in semiprofessional baseball in the 1890s, Strong gained control of New York-area ball fields like Dexter Park in Queens that hosted these games. He rented out these facilities to white and black teams alike and gradually expanded his empire to include a substantial portion of the East Coast. In 1905 Strong formed the National Association of

Colored Professional Clubs of the United States and Cuba, which booked games for the Philadelphia Giants, Cuban X Giants, Brooklyn Royal Giants, and other top eastern black squads.[56]

Any team hoping to schedule lucrative Sunday dates at a profitable site had to deal with Strong, who systematically attempted to secure a monopoly over black professional baseball. Teams that defied Strong found themselves barred from the best bookings. When John Connors, the black owner of the Royal Giants, obtained a playing field in 1911 and attempted to arrange his own games, Strong blacklisted teams that dealt with Connors. Within two years Strong had wrested control of the rebellious franchise from Connors.[57] Black teams also resented the fact that Strong paid a flat guarantee rather than a percentage of the gate, allowing him to reap the profits from large crowds. Behavior like this led former player and organizer Sol White to remark in 1929, "There is not a man in the country who has made as much money from colored ballplaying as Nat Strong, and yet he is the least interested in its welfare."[58]

The creation of the original Negro Leagues in the 1920s occurred against this backdrop. Historians have usually accepted Rube Foster's descriptions of his Negro National League (NNL) as a purer circuit than the rival Eastern Colored League (ECL). Black owners predominated in the NNL; white owners, particularly Strong, prevailed in the ECL. Foster vehemently dismissed the ECL as a tool of Strong. Yet, the reality of the two leagues was more complex.

As Neil Lanctot has demonstrated, the key figure of the ECL was not Strong, but its president, Ed Bolden. Bolden, a black Philadelphia-area postal worker, had elevated the Hilldale Club of Darby, Pennsylvania, from a sandlot team into a frontline independent competitor. In 1918, when Strong had attempted to gain control of the Hilldale Club, Bolden sent an open letter to the *Philadelphia Tribune*, proclaiming, "The race people of Philadelphia and vicinity are proud to proclaim Hilldale the biggest thing in the baseball world owned fostered and controlled by race men. . . . To affiliate ourselves with other than race men would be a mark against our name that could never be eradicated."[59] Yet, five years later Bolden allied with Strong to form the ECL. Bolden, heavily dependent on scheduling nonleague games at locales like Dexter Park, owned or controlled by Strong, recognized the benefits of amalgamation. "Close analysis will prove that only where the color line fades and co-operation instituted are our business advances gratified," wrote Bolden in 1925.[60]

If, as Foster and black sportswriters alleged, Strong "was the league and ran the league," his conduct certainly belied this accusation. The ECL failed, in no small measure, because Strong's Brooklyn Royal Giants refused to adhere to the league schedule. A traveling team with no home base, the Royal Giants frequently bypassed games with league opponents if offered more lucrative bookings. In 1924 the league commissioners voted the Royal Giants out of the ECL, but relented when Strong promised his team would play all scheduled games. His failure to adhere to this pledge greatly weakened the league.[61]

As Bolden noted, however, the Negro National League also had a "few [white] skeletons lurking in the closet."[62] The most visible white presence in the NNL was league secretary J. L. Wilkinson, the owner of the Kansas City Monarchs. Wilkinson represented the best in Negro League ownership, white or black. As Wendell Smith later saluted, he "not only invested his money, but his very heart and soul" in black baseball. But Wilkinson always remained conscious of the need to portray the Monarchs as a black institution. African Americans Dr. Howard Smith and Quincy J. Gilmore became the public faces of the Monarchs, attending league meetings and riding in the lead car at the opening game festivities.[63] In Detroit, first Tenny Blount and later Mose Walker fronted for white businessman John Roesink as owner of the Stars. Most significantly, Foster himself was not the sole owner of the Chicago American Giants. John Schorling, owner of Schorling Stadium, the team's home grounds, underwrote the American Giants and split all profits evenly with Foster. After the *Chicago Broad Ax* protested in 1912 that Schorling received proceeds that "should be received by the Race to whom the patrons of the game belong," Foster concealed Schorling's role. Nonetheless, other NNL owners remained suspicious of Schorling's influence and, when Foster became ill in 1926, Schorling assumed sole ownership of the team.[64]

Nor was the NNL free from the tyranny of booking agents. In this instance, however, the key figure was Foster. As early as 1917 Foster had seized control of scheduling in the Midwest. As president of the NNL, Foster booked all league games and received 5 percent of the gate. Critics leveled charges against Foster's domination similar to those directed at Nat Strong in the East. St. Louis Giants secretary W. S. Ferrance protested Foster's profits, noting, "There was not a man connected [with the league] that was not in a position to book his own club and had been doing so for years." Others charged that Foster guaranteed lucrative Sunday home games for his American Giants. One black writer charged that Foster's "Race baseball league" was designed to "extend his booking agency," just as Foster accused Strong of manipulating the ECL.[65]

Racial controversies also arose in the operations of both leagues, most notably over the issue of employing white umpires. Fay Young protested in 1922, "It isn't necessary for us to sit by the thousands watching eighteen men perform in the national pastime, using every bit of strategy and brain work, to have it all spoiled by thinking it is impossible to have any other man officiating but pale faces."[66] Many owners believed that white arbiters could exercise more authority and better control player rowdiness. They also argued that few blacks had the requisite experience to offer competent officiating. "The colored umpire does not have the advantage that the white umpire has, in passing from sandlot ball to the minor leagues and then to the majors," contended Baltimore Black Sox owner George Rossiter. "As a result of his inexperience he is not able to deliver the goods." Nonetheless, many fans and sportswriters agreed with the verdict of the *Philadelphia Tribune*, which argued, "Regardless of the reason for colored ball games having white umpires it is a disgusting and indefensible practice" and "a reflection on the ability and intelligence of colored people."[67]

The very presence of white owners also continued to rankle many in the African-American community. After a tragic fire injured 219 black fans at Mack Park in Detroit in 1929, some blacks organized a boycott protesting white owner John Roesink's "failure to advertise in 'shine' newspapers, his arrogant, insulting attitude toward patrons of the game" and "his failure to compensate, or visit or even speak kindly to any of the persons injured in the catastrophe at Mack Park." The boycott reportedly "brought Roesink down from his 'high horse'" and elicited a promise that he would stay away from the park and allow his black assistant Mose Walker to operate the Stars.[68] That same year the *Baltimore Afro-American* attacked the local Black Sox on the umpire issue. Ignoring the fact that both white-owned and black-owned teams employed whites, the *Afro-American* maintained, "If the Sox management were colored, we'd have colored umpires tomorrow."[69]

Both the NNL and ECL collapsed with the onset of the Great Depression. By this time a group of unorthodox, but highly successful, black businessmen wealthy enough to finance black professional baseball had arisen in many cities. Cuban Stars' impresario Alessandro (Alex) Pompez pioneered this new breed of owner in the 1920s. Pompez, a Cuban American born in Florida, reigned as the numbers king of Harlem. The numbers game was a poor man's lottery. For as little as a nickel, individuals could gamble on hitting a lucky combination of three numbers and winning a payoff of 600 to 1. Since the true odds of winning were 999 to 1, considerable profits awaited a resourceful and reliable man who could oversee the operation. Pompez reportedly grossed as much as $7,000 to $8,000 a day from his organization. In the 1920s Pompez purchased Dyckman's Oval, a park and stadium in Harlem, and staged a variety of sports events including boxing, wrestling, and motorcycle racing. Pompez, who had strong connections in Cuba and a keen eye for baseball talent, formed the Cuban Stars to play at Dyckman's Oval. In 1923 they joined the ECL, one of only two black-owned clubs in the league. During the 1930s he owned the New York Cubans. Pompez imported top Cuban players like Martin Dihigo and Luis Tiant, Sr., to perform for his teams.[70]

The numbers operations run by Pompez and others were illegal but widely accepted in black America. In a world in which African Americans had few legitimate business opportunities, many of the most talented and resourceful entrepreneurs, men who, according to novelist Richard Wright, "would have been steel tycoons, Wall street brokers, auto moguls had they been white,"[71] entered the numbers racket. Some, like Jim "Soldier Boy" Semler of New York or Dick Kent of St. Louis, were ruthless gangsters, prone to violence and intimidation.[72] Others, like Pompez and Gus Greenlee of Pittsburgh, although not averse to using strong-arm methods to expand and defend their empires, won reputations as community benefactors. Often these numbers kings turned a portion of their profits back into the black community through loans, charity, and investments.[73]

In the 1930s black gambling barons throughout the nation began to follow Pompez into baseball. In Pittsburgh Gus Greenlee, a Pompez friend and protégé whose peak income has been estimated at $20,000 to $25,000 a day, launched the Pittsburgh Crawfords. In Detroit Everett Wilson, numbers partner of John Roxborough who managed Joe Louis, bought the Detroit Stars from John Roesink. Abe Manley, a retired numbers banker from Camden, owned first the Brooklyn and then the Newark Eagles. Semler ran the New York Black Yankees and Rufus "Sonnyman" Jackson supplied needed capital for Cum Posey's Homestead Grays. When Greenlee united the eastern teams into a new Negro National League in 1933, league meetings, according to Donn Rogosin, brought together "the most powerful black gangsters in the nation."[74]

Their wealth, power, and influence within the black community notwithstanding, the numbers kings still had to make their way in a white-dominated world. Of the Negro National League teams of the 1930s and 1940s, only the Pittsburgh Crawfords owned and operated their own stadium. All teams still relied heavily on white booking agents for scheduling. Nat Strong had died in the early

1930s, but William Leuchsner who ran Nat C. Strong Baseball Enterprises in the New York area, and Eddie Gottlieb, who operated out of Philadelphia, now ruled Strong's domain.[75] In the Midwest, where a new Negro American League formed in 1937, Abe Saperstein, better known as the founder of the Harlem Globetrotters, had succeeded Rube Foster as the preeminent booking agent. Saperstein even received 5 percent of the substantial gate at the East-West showcase.[76] These arrangements were not without benefits for Negro League teams. Gottlieb, for example, coordinated ticket sales and newspaper and poster publicity for events he booked, enabling teams to reduce their overhead and maintain fewer employees. The booking agents also negotiated reduced rental, operating, and insurance fees from major and minor league ballparks. The Homestead Grays reported that Gottlieb's intervention with the New York Yankees saved league owners $10,000 in 1940.[77]

Nonetheless, many owners bridled at the influence of white booking agents and repeatedly sought to be free of them. According to Effa Manley, who owned the Newark Eagles with her husband Abe, "[We] fought a . . . war against the booking agents from the first day [we] entered the picture . . . but [we] fought a losing battle. The tentacle-like grip of the booking agents proved impossible to break." Their resistance cost the Eagles their Yankee Stadium playing dates in 1939 and 1940. At the 1940 league meetings, the Manleys demanded the removal of Gottlieb as booking agent for Yankee Stadium. According to *Baltimore Afro-American* sports editor Art Carter, Effa Manley "assumed the position that the league was a colored organization and that she wanted to see all the money kept within the group." When Posey defended Gottlieb, Manley (who, although she lived as a black woman, later claimed to be white) denounced the Gray's owner as a "handkerchief head," a street-slang variation on "Uncle Tom."[78] That same year black sportswriters at the East–West game organized the American Sportswriters Association to protest Saperstein's domination of that event and the Negro American League removed Saperstein as its official booking agent. The fact that Strong,

Leuchsner, Gottlieb, and Saperstein were all Jewish injected elements of anti-Semitism into these disputes.[79]

The race issue also reared its head in hiring decisions. On several occasions teams hired whites to handle publicity in hopes that they might be able to better attract more whites to the games, much to the chagrin of black sportswriters. In the 1920s, when Ed Bolden hired a local white sportswriter as the ECL umpire supervisor to garner attention, John Howe of the *Philadelphia Tribune* called it inappropriate to hire whites in a league "of . . . for . . . and by Negroes." Greenlee employed Saperstein to publicize the East-West game in the 1930s, but the move brought out few white fans.[80] Even the Manleys, who demanded black control, had, in the words of sportswriter Ed Harris, "the temerity to hire a white press agent to do their work," evoking widespread criticism. One columnist noted, "Speaking of unholy alliances, how about the one between . . . the Negro owner of a Negro baseball team who hires a white press agent." Oliver "Butts" Brown of the *New Jersey Herald News*, protested: "No white publicity man could be of much assistance to you in the many things you hope to do to improve the condition of Negro baseball. In fact he would be a detriment."[81]

These conflicts and debates over the role of whites in black baseball revealed not just the racial tensions that always existed in the age of segregation, but the stake of African Americans in successful black-owned and -operated institutions. "Who owns the Grays?" reflected the *Washington Afro-American* in 1943. "It is a pleasure to inform the fans of Washington that the Washington Homestead Grays are owned and operated by three colored gentleman."[82] A scene at the opening game of the 1946 Negro League World Series captured this sense of pride. When heavyweight champion Joe Louis threw out the first pitch, he tossed a silver ball that had been awarded to the Cuban Giants, the first great black professional team, for winning a tournament in 1888. As James Overmyer writes, "With a sweep of his right arm, Louis, the greatest black athlete of his day, symbolically linked the earliest era of Negro baseball with its most recent high point."[83]

The World Series ceremony occurred at a critical juncture in the history of black baseball. In September 1946 Jackie Robinson was completing his successful first season in Organized Baseball. The response to Robinson revealed the fragile hold that all-black baseball held on the African-American psyche. From its earliest days, the promoters of the African-American game had made its transitional nature clear. In *The History of Colored Baseball* in 1906, Sol White advised the black ballplayer to take the game "seriously . . . as honest efforts with his great ability will open an avenue in the near future wherein he might walk hand-in-hand with the opposite race in the greatest of all American games." In a remarkably prescient passage, White added, "There are grounds for hoping that some day the bar will drop and some good man will be chosen out of the colored profession that will be a credit to all, and pave the way for others to follow."[84] Rube Foster had another vision, wherein an all-black team would pierce the ranks of the white professional leagues, but the model of ultimate integration remained. *The Crisis*, the journal of the National Association for the Advancement of Colored People, left no doubt as to the ultimate purpose of the Negro Leagues. "It is only through the elevation of our Negro league baseball that colored ballplayers will break into white major league ball," avowed *The Crisis* in 1938. Even as strong an advocate of "Race baseball" as Fay Young who railed against white umpires, publicity men, and booking agents, joined the chorus. "We want Negroes in the major leagues if they have to crawl to get there," wrote Young in 1945.[85]

Most people involved with black baseball had few illusions as to what the impact of integration would be. Asked about the prospect of blacks in the major leagues in 1939, Homestead Grays Manager Vic Harris replied, "If they start picking them up, what are the remaining players going to do to make a living? . . . And suppose our stars—the fellows who do draw well—are gobbled up by the big clubs. How could the other 75 or 80% survive?" Black sportswriters like Sam Lacy "knew [that integration] would have a devastating effect on black baseball."[86] Joe Bostic wrote in 1942:

Today, there are two Negro organized leagues, just on the threshold of emergence as real financial factors. . . . To kill [them] would be criminal and that's just what the entry of their players into the American and National Leagues would do.

Nor should money from the byproducts be overlooked such as the printers, the Negro papers and the other advertising media, which get their taste: the officials, scorekeepers, announcers, secretaries and a host of others. These monies are coming into Negro pockets. You can rest assured that we'd get none of those jobs in the other leagues, *even with a player or two in their leagues.*

In sum: From an idealist and democratic point of view, we say "yes" to Negroes in the two other leagues. From the point of practicality: "No."[87]

But for Lacy, Bostic, and others, "the idealistic and democratic point of view" won out. Less than three years after issuing his admonition, Bostic ardently pursued the policy he had condemned, confronting Branch Rickey with Negro League players Terris McDuffie and Dave Thomas and demanding a tryout with the Dodgers during spring training in 1945. Wendell Smith might criticize black fans for attending white games, but, working alongside Rickey, he became one of the key architects of baseball integration. Sam Lacy acknowledged, "After Jackie, the Negro Leagues [became] a symbol I couldn't live with anymore." For these sportswriters, as James Overmyer points out, "covering baseball integration [was] the biggest story of their lives" and they pursued it wholeheartedly.[88]

Throughout black America the focus shifted from the Negro Leagues to the major leagues. The African-American press reduced its coverage of the Negro Leagues to make room for updates and statistics about Robinson and other black players in Organized Baseball. Advertisements appeared for special rail excursions to National League cities to see Robinson play. Even the Negro Leagues themselves attempted to capitalize on Robinson's popularity. The cover of the 1946 Negro League yearbook featured Robinson rather than one of the established league stars. A program for the Philadelphia Stars in the late 1940s pictured Robinson in his Dodger uniform.[89]

Negro League fans voted with their dollars decisively in favor of integration. In 1946 Effa Manley found that "our fans would go as far as Baltimore" to see Robinson play for the Montreal Royals.[90] Once he joined the Dodgers and New York-area fans could see Robinson in eighty-eight games at Ebbets Field and the Polo Grounds, attendance plummeted for the Newark Eagles and New York Black Yankees. Other teams also felt the pinch. "People wanted to go to see the Brooklynites," recalled Monarch pitcher Hilton Smith. "Even if we were playing here in Kansas City, people wanted to go over to St. Louis to see Jackie."[91]

Occasionally critics raised their voices to protest the abandonment of black baseball. "Around 400 players are involved in the Negro version of the national pastime," warned Dan Burley in *The Amsterdam News* in 1948. "If there are no customers out to see them, they don't earn a living. In enriching the coffers of the major league clubs, we put the cart before the horse for no purpose."[92] But most commentators were less sympathetic. In response to Manley's complaints about declining fan support, the *Kansas City Call* cajoled, "The day of loyalty to Jim Crow anything is fast passing away. Sister, haven't you heard the news? Democracy is a-coming fast."[93] The Manleys sold the Eagles after the 1948 season. By the early 1950s all but a handful of the Negro League clubs had disbanded.

As Burley, Manley, and others had predicted, the end of segregation would mean that fewer, rather than more, African Americans would earn their living from baseball in the latter half of the twentieth century. The failure of major league teams to hire black managers, coaches, and front-office personnel compounded this problem. The nearly universal celebration of Jackie Robinson's triumph notwithstanding, integration would produce negative as well as positive consequences.

Cultural critic Gerald Early sees the demise of the Negro Leagues as the destruction of "an important black economic and cultural institution" that encompassed many of the best and worst elements of African-American life. Blacks, writes Early, "have never gotten over the loss of the Negro Leagues because they have never completely understood the ironically compressed expression of shame and pride, of degradation and achievement that those leagues represented."[94] In the final analysis, the black baseball experience captured the "twoness" in the "souls of black folk" as well as the "dogged strength" that kept them "from being torn asunder."

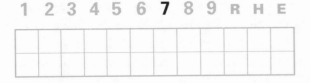

The Shot Heard
'Round the World

At 3:58 P.M. on October 3, 1951, New York Giants third base-man Bobby Thomson launched the most famous home run in baseball history. With two men on base in the bottom of the ninth inning of the third and final game of a playoff series between the Giants and their interborough rivals, the Brooklyn Dodgers, Thomson drove Ralph Branca's second pitch into the left field stands, lifting New York from a 4–2 deficit to a 5–4 victory, cap-ping perhaps the most dramatic pennant race ever staged. The feat instantly entered the nation's folklore, a symbolic signpost for a generation of Americans. "It was likely the most dramatic and shocking event in American sports and has since taken on the tran-scendent historic character of Pearl Harbor and the Kennedy As-sassination," observed journalist George W. Hunt in 1990. "Any-one alive then and vaguely interested can answer with tedious exactitude the question: 'Where were you when you heard it?'" Roger Angell calls it "baseball's grand exclamation point." Novelist Don Delillo used it to introduce *Underworld*, his fictional inquiry into the meaning of modern America. "Isn't it possible," mused Delillo, "that this midcentury moment enters the skin more last-ingly than the vast shaping strategies of eminent leaders, generals steely in their sunglasses—the mapped visions that pierce our dreams?"[1]

On the day after the home run, the *New York Daily News*, recalling Ralph Waldo Emerson's patriotic hymn, called Thomson's hit "the Shot Heard 'Round the Baseball World." A *New York Times* editorial invoked the same imagery, dubbing it "the home run heard 'round the world."[2] The two similar phrases merged in the popular memory, forever celebrating Thomson's triumph, in Emerson's exact phrase, as "the shot heard 'round the world."

Labeling Bobby Thomson's home run in this manner endowed the moment with several enduring, yet unintended ironies. In one sense it reflected American postwar arrogance about the country's centrality in world affairs: that people across the globe cared about all things American, including its idiosyncratic national pastime. Yet it also reflected Cold War reality. Hundreds of thousands of American military personnel stationed " 'round the world," in Europe and Asia, heard "the shot" via Armed Forces Radio. Millions of others who experienced the event as it occurred also literally *heard* it on radio broadcasts beamed not merely across the New York metropolitan area, but throughout the nation. Significantly, still others *saw*, rather than *heard* the shot in homes, in bars, or standing on the street outside store windows with television sets, many of them watching their first televised baseball game. Thus, Thomson's home run, the last great moment of radio sportscasting, simultaneously offered the first nationally televised sports highlight. These radio and television witnesses included untold numbers of African Americans drawn to a contest pitting the National League's two most racially integrated teams—the Jackie Robinson Dodgers and the Willie Mays Giants. Thus, baseball's "home run heard 'round the world"—stroked against Cold War and civil rights backdrops, situated at a crucial communication crossroads, and occurring at a juncture of critical changes in both baseball and society—offers a revealing glimpse of mid-century America.

For many fans and historians the 1951 playoffs mark the premiere highlight of a golden age of baseball that extended from the arrival of Jackie Robinson in 1947 to the uprooting of the Dodgers and Giants from New York to California a decade later. To a great extent, the retrospective romance of the era reflects the centrality of New York in both the baseball and American universe at mid-century. Although perhaps not as dominant as its provincial residents believed, and increasingly challenged by developments in Washington, D.C., Los Angeles, and other large cities, New York City at that moment remained the center of radio, television, publishing, and recording and theatrical culture. Events taking place in New York assumed an often-exaggerated significance. Furthermore, in no other era would New York baseball teams achieve the success they had over these eleven seasons. Between 1947 and 1957 a New York team appeared in the World Series every year but one. Seven of the eleven World Series pitted the Yankees against either the Dodgers or the Giants. The 1951 playoffs possessed a particular resonance. Despite baseball folklore about the great Giant-Dodger rivalry, the two teams had rarely battled for a pennant. Only in 1920, when the Dodgers finished first by seven games, and 1924, when the Giants edged the Brooks by a game and a half, had the teams finished in the top two slots in the National League. Played against the backdrop of the Jackie Robinson experiment, these matchups proved a formative signpost for an entire generation of New Yorkers.

There remains much to commend this idealized view. The game in 1951 seemed, both figuratively and literally, closer to the fans than later editions. Baseball still maintained the limited geographical configuration established a half-century earlier. Ten cities, none further south or west than St. Louis, hosted sixteen teams. Teams played in stadiums largely built in the teens and early twenties, located amid urban neighborhoods, within walking distance or streetcar and subway rides of most fans. The ballparks, most of which, like Ebbets Field, held between 30,000 to 40,000 fans, brought fans close to the action.

The players themselves were less remote and more accessible. Bobby Thomson and Ralph Branca, the two pivotal figures in the final game's final play, epitomized this link. Both came from large immigrant working-class families; both had been raised and lived in the New York area, and, according to legend, had kissed their mothers good-bye when they left for the game that morning. Thomson, born in Scotland, had come to the United States at the age of two. His family had settled in Staten Island, where he still lived. On the day of the game he commuted to Manhattan on the Staten Island Ferry. Branca, one of thirteen surviving children of an Italian father and Hungarian mother, had been born and raised and resided in Mount Vernon, New York. A local boy who made good, Branca was even engaged to marry the boss's daughter (Ann Mulvey, whose father owned 25 percent of the Dodgers) at the end of the season.[3]

Other Dodgers and Giants also had direct links with the metropolitan area. The Dodgers routinely scouted local prospects at the Parade Grounds, a complex of twenty-six baseball diamonds not far from Ebbets Field. As a goodwill gesture the Dodger club routinely signed about ten Brooklyn boys a year to play in its farm system. Although few of these aspirants ever made the Dodgers, those who did became local heroes. Reserve outfielder Cal Abrams, a graduate of James Madison High School and veteran of the Parade Grounds, was a particular favorite among the Jewish fans who honored him on a special "night" during the 1951 season.[4]

Even those who did not hail from the New York metropolitan area often seemed a part of the community. Players tended to live during the season, and sometimes all year, in the cities in which they appeared, rather than in affluent suburbs. Their salaries, although higher than the average workingman, rarely elevated them out of the working class. Most sought off-season employment to supplement their incomes. Physically, as well as financially, they weighed in only slightly above average. Relatively few exceeded six feet in height or 200 pounds in weight. Reporters described former Cleveland third baseman Al Rosen at five feet ten inches and 175 pounds as "big and burly."[5]

Like Thomson and Branca, the athletes on the 1951 Dodgers and Giants captured the polyglot makeup of postwar urban America. In addition to the distinctive racial mix, the teams included players representing a wide variety of ethnicities. A majority of the players hailed from the American South and Midwest. But the Giants' lineup—with Whitey Lockman, Don Mueller, and Larry Jansen—had a substantial contingent of German extraction. Sal Maglie, Carl Furillo, Branca, and Roy Campanella were the sons of Italian immigrants. Clem Labine was of French-Canadian heritage; Andy Pafko, Hungarian; Ray Noble, Cuban. Along the bench sat players with ethnic surnames like Abrams, Hermanski, Palica, Miksis, Koslo, and Podbielan. Many had served in the military during World War II. Several, like Gil Hodges, Monte Irvin, Billy Cox, and Furillo, had experienced active combat.

Yet the roseate glow adhering to these seasons obscures other more sobering truths. It is telling that the third game of the 1951 playoffs, despite the massive hype surrounding it, attracted only 34,320 fans, filling just two-thirds of the seats at the Polo Grounds. Threatening weather and the last-minute availability of tickets partially explain the attendance shortfall. But the less than capacity crowd also reflected baseball's new economic reality. At least when measured at the box office, baseball experienced a staggering decline in the early 1950s. From 1947 through 1949 the major leagues had drawn approximately 20 million fans a season. In 1951 the sixteen teams barely topped the 16 million mark (a figure that would further sag to 14.3 million in 1953.) The New York teams were not immune to the plague. Whereas 5.6 million people had attended Yankee, Dodger, and Giant games in 1947, in 1951, despite the great pennant race, only 4.3 million fans went through the turnstiles. Crowds were surprisingly small at several key junctures of the season. On August 28, after the Giants had won sixteen straight games to propel them back into contention, only 9,000 fans appeared at the Polo Grounds to see if they could extend this streak. At the home finales for the two clubs on September 22, only 19,000 people appeared at Ebbets Field; a scant 6,000 at the Polo Grounds.[6]

Commentators have advanced many explanations for baseball's mid-century attendance woes. Suburbanization drew fans away from the old ballparks, with automobiles replacing streetcars for many as the primary mode of access. With few stadiums equipped with adequate parking (Ebbets Field had only 750 spaces)[7] and most games now played at night and often televised, suburbanites found a trip to the ballpark a chore rather than an escape. Historian Ben Rader also attributes the decline to a "fundamental shift in urban leisure patterns," in which the suburban home, revolving around the television set, "became a self-sufficient recreation center," and the rapid growth of the suburbs drew people not just distant from inner-city ballparks, but into rival leisure pastimes. Charles Alexander notes that while urban Americans spent two-thirds of their recreation dollars on baseball in 1948, just two years later baseball accounted for less than half of these expenditures.[8]

Often lost in these discussions is the uniqueness of the post–World War II baseball boom. Before 1945 major league teams had never drawn consistently large crowds. Game attendance during the boom years of the 1920s averaged only 7,531 fans. During the Depression years it dropped to 6,578. In 1945, as the war drew to a close, the 10.8 million fans who attended games established a new record. In 1946 baseball, a symbol of the euphoric postwar celebration, nearly doubled its attendance as 18.5 million people flocked to ballparks. The figure rose to 19.8 million in 1947 and 20.8 million in 1948. Average game attendance between 1946 and 1949 jumped to an unprecedented 16,027.[9]

In retrospect, this bulge, which created new standards for major league attendance, was clearly an aberration rather than a new yardstick. The decline of the 1950s represented a correction to baseball's postwar bull market. Nor did this drop necessarily mean a corresponding decline in devotion. As Roger Kahn has noted, "The crowds watching television baseball multiplied and grew. Interest as opposed to attendance never flagged."[10] Even in 1953, when fan support slipped to its lowest level in the postwar era, attendance hovered almost one-third higher than in 1945 and 50 percent higher than most wartime and prewar seasons.

Yet major league owners drew several lessons from the attendance dip: most cities could not maintain more than one team; many of the older stadiums needed to be replaced, preferably with arenas with easier access to the suburbs and adequate parking; and cities outside the sacred circle of the Northeast and Midwest could offer new markets and larger crowds. In 1953 the Braves migrated from Boston to Milwaukee launching an era of relocation and expansion that would transform not just the map of baseball, but the game itself. By 1958, both the Dodgers and Giants would be in California. Although they did not realize it at the time, the fans watching and listening to the final game of the 1951 playoffs were bearing witness to the end of an era.

Two memorable artifacts of Thomson's shot have left the game indelibly etched in the nation's soul. The first is the remaining newsreel footage of the game, showing Branca's pitch, Thomson's swing, Dodger outfielder Andy Pafko standing at the wall looking up, and Thomson exuberantly romping around the bases, stomping on home plate into the jubilant arms of his Giant teammates. The second is a recording of Giants' radio announcer Russ Hodges's famous home run call:

> Branca throws again . . . there's a long fly . . . it's gonna be . . . I believe . . . the Giants win the pennant . . . the Giants win the pennant . . . the Giants win the pennant . . . the Giants win the pennant.

This description has been replayed so often as to create the illusion that most Americans who experienced the Thomson home run did so through Hodges's impassioned exclamations. In reality, if not for the improbable actions of a Dodger fan, Hodges's broadcast would long since have been forgotten. Neither teams nor radio stations routinely taped or preserved broadcasts in the early fifties. Thus, no full record of Hodges's work in the radio booth on October 3, 1951, has survived. However, Lawrence Goldberg, a Dodger fan listening to the game in Brooklyn, confident of a Dodger victory, decided to record Hodges's call of the final half-inning so that he could relive Hodges's anguish in defeat. Placing a primitive tape recorder next to his radio, Goldberg instead captured the classic home run call. A lesser man, or a more devious

Dodger diehard, might have destroyed the tape, but Goldberg called Hodges the next day. "I want you to have this tape," explained Goldberg, unwittingly creating a piece of Americana.[11]

If not for Goldberg's recording, our memories of Thomson's home run would be quite different. Only a small proportion of those experiencing the game did so via Hodges's broadcast. Indeed, Americans in general, and New Yorkers in particular, had an unprecedented range of options for partaking in the playoffs. The *New York Times* called the decision about which version of the game to tune in on, "the great schism of 1951. . . . The metropolis went quietly mad trying to figure out which radio station to listen to."[12] In New York City the playoffs were broadcast by Hodges and Ernie Harwell on WMCA, the Giant station, while Red Barber and twenty-three-year-old Vince Scully handled the Dodger accounts on WMGM. A group of radicals at CCNY heatedly debated the issue of Barber v. Hodges, finally compromising by alternating stations after each inning. Those opting for neutrality could settle for national broadcasts on the Mutual Network with "Brother Al" Helfer, a former Dodger and Giant announcer.[13]

Television offered yet another alternative. The Dodgers had televised the first playoff game, played at Ebbets Field, on Channel 9. The second and third games, at the Polo Grounds, were televised on Channel 11, the Giant station. Hodges and Harwell alternated the radio and television announcing chores. As the senior announcer, Hodges covered the middle three innings on television, allowing him to deliver the more crucial first and last three innings on the radio.[14]

As Yankee announcer Mel Allen later noted, the early fifties were an experimental era for radio and television. "In '51 and '52 they were both giants — both hating each other's guts, and the competition was conducive to baseball because they were both great vehicles for the game," commented Allen.[15] For those in the New York area, television had lost some, though not all, of its uniqueness by 1951. Many, if not most, New York homes possessed televisions. Others could partake in the "World Series special" offered by General Electric, allowing them to buy a seventeen-inch television for just $299.95 with weekly payments as low as $2.72. Those who did not own sets could watch with neighbors or relatives or in a variety of other venues. Bars and restaurants had long since discovered that televisions broadcasting sports events attracted patrons. As early as 1947 an estimated 3,000 New York City bars and grills had added televisions, prompting *Newsweek* to observe "Television is the best thing to happen to the neighborhood bar since the free lunch." Many watched the game in small crowds around televisions placed in windows of appliance and other stores. One twelve-year-old New Jersey boy later recalled watching the Thomson game on a television set up in a local Passaic bank.[16]

Nor was televised baseball a novelty. New Yorkers had watched the World Series on television since 1947. All three New York teams broadcast many of their home games during the regular season. In August 1951 the Dodgers had even experimented with color television. Ten thousand viewers received color wheels, allowing them to convert the images on their screens. Red Smith, who watched the game at CBS headquarters, found "the reproduction . . . excellent, striking, and only faintly phony." Gil Hodges's well-muscled arms "were encased in a pelt of somewhat lovelier tone—about the shade of medium roast beef—than Gil wears in real life." Dodger Manager Charlie Dressen's white uniform appeared "as immaculate as a prom queen's gown," until when walking along the grass, "he turned green, like cheap jewelry."[17]

Outside New York City fans had fewer options, but a nonetheless impressive array of choices. The dramatic expansion of television in the postwar era obscures the corresponding boom in radio broadcasting. The number of local radio stations in the nation doubled between 1945 and 1950. Baseball became a major staple of radio programming on the local, regional, and national levels. Several major league clubs, including the Dodgers and Giants, had established regional networks to carry their games. The St. Louis Cardinals, whose network encompassed over 120 stations in nine states, dispatched Harry Caray to the Polo Grounds to call the game live. The Giants network broadcast games over thirty-eight stations to an estimated audience of 3 to 4 million people.[18]

The Dodgers, in addition to a local regional network that re-produced Barber's broadcasts, had established a second innovative Dodger Network in 1950. This network broadcast Dodger games recreated by announcer Nat Allbright in a Washington, D.C., stu-dio. It primarily targeted the South, where the Dodgers as the pioneers of baseball integration attracted a wide audience, primar-ily, although not solely, among African Americans. "They were . . . even in the South almost a matter of life and death," recalled All-bright. "You had whites who were praying for Big Newk (Don Newcombe) and Jackie Robinson to lose. You had blacks who wanted them to win." In Washington, D.C., broadcasts over the Dodger Network reportedly garnered higher radio ratings than Senators games.[19]

On the national level most fans absorbed their baseball on one of two networks: the Mutual Broadcasting System and the Liberty Broadcasting Network. In 1949 Mutual, the nation's largest net-work with 350 affiliates, contracted with major league baseball to air a Game of the Day every afternoon of the baseball season except Sundays. During the 1951 season Mutual carried 145 major league games over 520 stations, many of which had signed on specifically to carry its baseball programming.[20] Liberty was the creation of Texan Gordon McClendon. Beginning in 1949 McClendon, who dubbed himself "the Old Scotchman," bypassed major league li-censing by purchasing game transcripts from Western Union and recreating his own games of the day from his studio in a Dallas suburb. By 1950 McClendon had established a network of 430 sta-tions, mostly in the South and Southwest. Unlike Mutual, Liberty aired games on Sundays, and in 1950 added a "Game of the Night."[21]

McClendon became an institution in the postwar American South. Author Willie Morris, who grew up in Yazoo, Mississippi, recalled, "By two o'clock almost every radio in town was tuned in to the Old Scotchman. His rhetoric dominated the place. It hov-ered in the branches of the trees, bounced off the hills, and came out of the darkened stores." One out of four weeks each month, Liberty would broadcast live from a major league ballpark. In 1951 the *Sporting News* named McClendon its broadcaster of the year. By that time his empire had grown so large that McClendon had begun to limit his own on-air time to major events, turning over the daily broadcasts to young announcers like Lindsay Nelson, Jerry Doggett, and Buddy Blattner. On October 3, however, McClendon manned a mike at the Polo Grounds, broadcasting live to his devoted following. Indeed, more Americans may have heard McClendon's home run call than either Hodges's or Barber's or Helfer's on Mutual. Like Hodges, McClendon barked out, "The Giants win the pennant!" Then after several moments of crowd noise, the Old Scotchman added, "Well, I'll be a son of a mule."[22]

Television, not radio, however, had emerged as the major media issue facing baseball in 1951. Four years earlier New York Yankee General Manager Larry MacPhail, who had pioneered radio and television broadcasts, had unsuccessfully attempted to block the sale of television rights to the 1947 World Series, fearing that telecasts would drive down attendance. World Series attendance nonetheless remained high, but Dodger President Branch Rickey concurred in his arch-rival MacPhail's assessment of the impact of television on the gate. When offered $150,000 to televise Dodger games, Rickey rejected the proposed deal. "Radio stimulates interest. Television satisfies it," pronounced Rickey, predicting an erosion of the fan base. Yet within a short time both the Yankees and Dodgers (as well as the Giants) had capitulated to the lure of television revenues. From a business standpoint the choice was not hard to make. By the mid-fifties the Dodgers earned more than $750,000 for television and radio rights, a figure that exceeded the player payroll by $250,000. "We were in the black before Opening Day," allowed Dodger executive Buzzie Bavasi.[23]

Yet baseball, at least in the short run, had entered into a Faustian bargain. Many observers blamed television for the decline in attendance in the early fifties. Veteran sportswriter Grantland Rice opened the 1951 season with a *Sport* magazine broadside entitled "Is Baseball Afraid of Television?," identifying television as "by all odds the greatest problem baseball has faced in these 75 years." The following season prompted articles by St. Louis Browns owner Bill

Veeck and sportswriter Dan Daniel, both of whom had advocated baseball telecasts in 1948, entitled "Don't Let TV Kill Baseball" and "TV Must Go—Or Baseball Will." "All we've got to sell are seats," argued Veeck. "If our ballparks are empty, what good does a TV sponsor's fee mean." Veeck also presciently predicted that "television would help widen the inequality that has existed for too long in baseball . . . the rich are getting richer and the poor are getting poorer."[24]

The 1951 Dodger-Giant playoffs added a new dimension to these debates. Prior to 1951 television shows could not be transmitted live from coast to coast. Programs produced in New York were filmed and then flown to California for western distribution. This hardly diminished the appeal of most early television, but it proved a poor substitute for live sports events. Several months prior to the playoffs, however, American Telephone and Telegraph had installed a coaxial cable allowing nationwide broadcasts. The 1951 World Series, scheduled to begin on October 2, was to be the first nationally televised sports event. Taking advantage of the new technology, the Dodger-Giant playoffs supplanted the Series as the pioneer programming. This development was so unexpected that CBS televised the regular Dodger broadcast of the first playoff game from Ebbets Field on October 1 nationally without a commercial sponsor. For games two and three from the Polo Grounds, however, Chesterfield cigarettes, the Giants' regular sponsor, agreed to pay the coast-to-coast transmission costs in exchange for commercial rights over NBC.[25]

The playoffs thus found a ready national audience. *Time* reported that in Los Angeles, where people "never used to get excited about the World Series," television purchases skyrocketed. Denver, according to *Time*, was experiencing not only its first live World Series, but its first television of any kind. Denver's Grand Palace Department store installed sets in its show windows and hotels placed televisions in their lobbies for the week. Other cities replicated the pattern found in earlier years in New York. When the Series began, "TV watchers . . . clotted around dealers' show windows, jockeyed cunningly for position at bars, ate with their eyes upraised in restaurants which had a video screen." Police erected barricades to control crowds watching the games.[26]

It is difficult to gauge how many people in the United States watched the third game of the 1951 playoffs on television. Many people still lived in areas that could not receive television transmissions, and most Americans outside the New York metropolitan area probably did not own televisions. Media reports focused primarily on the World Series, rather than the playoff television experience. *Look*, in an article entitled "The World Series Stare," estimated that 70 million people watched the first game of the 1951 World Series.[27] A lesser, but nonetheless unprecedented number probably saw Bobby Thomson instantaneously dash the Dodger pennant hopes, undoubtedly whetting their appetites for more televised baseball.

The phrase "shot heard 'round the world" possessed yet another irony. Although the vast majority of people in the world paid no heed to the events at the Polo Grounds, baseball, like the nation as a whole, seemed unusually focused on world affairs. The entire 1951 season had been played out against the backdrop of Cold War and Korean War tensions. The season opened on the day that General Douglas MacArthur, recently relieved from his command in Korea by President Harry S. Truman, arrived in the United States for his triumphal farewell tour. Thomson's home run coincided with President Truman's acknowledgment that the Soviet Union had detonated a second atomic bomb, confirming the end to the American nuclear monopoly.

These concerns never seemed far removed from the baseball diamond. MacArthur delivered his famous "Old soldiers never die" speech on April 19, the third day of the baseball season. He then faded not away, but into the midst of the first Dodger–Giant series of the season. On April 20, as President Truman threw out the first ball in Washington, D.C., to a chorus of boos, New York City held a massive ticker-tape parade honoring MacArthur. At the Polo Grounds the Giants delayed the starting time for their first game against the Dodgers by one hour to accommodate parade goers and recruited a marine wounded three times in Korea to throw out the first ball. MacArthur, who on arrival in the United States after a two-decade absence had listed baseball among the things he missed most, made a well-publicized appearance at the Polo Grounds on April 21. Forty-six thousand fans watched the general's son Arthur, seated alongside the general, throw out the first ball.[28]

MacArthur became a familiar figure at New York City ballparks, attending games at Yankee Stadium and Ebbets Field as well as the Polo Grounds. In May Dodger publicist Irving Rudd orchestrated MacArthur's Brooklyn debut with a lavish ceremony, featuring the World War II Nisei "go-for-broke" battalion and MacArthur materializing in full-dress uniform out of a limousine driven through a gate in the right field fence. MacArthur told the crowd, "I have been told that one hasn't really lived until he has been to Ebbets Field. I am delighted to be here." Nor was this mere rhetoric. The deposed general returned to Ebbets Field twelve more times in the course of the season and attended the playoff series as well. Major league owners joined the MacArthur mania, floating his name as a replacement for Commissioner Happy Chandler, who, like MacArthur, had been dismissed when he failed to please his superiors. When MacArthur declined, the owners offered the job to his colleague, Major General Emmett "Rosey" O'Donnell. President Truman, however, refused to release O'Donnell from active service.[29]

Cold War themes reverberated throughout the 1951 season. Sportswriters took to calling Giant second baseman Eddie Stanky, who in 1949 had set a National League record for walks, "Gromyko" for the Russian diplomat who had stormed out of the United Nations. When Dodger Manager Charlie Dressen chastised pitcher Irv Palica for lacking guts, a *New York Post* editorial challenged this "unfortunate statement." "The public does not readily associate courage with a game that children can play, especially when they turn the page and read the latest casualty lists from Korea," commented the *Post*. Dressen later blamed the Dodger collapse, in part, on the shortage of reserves created by the Korean War draft that had claimed 190 players out of the Dodger system. Those recalling the playoffs often did so within the context of the war. One group of Dodger fans watched the first game on TV while waiting to give blood for American combatants. A group of antiwar protesters at CCNY unanimously voted to adjourn their strategy meeting to listen to the third game.[30]

The *New York Times* also joined the Cold War chorus. The *Times* lead editorial on October 4 dealt with "The Russian Bomb," calling "it news of gravest import in the whole world." The *Times* immediately followed this dire pronouncement with an editorial beginning, "Well, the Giants exploded a bomb, too," invoking the image of a "home run heard 'round the world."[31]

The notion that events in baseball might have bearing on the Cold War had already been introduced by the game's unfolding racial drama. Only four years had passed since Jackie Robinson's historic breakthrough and major league desegregation had progressed grudgingly. Only three teams in each league fielded black players in 1951. Yet many observers grasped on the imagery of an integrated game as a potent propaganda weapon. In 1949 when Paul Robeson had questioned whether African Americans would participate in a war against the Soviet Union, the House Un-American Activities Committee recruited Robinson to rebut his charges.[32] A group of promoters proposed a world tour by the Brooklyn Dodgers and the Cleveland Indians, the most integrated team in the American League. They considered it "most important that the Negro race be well represented, as living evidence of the opportunity to reach the top which America's No. 1 sport gives all participants regardless of race."[33]

The 1951 Dodgers and Giants symbolized baseball's, and America's, impending racial revolution. The two New York squads accounted for all but one of the black players in the National League. (Sam Jethroe, the 1950 Rookie of the Year, whom the Boston Braves had acquired from the Dodgers, was the sole black player on the remaining six teams.) Both the Dodgers and Giants fielded several African Americans, almost all of whom had played critical roles in the pennant drive. During spring training both clubs toured the South, breaking down color barriers in many cities, while attracting overflow crowds of both black and white fans. It was not lost on contemporary observers that the two most inte-grated teams in the National League had finished in a dead heat for the pennant.

According to most accounts, racial harmony prevailed on both clubs. But the unique element of race always percolated just be-neath the surface of the Giants and especially the Dodgers. The Giants began the season with four Negro League veterans: Monte Irvin, who would emerge as the team's leading slugger; Hank Thompson, the erratic, alcoholic third baseman; backup shortstop Artie Wilson; and journeyman Cuban catcher Ray Noble. Several key Giant performers including team leaders Stanky, Alvin Dark, and Whitey Lockman hailed from the South. Nonetheless, main-tains Irvin, "We got along with those guys just fine . . . there was absolutely nothing racial on the ball club."[34]

Several incidents, however, illustrated the uncertain dynamics of the newly integrated game. Announcer Ernie Harwell claimed that the "fun-loving" Stanky took to calling Noble "Bushman." The catcher warned manager Leo Durocher, "I'll kill him if he calls me that again."[35] Giant personnel decisions raised the specter of a quota system limiting the number of blacks on the team. In late May the Giants management promoted African-American sensa-tion Willie Mays to the major league club. The Giants had pur-chased Mays' contract from the Birmingham Black Barons of the Negro American League in 1950, and Mays had advanced through the Giants farm system at an unexpectedly rapid rate. Assigned to the Minneapolis Millers in 1951, just one step below the major leagues, Mays assaulted American Association pitching at a .477 rate while astounding eyewitnesses with his spectacular fielding. Giant Manager Durocher demanded that Mays be added to his squad. When the promotion came on May 27, the Giants demoted Artie Wilson, one of the four other African Americans, to make room for Mays. Several weeks later, the Giants sent slumping third baseman Hank Thompson to the minor leagues. For the third straight year they bypassed Negro League great Ray Dandridge as a solution to their perennial third base problem. The Giants left Dandridge stranded on their Minneapolis farm club and instead shifted outfielder Bobby Thomson, who had never played the position, to third.[36]

Had the Giants imposed a quota preventing them from keeping too many African Americans on the team? Many observers at the time and subsequent chroniclers of the 1951 Giants believe they had. "They'll deny it," Irvin later commented, "but I'm sure there was a quota system. . . . My feeling is they didn't want more than two or three blacks playing then."[37] Dandridge, arguably the greatest third baseman in baseball history and the American Association's Most Valuable Player in 1950, never made it to the majors.

The promotion of Mays injected yet another element into the racial mix. The twenty-year-old phenom captivated nearly everyone with his skills and exuberance. But responses to Mays, whose southern mannerisms and youthful naivete often reinforced racial stereotypes, revealed much about attitudes and assumptions of the time. The Giants assigned Irvin to room with Mays and, in Irvin's own words, to "look after him." Announcer Russ Hodges recalled that Irvin, "a man of quiet dignity and great pride . . . realized at once that Mays, as a potential national figure, must also be a credit to his race." Leo Durocher delighted in his own relationship with the young Mays, who always called him "Mr. Leo." Yet, as Roger Kahn notes, "There was always an Uncle Tom in Durocher's view of Mays. . . . He was the straw boss and Mays the plantation hand." Newspapers endowed Mays with a Stepin Fetchit discourse. One 1951 cartoon depicted Mays in action exclaiming, "Ah gives base runners the heave ho!" and "Ah aims to go up in the world."[38]

Revealingly, the three most important cogs of the 1951 Dodgers—Roy Campanella, who won the National League Most Valuable Player Award; twenty-game winner Don Newcombe; and Jackie Robinson—were the squad's only black players. Four years after Robinson's debut, all the reserves, other starting pitchers, and relief pitchers on the pioneer team of baseball integration were white. As always, the race issue on the Dodgers coalesced around Robinson. Robinson reigned at the peak of his playing prowess— batting .338, hitting a career-high nineteen home runs, scoring 106 runs, and setting National League records for second basemen in fielding percentage and double plays. On the final day of the regular season Robinson's heroics, including a game-saving catch in the eleventh inning and a game-winning home run in the fourteenth (prematurely dubbed by *New York Post* writer Arch Murray the "shot heard 'round the baseball world"), had forced the playoff series. In the aftermath of Thomson's home run a *New York Times* editorial addressed Robinson's almost supernatural mystique, acknowledging that "even the great Jackie Robinson must bow to miracles."[39]

Robinson was also at the peak of his talent for generating antagonism and controversy. On May 2 National League President Ford Frick chastised Robinson for his aggressive baserunning. When Robinson defiantly defended himself, Frick responded angrily, "I'm tired of Robinson's popping off. I have warned the Brooklyn club that if they don't control Robinson, I will." According to John Kiernan, Robinson, still unintimidated, countered, "And I'm getting tired of being thrown at. Let Mr. Frick change the color of his skin and go out and hit against Maglie." Three weeks later in Cincinnati Robinson received three letters threatening his life. After a close call at home plate and the ejection of Campanella in the ensuing argument cost the Dodgers a critical September contest against the Braves, newspapers falsely accused Robinson of smashing in the door to the umpire's dressing room. As Robinson later complained, the report led "millions of baseball fans to believe . . . that I am a foul-tempered character."[40]

One particular episode involving the Giants and Dodgers illustrates the pent-up racial undertones of the campaign. At Ebbets Field only a thin wall separated the clubhouses between the home and visiting teams. Losing players could hear the revelry in the other locker room. After one Dodger victory over the Giants, Robinson deliberately taunted his arch-rivals, tapping his bat against the wall and yelling insults. The enraged Giants began cursing back. Stanky shouted, "Stick that bat down your throat, you black nigger son of a bitch," only to find his teammate Irvin standing next to him. For Irvin it was a delicate situation. He had never been close to Robinson, and the Dodger-Giant rivalry rather than any racial solidarity dominated his thoughts. Angered by Robinson's tirade and anxious to retain harmony on the Giants, Irvin reassured his teammate. "That's just fine with me, Eddie," he told Stanky, later explaining, "I could have gone along with anything they said, I was that mad."[41]

The presence of Robinson, Irvin, Mays, and other black players reflected not just a social transition, but a profound change in the game on the field as well. As one sportswriter has noted, "Baseball in 1950 stood at the end of the era built by Babe Ruth," who had died two years earlier. It poised on the brink of an age forged by Robinson and, especially significant in 1951, by Willie Mays. Mays, with his indisputable excellence, convinced all but the most stalwart resisters to integration of the need to recruit African Americans. The Ruthian game had been characterized by what Bill James has described as a "one-dimensional offense . . . the baseball of the ticking bomb."[42] Black players would transform major league play. Led by Mays, they added the speed and flair that had characterized the Negro Leagues without sacrificing the power introduced by Ruth.

Indeed, in the fall of 1951 baseball, like America, seemed poised on the brink of change in many areas. In the nation's capital a House subcommittee launched the first congressional investigation into baseball's monopolistic practices, ending the game's isolation from government scrutiny. The season marked the first in which Walter O'Malley, who would emerge as the dominant personality of baseball's elite, guided the fortunes of the Dodgers. He had wrested control from Branch Rickey, architect of both baseball integration and its minor leagues, the symbol of an earlier era. The game also had a new commissioner, Ford Frick, named to the post just one week before the playoffs began. Frick, unlike his predecessors Kennesaw Mountain Landis and Happy Chandler, was a man drawn from the ranks of the game, not a politician. He would restore command over the game to the owners. In one of his first actions Frick limited unauthorized radio recreations of the game, dooming McLendon's Liberty Network. "Tonight, a chapter in the life of the American dream closes," lamented McLendon in his farewell broadcast.[43]

Another more subtle challenge to the traditions of the game was in evidence at the third game of the 1951 playoffs, though few people realized it at the time. Baseball, for all its fascination with statistics and recordkeeping, had always pursued a stalwartly unscientific and unsystematic course. Field managers guided the destinies of their teams "by the book," an unwritten compendium of arcane strategies and intuitive impulses. The two colorful, controversial managers at the Polo Grounds on October 3, 1951—Leo Durocher of the Giants and his former protégé, Charley Dressen of the Dodgers—personified this approach. Dressen, renowned for taking credit for victories but blaming his players for losses, summed up his leadership philosophy as, "Stay close to 'em. I'll think of something."[44]

Dressen rarely paid attention to an innovative young Canadian who had labored for the Dodgers since 1947. Allan Roth had approached then Dodger president Branch Rickey with a hobby he had developed as a child, tracking the game pitch-by-pitch and keeping detailed records of each player's strengths and weaknesses. Rickey, always attuned to the scientific approach, employed Roth and encouraged his efforts. With pencil and paper, Roth began to compile the most detailed analysis of baseball ever undertaken. "Back then my system was unique," he later explained. "I would record the types of pitches and location. I even had averages for players when they were ahead or behind on the count. My system showed the record for a hitter against a pitcher for the year and over his career." Roth's efforts, especially with the introduction of computers in the 1970s, would provide the basis for modern baseball statistics. Unfortunately, in 1951 his was a craft in the wilderness. "Charley Dressen didn't want to see it," said Roth. "The man didn't want help from anybody. He thought he could do it all himself."[45]

In the bottom of the ninth inning, with two men on base, the Dodgers leading 4–2 and Bobby Thomson scheduled to bat, Dressen made a pitching change. He called in Ralph Branca. Dodger publicist Irving Rudd turned to Roth. "Allan, Allan, what are the statistics on Ralph Branca pitching to Thomson?" asked the anxious Rudd. Roth did not even have to check his numbers. Branca, who had allowed just seven home runs to the rest of the league, had surrendered ten to the Giants. Five of his eleven losses had come against the Giants. Thomson had stroked two of those homers including one two days earlier in the first game of the playoff series. Roth, staring out at the field, just shook his head sadly.[46] Moments later, Thomson struck "the shot heard 'round the world."

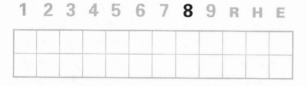

The Homes of the Braves
Baseball's Shifting Geography, 1953–1972

On April 14, 1953, Warren Spahn took the mound for the Braves' home opener against the St. Louis Cardinals. One month earlier Spahn had expected to be pitching at Braves Field, an aging, decaying ballpark in the heart of Boston. Instead, the lefthander unexpectedly found himself in Milwaukee County Stadium, the sparkling new home of the Braves. Spahn peered in at his catcher, kicked up his right leg, and fired a strike past the Cardinal leadoff man. "A tremendous roar went up," Spahn recalled. "I looked up to see what was going on, and then I stepped off the rubber and looked behind me." Everywhere he gazed Spahn saw not the empty seats that had grown commonplace at Braves Field, but wildly ecstatic baseball fans. A veteran of five all-star games and the 1948 World Series, Spahn was nonetheless stunned by the boisterous crowd reaction. "I realized that all they were screaming about was the first pitch. I have never experienced anything like it in an All-Star or in a crucial World Series game," marveled Spahn. "Those fans were welcoming our team as no team has ever been welcomed."[1]

The roar that greeted Warren Spahn and the Milwaukee Braves

proclaimed a new era for Organized Baseball. Fifty years had passed since the last franchise shift, the 1903 transfer of the Baltimore Orioles to New York City, where they would ultimately become the Yankees. In the interim, the nation's population had more than doubled and major urban areas had developed far beyond the traditional Northeast/Midwest industrial core. Yet baseball, as one executive later noted, had "stood still . . . while the country's population changed and baseball's market changed."[2] The number of major league ballplayers held steady at 400. The sixteen major league teams—the Boston Braves, Boston Red Sox, Brooklyn Dodgers, Chicago Cubs, Chicago White Sox, Cincinnati Reds, Cleveland Indians, Detroit Tigers, New York Giants, New York Yankees, Philadelphia Athletics, Philadelphia Phillies, Pittsburgh Pirates, St. Louis Browns, St. Louis Cardinals, and Washington Senators—remained anchored to ten metropolitan outposts. Four cities had two teams each; New York City had three; and St. Louis stood as both the westernmost and southernmost outpost of the "national" pastime. The spectacular success of the Braves in Milwaukee, however, launched a dramatic reconfiguration of the baseball map. In less than a decade six of the original sixteen teams would be playing in different cities. Within two decades expansion and additional franchise shifts would bring major league baseball to eight more communities. California hosted four teams, Texas two. Atlanta and Montreal expanded baseball's southeastern and northeastern boundaries.

Ironically, many remember this era as one of abandonment, rather than delivery, as cause for lamentation rather than celebration. Mayor John B. Hynes called the loss of the Braves "a body blow to Boston." Local fans labeled team owner Lou Perini "the Benedict Arnold of baseball."[3] The protests were even louder four years later when the New York Giants and Brooklyn Dodgers departed for California. New York City Council President Abe Stark condemned San Francisco Mayor George Christopher as a "pirate." Dodger fans like Doris Kearns Goodwin still denounce the club's exodus as "an invidious act of betrayal."[4] Yet, viewed from the perspective of those cities receiving teams, the franchise shifts, at least in their initial phase, provoked widespread jubilation. The acquisition of a major league team marked a sense of maturity, arrival, and acceptance, an acknowledgment of an elevated status in a newly emergent American constellation. These transfers reflected the broader changes affecting the nation as the country's economic and population base shifted from the Northeast and Midwest into the South, Southwest, and Far West. As with all dramatic transformations, the results were unpredictable and often disappointing, revealing a mosaic far more complex than any simple model of progress and loss might have augured.

The demographic shifts accelerated by World War II and its aftermath prompted a reexamination of baseball's limited geography in many quarters. In 1947 Californian H. D. Robins prepared a 115-page monograph, complete with diagrams, charts, and tables, analyzing baseball's increasingly irrational status quo. The sport, protested Robins, "had not responded to shifts in population or other pertinent changing factors." Given population increases and improved standards of health, he argued, "the number of men of major league caliber must not be twice but several times the number of men as were available at the turn of the century." Robins noted that although Cincinnati, the twentieth largest city in the United States, Canada, and the Caribbean, had a major league team, and St. Louis, the tenth largest city, had two teams, Los Angeles and San Francisco, the third and ninth ranking cities, had none. Montreal, Baltimore, Toronto, Buffalo, Havana, and Milwaukee, all larger than Cincinnati, also lacked representation, as did the burgeoning metropolises of Kansas City, Houston, and Minneapolis. Robins proposed a radical solution: the establishment of four eight-team major leagues, with a "Great Southern League" and a "Great Western League," joining the National and American Leagues, thus creating a truly national pastime.[5]

Although few embraced the bold scope of Robins's expansionist vision, he was not alone in reevaluating the baseball map. Both major and minor league turnstiles clicked at a record pace in the immediate postwar years, emboldening the baseball dreams of cities throughout the United States, most especially in California.

Pacific Coast League attendance nearly doubled between 1941 and 1946. Both the San Francisco Seals, who established a new minor league attendance mark, and the Oakland Oaks drew more fans than the St. Louis Browns and Kansas City Athletics. The Los Angeles Angels and Hollywood Stars combined to attract more than a million fans. "Is the West Coast Ready for Big League Baseball?" wondered a 1947 *Sport* magazine article. Pacific Coast League (PCL) President Clarence "Pants" Rowland, long an advocate of a third major league, proposed a new classification for the PCL, placing it above the triple-A level as a preliminary to big league status.[6]

The major leagues responded coolly to the PCL bid. Everyone recognized that both Los Angeles and San Francisco possessed legitimate major league potential, but many discounted PCL attendance figures as inflated by a long 186-game season and the practice of counting women and children who received free admission. Furthermore, Seattle, Portland, Oakland, and San Diego, saddled with inadequate ballparks and smaller populations, seemed dubious prospects. Baseball Commissioner Happy Chandler proposed that, rather than add an entire league, the two existing circuits should be expanded to ten teams each. The National League unanimously endorsed Chandler's suggestion, but the American rejected it, placing all expansion plans on hold.[7]

This lack of initiative and foresight on the part of the major league establishment was not surprising. None of the aspiring cities had viable major league facilities and, while all major league stadiums were privately built and owned, increased costs made new ballpark construction a daunting challenge unless underwritten by public funds. In addition, as David Voigt has noted, the traditional eight-team configuration produced a "marvelously balanced" 154-game schedule. Each team played the other twenty-two times, and Pullman trains easily accommodated "western" excursions.[8] Despite dramatic improvements in air travel, few owners could envision an alternative to this arrangement. In 1946 United Airlines had introduced the DC-6, capable of traveling 300 miles an hour and carrying more than fifty passengers; larger and faster planes were in development. As Dan Daniel noted in *Baseball Magazine*, a team could now travel from New York to Los Angeles in half the time it took to get to St. Louis by train. Larry MacPhail, always far ahead of his colleagues, signed an exclusive contract with United to transport the New York Yankees on most of their road trips. Most major league executives, however, some fearing the possibility of losing an entire squad to an air disaster, resisted plane travel.[9]

The unwillingness of the major leagues to expand or recognize a third major league left just one alternative for cities hoping to achieve major league status: to lure an existing team away from its long-standing home. But, the postwar attendance boom had seemingly secured the profitability of all franchises, save the lowly St. Louis Browns, and Organized Baseball had strict restrictions on the shifting of franchises. Any proposed transfer had to be approved by a unanimous vote of both leagues. Thus, as it approached mid-century, the baseball establishment seemed poised, as usual, on the brink of inaction.

By 1951, however, the pressure to change had intensified. The attendance bubble had burst, threatening the financial viability of not just the Browns, but the Boston Braves and Philadelphia Athletics, the other weak franchises in two-team markets. In addition, a congressional subcommittee, headed by Emmanuel Celler, launched an investigation of baseball's business practices. With Los Angeles Congressman Patrick J. Hillings leading the way, the committee challenged baseball's restrictions on rewarding and relocating franchises.[10] In response, National League President Ford Frick produced a report on "the Pacific Coast and its baseball potentialities," halfheartedly suggesting that while expansion was "the most practical solution," the major leagues had to tread carefully lest they violate minor league interests. The following year major league baseball, while still evidencing little interest in expansion, greatly eased its restrictions on franchise shifts. Instead of requiring a unanimous vote in both leagues, a move could be approved by a vote of the affected league.[11] This series of decisions guaranteed that baseball's adaptation to modern America would occur not in a planned or orderly manner, but rather in haphazard style, pitting city against city in a quest for major league status.

The carousel began spinning in spring 1953, not in Boston or Milwaukee but in St. Louis. Browns' owner Bill Veeck had struggled to make his perennially cellar-dwelling club into a viable rival to the more popular St. Louis Cardinals. A series of inspired promotions, including sending midget Eddie Gaedel to bat in a ball game, had doubled Browns attendance in two years, giving Veeck hope that he might seize the local initiative. In February 1953, however, the Annheuser-Busch brewery purchased the Cardinals, dashing any possibility that the team might ultimately be driven out of St. Louis. Veeck, taking advantage of the newly liberalized relocation rules, announced his intention to immediately move the Browns. Although many suitors savored his franchise, only Baltimore and Milwaukee, both of which had built publicly funded stadiums hoping to lure a big league team, had adequate facilities to host major league baseball. Veeck, who had once owned the minor league Milwaukee Brewers, favored the Midwestern city.[12] However, Boston Braves owner Lou Perini now controlled the Brewers and the territorial rights to baseball in Milwaukee. On March 3, 1953, Milwaukee fans learned that while proclaiming he would never stand in the way of the city getting a major league franchise, Perini had refused to allow Veeck to move the Browns into Milwaukee.[13]

The decision enraged the local populace. Milwaukee officials threatened to terminate the lease that allowed Perini's Brewers to play in County Stadium in 1953. Fans threatened to boycott the team. The local congressman vowed to reopen an investigation of baseball. Perini, whose Braves had drawn only 281,278 fans in 1952, had hoped to relocate the following year, but he had set his sights on larger cities with greater attendance potential. Faced now with the possibility of substantial financial losses in both Boston and Milwaukee, Perini caved in. On March 13, just ten days after rejecting Veeck's bid, Perini called for an emergency meeting of baseball owners to request a move to Milwaukee. On March 18, less than a month before the season was to start, the National League voted unanimously to approve the transfer.[14]

Perini was far from enthusiastic about the sudden and unexpected change. Although Milwaukee boasted a brand new stadium with 12,000 parking spaces and the city had offered him an extraordinarily generous lease, Perini expected no great bonanza. In Milwaukee he found himself in the second smallest city in the majors; the minor league Brewers had drawn fewer than 200,000 fans in a pennant-winning season in 1952. Privately, Perini confessed that he anticipated attendance reaching no more than 750,000. Seeking to protect his gate receipts, Perini refused to televise any games.[15]

Milwaukeeans, however, responded with what the *New York Times* described as an electric enthusiasm. Cheers rang out in downtown bars and restaurants. The news dominated the front pages of the Milwaukee newspapers under the headlines—WE'RE BIG LEAGUERS, and WE'RE HOME OF THE BRAVES. The Association of Commerce and others passionately endorsed the latter phrase as a promotional device. The city of Milwaukee cancelled its mail with a metered stamp reading, "Milwaukee, the home of the Braves." The local Photo Engravers Union stamped the slogan with an Indian head on its envelopes. Schoolchildren reportedly ended their daily national anthems, singing, "And the home of the Braves." Fans flocked to the stadium to sit in the stands and watch the final stages of construction, causing Sunday traffic jams in the weeks leading up to the season.[16]

On April 8 the Braves arrived to play an exhibition game against the Red Sox. Thirty models wearing Indian headdresses and 12,000 fans greeted the team at Milwaukee Station, where a red carpet had been laid out from the train shed to the street. An additional 50,000 fans lined Wisconsin Avenue as the players drove by in open cars, accompanied by marching bands and Native Americans on horseback. When the convoy reached the Shroeder Hotel, according to W. C. Heinz, "Every church bell, fire siren, factory and tugboat and railroad whistle in Milwaukee and vicinity let loose." In the hotel the players found a Christmas tree, decorated with bats and balls, and laden with gifts. A large banner read, YOU BROUGHT US CHRISTMAS IN APRIL.[17]

Civic leaders made no secret of the psychological impact of the Braves' arrival. Since the end of the war the Greater Milwaukee Committee for Development had laid out plans for over $200 million in public projects including highways, airport improvements, and a new zoo, library, museum, and war memorial. The stadium, built at a cost of $4,000,000 and viewed as the first phase of this program, had produced dividends within a few short years. "Once in the life of a city . . . there comes that wonderful golden opportunity for greatness," explained Mayor Frank Zeidler. "Milwaukee had its chance at greatness and it grasped and made splendid use of the opportunity."[18]

The phrase "big league" reverberated in the city's discourse. Visiting reporter Al Hirschberg discovered that the sudden appearance of the Braves had given Milwaukee a long-sought-after sense of identity. "Something happened to the ego of the people," reported Hirschberg. "They threw out their collective chest, looked the world squarely in the eye, and proclaimed, 'We're big league.' " A campaign to build a new public library succeeded on the platform, "We're a big league town, we have to have a big league library." Striking brewery workers lofted signs stating, "We're a big league town. We want big league wages." Milwaukee's "whole inferiority complex is gone," exclaimed a longtime resident.[19]

Sportswriter Shirley Povich attributed the commotion to a "mass brainwashing," in which "other values are replaced by a baseball hysteria."[20] The ferment escalated throughout the season. The Milwaukee Braves required only thirteen home games to surpass the previous season's attendance in Boston. The club passed one million paid admissions on July 31. The team's surprising performance fueled the passion. After finishing in seventh place in 1952, the Braves began the new season like pennant contenders. Behind the bats of second-year third baseman Eddie Mathews and newly acquired first baseman Joe Adcock, the glove of rookie centerfielder Billy Bruton, and the pitching of Warren Spahn and Lew Burdette, the Braves seized first place for a giddy twelve days in

June. Local fans embraced the team with an unprecedented ardor. "I've just seen a World Series in May," marveled a veteran Pittsburgh sportswriter. "Braves fans are the most rabid the game has ever seen." Milwaukee, stated a *New York Times* correspondent, is "more Brooklyn than Brooklyn."[21] Supporters swamped the players with affection and gifts. Milwaukee's heavily ethnic population regularly honored players of their respective nationalities. According to one report,

> Jews put on a night for Sid Gordon and Germans for Warren Spahn; Italians gave one for Sibbi Sisti; Negroes for (Bill) Bruton, Jim Pendleton and George Crowe; Iowans for (Jack) Dittmer. Lutherans turned out 10,000 strong to see Andy Pafko; Poles gave a birthday party at home plate for Max Surkont.

Gifts of cheese, pork sausage, and kielbasa descended on the clubhouse. "I've got to watch out they don't smother us with kindness, beer and sauerbraten," joked Manager Charlie Grimm.[22]

The excitement extended beyond the boundaries of Milwaukee. The Braves, located in the northwest reaches of the major leagues, tapped into a vast regional following. "Thousands of fans flocked to the games not only from all over Wisconsin, but from Minnesota, Milwaukee, Illinois, Iowa, the Dakotas and more distant points," reported *Business Week*. Trains and buses from all over the Midwest materialized at County Stadium. The Milwaukee Railroad built a passenger platform at the ballpark but frequently had to turn down excess requests for special trains. At a June night game 150 buses arrived overflowing the forty-slot bus parking lot.[23]

Even after the Braves dropped from the pennant race the frenzy continued. On the final day of the season Braves' attendance surpassed 1.8 million, establishing a new National League record. The total more than doubled the city's population. Only the limited seating capacity of County Stadium, which held only 33,000 fans, prevented the club from topping two million. The Association of Commerce boasted that the team had pumped between $5 million and $8 million into the local economy in increased taxi, restaurant, hotel, and retail revenues. "This is the greatest thing that has happened to Milwaukee since beer," crowed one merchant.[24]

Major league baseball had inadvertently stumbled into a gold mine. In a year in which attendance for all but two other clubs had sharply declined, the Braves had drawn 1.5 million extra fans. The Braves' triumph created a new blueprint for success. Teams suffering from poor attendance could reinvent themselves by moving to one of the many communities desperate for major league baseball. The Milwaukee experience also awakened baseball owners to the possibilities of regional franchises and the Braves second-place finish raised the chimera of new surroundings enhancing on-field performance. For cities aspiring to big league status, netting a major league team hooked with the lure of a publicly funded stadium meant profits and prestige, financial rewards and spiritual benefits.

The euphoria in Milwaukee obscured the potential downside lessons of the transfer. Much of the vaunted economic impact involved not a stimulus, but a shifting of spending patterns. Some local merchants, notably restaurants, complained that business fell on game days, as fans hovered near home and office radios to hear the action.[25] Money brought into Milwaukee was drained from nearby communities. Indeed, both the Chicago Cubs and Detroit Tigers saw sharp attendance drops in 1953, possibly related to the Braves' relocation. (Nor did the Boston Red Sox benefit from the Braves' departure; patronage declined by 8 percent.) Furthermore, the "Milwaukee Miracle" established an important precedent. "Any city that wants to get a big-league team nowadays is going to have to provide a stadium," commented a baseball executive.[26] Cities seeking teams would have to spend tax dollars to build stadiums, subsidizing private enterprises from the public coffer. Finally, the abandonment of Boston raised the issue of a team's responsibility and relationship to a community. If the Braves could leave Boston, where they had drawn over a million fans just four years earlier, couldn't they also leave Milwaukee when the novelty of major league baseball wore off and attendance declined?

Few observers raised these questions in 1953. The path had cleared for additional franchise shifts. In 1954 the St. Louis Browns migrated to Baltimore, where they became the Orioles. The Maryland seaport seemed an ideal solution to the Browns' perennial attendance woes. Baltimore was the ninth largest city in the United States, able to draw on a metropolitan population of 1.5 million people. The city had a long-standing baseball tradition and had ardently supported its minor league Orioles. In 1947 voters had approved a $2.5 million bond issue to build Memorial Stadium. Three years later they authorized the addition of a second deck, raising the seating capacity to 50,000. City officials surrendered the showcase ballpark to the Orioles for a minimal rent and promised free office space and stadium maintenance, while allocating all parking and food revenues to the team.[27]

Both local politicians and baseball officials ignored the scattered protests accompanying the move. The arrival of the Orioles threatened to further weaken the struggling Washington Senators, less than an hour's drive to the south. In addition, civil rights leaders questioned whether Baltimore, a segregated city, deserved major league status. The Orioles did little to allay these fears when the club failed to resign Satchel Paige, its only black star, and cut pitcher Jesse Heard, the only black player on the roster, during spring training. Nor did the Orioles support Governor Thomas McKeldin's plea for local hotels to welcome visiting black players on other teams.[28]

These drawbacks notwithstanding, the 1954 season opened with visions of a replication of the Milwaukee scenario. "We stand on the eve of the Great Day we have anticipated so keenly," crowed the *Baltimore News-Post*. In 1953 the local Association of Commerce had hailed the promise of a major league team as "a development of great importance to our economic and community progress and a proper and overdue recognition of our city's national stature." With the Birds in hand, the Association celebrated "the amazing amount of favorable publicity—the kind that can't be bought," and predicted a buoying of "all aspects of the city's economy." An early flood of ticket orders boosted hopes that the Orioles would match or exceed Milwaukee's attendance figures. "I believe we'll come close to 2,000,000 admissions for the season," forecast club president Clarence Miles.[29]

Baltimore, reported the *New Yorker*, "was going slightly wacky" amid a recurrent theme of "Back in the Big League." Throughout the city, "the orange and black colors of the team floated everywhere, like the banners of the ancient artisans' guilds."[30] The town greeted its new club with a parade described by *Life* magazine as the "most exuberant demonstration since the Civil War." A half-million people joined Vice President Richard Nixon and baseball's last remaining links to Baltimore's earlier major league incarnation, ninety-one-year-old Connie Mack and eighty-five-year-old Clark Griffith, to welcome the team. The procession featured marching bands, women garbed as Orioles and baseballs, and a twelve-foot papier-mâché float of Baltimore native Babe Ruth rotating on a pedestal. The ballplayers threw 20,000 plastic baseballs into the cheering crowd.[31]

The Orioles played before a sellout crowd on opening day and attracted 43,383 fans to the first night game, creating "the most glorious traffic jam in the history" of Memorial Stadium. After the first five home games the Orioles had drawn 130,506 fans.[32] Unlike the Braves in Milwaukee, however, the change of scenery failed to improve the club's fortunes on the field. In 1953 the Browns had won fifty-four games, lost 100 and finished in last place, forty-six-and-a-half games behind the pennant-winning Yankees. The Orioles posted an identical record in 1954 and trailed the high-flying Cleveland Indians by fifty-seven games. Only the woeful performance of the hapless Philadelphia Athletics kept Baltimore out of the cellar. By midseason fans began to lose interest in the inept performance. Attendance tailed off far below preseason expectations. Nonetheless, the Orioles attracted 1,060,910 paid admissions. The total more than tripled the Browns' 1953 season and exceeded the highest figures ever recorded by the Browns, Senators, or Athletics. An economic survey reported that more than one in four patrons had come from out of town and spent an average of $30 each in Baltimore each time they attended a game, pumping $5 million into the local economy. Echoing the conventional wisdom, *U.S. News and World Report* would conclude, "A big league team is a financial asset to a city."[33]

In 1955 the scene shifted to Kansas City, where *Kansas City Star* sports editor Ernie Mehl had long waged a campaign for a major league team. Mehl approached Chicago businessman Arnold Johnson, who owned the local minor league stadium, and, according to Arthur Mann, assured Johnson "he could write his own ticket if he brought a big league team to Kansas City." The city would buy his ballpark for a generous price, raze it, and build a major league arena on the foundations. Johnson could rent back the new arena for a nominal fee.[34] Johnson, a business associate of New York Yankee owners Del Webb and Dan Topping, then offered to buy the Philadelphia Athletics from the Mack family and move the team to Kansas City. Connie Mack had reigned in Philadelphia since 1901 and his family had strong ties to the community, but team attendance had dropped to 362,113 in 1953. "The last thing we want to do is move the team out of Philadelphia," stated his son Roy. "But we can't afford another year as bad as last year." A "Save the A's" campaign ignited but quickly extinguished in Philadelphia and attendance plummeted to 304,666.[35] The Macks sold out to Johnson, who brought the Athletics to Kansas City.

For Kansas City baseball fans, the acquisition of a major league team, even one as lowly as the Athletics, inspired what one writer recalled as "an emotional binge of pride and optimism." Ernie Mehl explained, "The important thing is that we've gone big league, you've got to take the best you can get. The successful ball clubs aren't on the market." Voters approved the stadium bond issue by a five-to-one margin, and builders completed the reconstruction in only twenty-two weeks. In April 1955 Kansas City staged its own version of the ritual welcoming parade, with 200,000 "applauding, cheering, beaming friends" lining the streets to cheer the players. Governor Fred Hall of Kansas, Lt. Governor James T. Blair of Missouri, and a host of mayors from nearby cities joined the festivities. Regional enthusiasm for the team surfaced immediately. "Baseball fans swarmed in on the city like settlers bound for a house raising in pioneer days," reported Gerald Holland in *Sports Illustrated*. "They came by car, bus and plane, and by excursion trains. . . . They came from Arkansas, Oklahoma, Texas, Colorado, Nebraska and from deep into what used to be St. Louis Cardinal Missouri territory."[36] Moving up to sixth place, the Athletics drew 1,393,054 paid admissions, trailing only the Yankees in American League attendance.

From the perspective of 1955 the revamping of the major leagues seemed an unqualified success. The Braves had drawn in excess of two million fans to an enlarged Milwaukee County Stadium in both 1954 and 1955 and, although attendance in Baltimore had dropped to 852,039 in the Orioles' second year, this still marked a dramatic improvement over the St. Louis years. As Charles C. Euchner has commented, baseball had "replaced three over-saturated markets with six well-served markets." Yet this trio of transfers had scarcely broadened the boundaries of the national pastime. Although Kansas City was a few hundred miles west of St. Louis, notes G. Edward White, all the newly relocated clubs fit comfortably into the established train-travel networks.[37] With the logical candidates for transplantation accounted for, the West Coast metropolises of Los Angeles and San Francisco remained outside the major league orbit.

These early transfers had each involved money-losing franchises, the weaker club in a two-team market. Other teams, however, even profitable ones, shared the problems that had driven the Braves, Browns, and Athletics from their homes — declining patronage and aging stadiums with minimal parking spaces for a suburban population increasingly inclined to drive to games. New York City's two National League clubs, the Dodgers and Giants, both remained remunerative ventures, but each had experienced dramatic drops in attendance and required new ballparks to attract more fans. The Giants had drawn more than 1.1 million fans during their pennant-winning season of 1954, but in 1956, despite the attraction of Willie Mays, only 653,923 people came to the venerable Polo Grounds. Games against the Dodgers accounted for a third of this total, leaving them heavily dependent on their interborough rivals.

Television revenues virtually guaranteed an annual profit, but, rebuffed in his efforts to build a new stadium or share Yankee Stadium with the Yankees, Giant owner Horace Stoneham decided to move his club. Stoneham chose Minneapolis, where he owned the minor league franchise and the city had built a new stadium.[38] In Brooklyn, owner Walter O'Malley presided over the most profitable franchise in the major leagues, but New York City politics had frustrated his attempts to secure land rights for a new downtown ballpark. O'Malley also cast a fearful eye in the direction of Milwaukee, where the Braves had drawn more than twice as many fans as the Dodgers in 1954 and 1955. "I want to produce winning ball clubs and to continue to do so, I must be able to compete, dollar-for-dollar, with the Braves," O'Malley worried openly.[39]

In 1956 public officials in Los Angeles and San Francisco began to court the New York clubs. Los Angeles City Supervisor Kenneth Hahn, attending the World Series in hopes of luring the Washington Senators to Los Angeles, discovered that the Dodgers might be available. Shortly thereafter, O'Malley stopped in Los Angeles to meet with city officials.[40] San Francisco Mayor George Christopher began a secret weekend shuttle to New York to convince Stoneham that his city offered a preferable alternative to Minneapolis. "Getting a major league team into San Francisco is a crusade with us," confessed Christopher.[41] On February 21, 1957, the Dodgers purchased the Pacific Coast League Los Angeles Angels from the Cubs, securing territorial rights to the city. The following day Stoneham announced that if the Dodgers headed West, the Giants would also depart. Shortly thereafter Stoneham acquired the San Francisco Seals from the Red Sox.[42]

These actions notwithstanding, neither team had made a firm commitment to move to the West Coast. Both continued to negotiate with the California cities over proposals to build new stadiums. Stoneham announced on July 17 that the Giants would definitely leave New York, but left their ultimate destination open. O'Malley meanwhile continued to insist that a new stadium in Brooklyn would keep the Dodgers at home. On August 9 San Francisco formally offered to build a 40,000- to 50,000-seat stadium with 12,000 parking spaces for the Giants. Nine days later the Giants' Board of Directors approved the move to San Francisco. "Whether or not the Dodgers move to Los Angeles," stated Stoneham, "the Giants are definitely going—even if we have to go it alone." The fate of the Dodgers seemed almost assured, but not until October 7, when the Los Angeles City Council formally agreed to turn over 300 acres to O'Malley, where he could build a new ballpark, did the Dodgers officially confirm the move.[43]

Most New Yorkers conceded the inevitability of the Giants move. When asked how he felt about depriving New York's children of their beloved Giants, Stoneham commented, "I feel bad about the kids, but I haven't seen many of their fathers lately."[44] Few could fault his logic. The flight of the Dodgers, however, was another thing. "It's no laughing matter," wrote sportswriter Dick Young. "Yank this ball club out of Brooklyn where the people have been living and dying with it for three generations, and you tamper seriously with the fabric of their lives. What of the ball club's responsibility to the fan?"[45] The abandonment of Brooklyn secured O'Malley a permanent mantle of villainy in local folklore.

Across the continent, the arrival of major league teams set off the celebrations already familiar from Milwaukee, Baltimore, and Kansas City. The Giants instantly carved out a place in the hearts of San Franciscans. Billboards reading "Welcome San Francisco Giants. Swat those Bums" greeted the team. Mannequins in downtown store windows appeared in Giants' uniforms and the welcoming ticker-tape parade down Market Street attracted hundreds of thousands of people. "Major league ball . . . has taken its place alongside the famous fogs and the earthquake of '06 as a prime topic of conversation," asserted a longtime resident. Local baseball legend Lefty O'Doul opened a new restaurant near Union Square, anticipating a boom in baseball-related business. The Dimaggio Brothers doubled the size of their Fisherman's Wharf eating establishment. Newspaper columnist Charles McCabe observed, "The Giants . . . have given us all a notable civic strut. San Francisco has been saying for decades that it is big league. In its secret heart it has never been quite sure. These days it is."[46]

The Dodgers evoked the same sense of exhilaration and affirmation, offering "the first focal point on which everyone can unite." The team, claimed the *Los Angeles Times*, made Los Angeles "a great city, with common interests, and the civic unity which gives a city great character." Two months into the 1958 season, sportswriter Jim Murray proclaimed the Dodgers, "quite clearly a part of Los Angeles and Los Angeles a part of baseball."[47]

Before the 1958 season began, the general consensus held that the Dodgers, landing in the more populous city, had attained a far better deal than the Giants. As Tim Cohane explained the popular perception, "O'Malley, regarded as masterfully shrewd, planned the move west for both teams. He sold the idea to Stoneham who is supposed to be less shrewd." Yet, from the moment the season opened and the Giants trounced the Dodgers 8–0 at San Francisco's Seals Stadium, the opinion began to spread that the Giants had stumbled into Nirvana, while the Dodgers, according to Cohane, had "wandered into the original Valley of Migraine."[48] The Dodgers, perennial pennant contenders and third-place finishers in 1957, immediately sank to the bottom of the standings. The Giants, expected to duplicate their sixth-place status, unexpectedly rose to the top. Los Angeles fans watched fabled Dodger stars Gil Hodges, Pee Wee Reese, Duke Snider, and Carl Furillo on the decline. In San Francisco, rookies Orlando Cepeda, Jim Davenport, and Willie Kirkland joined twenty-seven-year-old Willie Mays as a promising core for the future.

The contrast extended beyond the playing field. Both teams had been promised new stadiums, but in 1958 they settled into temporary headquarters. The Giants moved into Seals Stadium in the city's Mission District, one of the nation's finest minor league ballparks. Although Seals Stadium seated only 23,000 fans, it offered convenient access and an intimate charm for players and fans alike. The Dodgers, forced to choose between the old Angels' home of Wrigley Field, which seated 10,000 fewer fans than Ebbets Field and offered no parking, or the Los Angeles Coliseum, described by Arthur Daley as "a huge oval with plenty of room for customers but no room for a playing field," opted for the latter. The result was a ballpark like no other that irredeemably distorted the games played within its confines. The right-field fence lay a distant 390 feet from home plate; centerfield a daunting 435 feet away; and the asymmetric left field stood only 250 feet deep. To compensate for the difference, the Dodgers erected a forty-foot high "queer-looking meshed" screen in left field. The configuration had a devastating effect on left-handed power hitters like Dodger star Duke Snider. Of the 193 home runs hit at the Coliseum in 1958, only eight were hit to right field and two to center. Snider's home run output fell from forty in 1957 to fifteen in 1958.[49]

The Giants seemed to have gotten the better of the political wars as well. After Stoneham rejected a downtown location for a new ballpark, San Francisco had promised to build a stadium at Candlestick Point, just south of the city. Although visiting newsmen like Arthur Daley complained about the cold weather at Seals Stadium ("This reporter froze to death . . . during the first night game of the season in San Francisco. He was wearing an overcoat too," recounted Daley), they were reassured that "the new Giant park . . . is being hollowed out of a hill that will serve as protection from both fog and winds." Candlestick Park, promised Mayor Christopher, would be located at a site where fog would not be "troublesome." The new $15-million arena, constructed entirely with public funds, constituted a massive giveaway to a private corporation, but despite a short-lived taxpayer suit, San Franciscans voiced minimal opposition. Construction began on schedule, and the Giants would have their new home in time for the 1960 season.[50]

The situation in Los Angeles evolved in a diametrically opposite fashion. Unlike Stoneham, Dodger owner Walter O'Malley proposed building a new ballpark with his private funds. The City Council agreed to turn over Chavez Ravine, a 315-acre site near downtown Los Angeles and its central freeways, to the Dodgers for this purpose. Once the home of an impoverished but thriving Mexican community, Chavez Ravine was the largest undeveloped parcel of land close to the downtown area. Most residents had left in the early 1950s when the federal government had acquired the land for public housing. In 1952, however, Los Angeles voters blocked this project, so the land reverted to the city under the stipulation that it must be used for an appropriate public purpose. This requirement had left the land not only undeveloped, but also seemingly undevelopable. The Council traded the problematic gulch to the Dodgers in exchange for the less valuable Wrigley Field property, promising to use public funds to grade the canyon and build access roads.[51]

Opposition to the Chavez Ravine deal arose immediately. Several City Council members protested awarding the Dodgers land and services worth millions of dollars. Professional baseball, they contended, was not an appropriate public purpose. Underwritten with monies provided by John A. Smith, who owned the Pacific Coast League San Diego Padres and feared the arrival of the Dodgers would weaken his franchise, opponents placed an initiative on the June 1958 ballot seeking to reverse the City Council's agreement with the Dodgers. The action took O'Malley by surprise. "I never anticipated a referendum," he observed. "In fact, I was completely unaware of the thing they called a referendum because they never had that in New York." O'Malley grew even more concerned when polls began to show voters, especially those in outlying districts, tilting against the land deal. In desperation, Los Angeles Mayor Norris Poulson suggested a "scare campaign," portraying the election as an unalterable "yes-or-no vote for baseball." Hollywood celebrities, headed by comedian Joe E. Brown, formed a city's committee for "Yea on Baseball." The committee staged a telethon shortly before the balloting. The cast included George Burns, Groucho Marx, Jack Benny, and Debbie Reynolds. The highlight came when Ronald Reagan, an actor en route to a political career, derided the argument against the Chavez Ravine deal as "One of the most dishonest documents I ever read in my life." O'Malley, observed the future president, was getting a good deal, but so was the city.[52]

The June 3 balloting proved remarkably close. "On the day of the vote we were uncertain of the outcome until about midnight," recalled Dodger executive Buzzy Bavasi. The voters approved the stadium contract by a narrow margin of 51.8 percent to 48.2 percent. According to Charles Alexander, African Americans, loyal to the Dodgers since the days of Jackie Robinson, may have cast the decisive ballots.[53] The Dodgers experienced only fleeting jubilation. Opponents had filed a taxpayers' suit seeking to prevent the transfer of Chavez Ravine. Three days after the election, a superior court judge issued a preliminary injunction blocking consummation of the agreement. One month later another judge declared the contract "an illegal delegation of the duty of the City Council, an abdication of its public trust, and a manifest gross abuse of discretion." The decision dealt the Dodgers and the prospect of a ballpark at Chavez Ravine a severe blow.[54]

The Dodgers drew consolation from the team's splendid showing at the box office. Despite the bizarre dimensions of the Coliseum and the poorest Dodger finish since World War II, the team attracted 1,845,268 fans. Dodger radio broadcasts featuring the extraordinary Vince Scully became a staple of Southern California listening, receiving the highest local radio ratings since the advent of television. The Dodgers had outdrawn the Giants, whose attendance had been limited by the lesser capacity of Seals Stadium, by more than a half million fans. Nonetheless, the move had proved a financial success for both clubs. The Giants, behind a strong third-place finish, had doubled their New York draw. "I'm positive that I picked the better city," Stoneham told *New York Times* sportswriter Arthur Daley. Daley "fully" agreed with Stoneham. "He's more set than O'Malley is because his stadium is already in the process of construction," affirmed the reporter.[55]

The travails of the Dodgers began to lift in 1959. In January the California Supreme Court issued a writ of prohibition, which in effect overruled the superior court ruling on the Chavez Ravine controversy. In April the state supreme court declared the original contract constitutional, allowing the Dodgers to proceed with construction. The Dodgers, however, would suffer one further humiliation. In May they proceeded to remove the last remaining residents of Chavez Ravine. Only twenty families were left of the hundreds who had once shared the gullies and hillsides. Most departed willingly, but the Arechiga family, who had lived in the arroyo for thirty-six years and had turned down a $10,500 federal buyout in 1951, refused to leave. Police deputies forcibly evicted the recalcitrant squatters, with the women kicking and screaming, and bulldozed their home. Television news cameramen reported and repeatedly rebroadcast the scene, provoking an outpouring of sympathy, particularly in the Mexican-American community. The Arechigas, claiming that they now had no place to live, pitched a tent nearby and continued their defiance for ten days. Public sympathy, and the family's resistance, collapsed when a local newspaper revealed that far from being destitute, patriarch Manuel Arechiga owned at least nine houses, including one vacant property.[56] The Dodgers were finally free to move ahead with their Los Angeles pleasure palace.

The Dodgers also experienced an on-the-field rebirth in 1959. A mild reconfiguration of the Coliseum, bringing in the right-field fence, and a rejuvenation of the lineup produced an unlikely National League pennant and a World Series Championship. Attendance soared over 2 million. Crowds exceeding 92,000 fans also turned out for three World Series contests and a Dodger–Yankee exhibition game honoring paralyzed Dodger catcher Roy Campanella. A Chicago reporter decried the spectacle of the World Series at the Coliseum as a "travesty." But in Los Angeles, wrote Sid Ziff, where people had "grown to enjoy their weird ball park . . . [t]he whole community has gone Dodger nuts." "Who will have the effrontery to tells us now," crowed the *Los Angeles Times*, "that the movement to supply the Dodgers with a decent playing yard was against the public interest. Their triumph is that they have created one of those centers of attachment that the metropolitan area of Los Angeles has needed so desperately."[57]

The Giants also continued to prosper. In 1959 attendance jumped to 1.42 million. Candlestick Park debuted in 1960. Built entirely with reinforced concrete, it became the first stadium without a single obstructed seat. However, it quickly became apparent that Candlestick's deficiencies far outweighed its virtues. A June 1960 report in the *Californian* criticized the cold, harsh winds blowing in off the bay, the smell of sewage, and "Cardiac Hill," the long climb from the parking lot to the ballpark, which it claimed had already caused six deaths from heart attacks.[58] Nonetheless, just under 1.8 million people visited the 'Stick during its inaugural season.

The Dodgers finally unveiled Dodger Stadium in 1962. The only privately funded stadium built in the postwar era, Dodger Stadium proved to be, in the classically hyperbolic words of Jim Murray, "not just any baseball park, but the Taj Mahal, the Parthenon, and Westminster Abbey of baseball." Two million seven hundred thousand fans attended Dodger games in 1962 and Dodger profits exceeded $4 million. The Dodgers had become what economist Roger Noll would later call "baseball's answer to the Denver Mint."[59]

The 1958 transcontinental migration of the Dodgers and Giants whet the appetites of other communities for major league baseball. New York City formed a committee to secure a team to replace the departed franchises. With few of the original clubs still candidates for relocation, the only hope for most major league aspirants was the expansion of the existing leagues, but organized baseball stubbornly refused to abandon its sixteen-team tradition. "If baseball owners ran Congress," observed Bill Veeck, "Kansas and Nebraska would still be trying to get into the union."[60] The solution, according to William Shea, chairman of the New York baseball committee, was to revive the idea of a third baseball league. On November 13, 1958, he announced the creation of a new Continental League with franchises in Houston, Dallas–Fort Worth, Atlanta, Denver, Toronto, Minneapolis–St. Paul, and second teams in New York and Detroit. Representatives from each of these cities posted $50,000 to indicate their sincerity.[61]

The league gained added credibility when Shea introduced Branch Rickey as the commissioner. Rickey, long an advocate of expansion, argued that a third circuit was preferable to piecemeal expansion of the National and American Leagues. Rickey argued that expansion teams would be overmatched in the existing leagues. "It may seem illogical and paradoxical that you can't get manpower for four extra clubs but you can for eight," reasoned Rickey. "New ones can't compete on a basis of equality with old ones. But eight teams can compete equally while recognized as a third major league. Our new league would not pretend to be major the first year. But by the end of the third year that would not be unthinkable."[62]

The Continental League, seeking to neutralize opposition from Organized Baseball, lobbied Congress to pass legislation eliminating baseball's antitrust exemption. Senator Estes Kefauver introduced a bill in the Senate placing baseball under the purview of the Federal Trade Commission and the Sherman and Clayton Antitrust Acts. The Kefauver bill also proposed to outlaw any efforts "preventing, hindering, obstructing, or adversely affecting the formation and operation of a new major league," a proscription that might be construed to include baseball's treasured reserve clause. Kefauver's measure failed to pass by only four votes.[63]

The Continental League may have been no more than a grand bluff. As Houston advocates admitted, "What fans in Houston and every other expansion city wanted was their team playing the Dodgers or the Yankees, Red Sox or Pirates."[64] The aggressive third league threat, however, crushed Organized Baseball's stubborn resistance to expansion. Several days after the perilously close Senate vote, Commissioner Ford Frick announced that the American and National Leagues would each add two new franchises in the near future. To ensure the collapse of the Continental League, the majors offered National League franchises to New York and Houston. In addition, the American League allowed Clark Griffith to move the Washington Senators to Minneapolis–St. Paul and awarded the nation's capital an expansion team. Hoping to cash in on the vast Southern California market, the American League created a second team for Los Angeles.

The fiery enthusiasm inspired by relocated teams burned less brightly for the expansion squads. As Rickey had predicted, none of the squads proved competitive with the older clubs, dampening fan enthusiasm and attendance figures. The American League introduced its new ten-team format in 1961. The Senators finished tied for last with the Athletics, and the Angels landed in eighth place. Both franchises recorded disappointing attendance. The Angels, playing in tiny Wrigley Field, attracted just over 600,000 patrons. The new Senators fared worse than either the Angels or their 1960 Washington predecessors, drawing only 597,000 fans. On the other hand, the transplanted Senators became the success story of 1961. To avoid alienating the citizens of either Minneapolis or St. Paul, owner Clark Griffith christened the club the Twins and named his team after the state of Minnesota rather than one of the cities. The appellation captured the regional attraction of the team. Fans reportedly came from seven states and three Canadian provinces to see the Twins, arriving by the busload and trainload from as far away as Billings, Montana. Fans sang a special fight song, *We're Going to Win, Twins* and, although the team failed to comply, the club drew 1,256,723 fans.[65]

National League expansion arrived in 1962. The bonanza attendance figures that had rewarded the relocated teams did not automatically carry over to the expansion clubs. Both of the new clubs were shackled with inadequate stadiums and neither reached the million mark in attendance during their first year. Houston, now the seventh largest city in the majors, had waged a six-year campaign for big league recognition. Voters had repeatedly approved bills to build a big league ballpark, but public officials had hesitated to start construction before the city secured a team. To accommodate the new Colt 45's, the city hastily built a temporary open-air stadium seating 32,000 people. The heat of the day forced most games into the nighttime, the hunting hours for the city's voracious mosquitoes. Colts Pitcher Hal Woodeschick recalled: "We'd get to the ballpark and watch it rain every day between four and five in the afternoon. Then the groundskeepers would go through the stands with an insecticide fogger to kill the mosquitoes. The ballplayers would have to be sprayed before every game. If we didn't have the stuff on our bodies, they would eat us up in the bullpen."[66] A healthy but unspectacular 924,456 fans braved the heat and mosquitoes to watch the eighth-place team play.

In New York, the fledging Mets, playing in the decaying Polo

Grounds, erected a monument to ineptitude. The team, managed by the inimitable Casey Stengel and stocked with aging former all-stars like Gil Hodges and Richie Ashburn and soon-to-be legendary underachievers Marv Throneberrry and Choo Choo Coleman, staggered out of the gate, losing their first nine games. They improved only minimally, triumphing in only forty of 160 games to post the worst winning percentage in major league history. "The youth of America," as Stengel referred to the dedicated and surprisingly rabid fans, turned out to see the team, but in less than stellar numbers. The Dodgers and Giants in their last year of residence had drawn a total of almost 1.7 million fans. Only 922,530 paid to see the Mets in 1962, fewer than had watched the Dodgers in 1957. Games with the prodigal Dodgers and Giants accounted for a disproportionate percentage of the Mets' draw.

Having reluctantly created four new franchises, three of them in cities that already or previously had teams, Organized Baseball evidenced no inclination to further enlarge its domain. The major league hopes of other cities once again rested with snaring an existing franchise by building a new stadium and promising greener pastures. Ironically, the teams most available for relocation were the Braves and Athletics, two of the clubs that had begun baseball's reconfiguration less than a decade earlier. Astonishingly, the Braves had fallen on hard times in Milwaukee. The Braves had won pennants in 1957 and 1958 and attracted two million fans for four consecutive seasons. In the early 1960s, however, the enthusiasm evaporated when the Braves dropped from contention. Ownership policies exacerbated the situation. The team converted general admission seats into higher-priced reserve seats and, perhaps more offensive to Milwaukeeans, barred fans from bringing their own beer into the ballpark.[67] In 1961 attendance dropped to 1.1 million; in 1962 it fell to 766,921.

Meanwhile, the situation in Kansas City had degenerated into farce. The Athletics had finished in sixth place during their inaugural 1955 season, but only reached that less than dizzy elevation once over the next decade. Baseball expert Bill James, who grew up rooting for the Athletics in those years, laments, "It would be very difficult, if not impossible for any team to become as bad as the Kansas City Athletics were. . . . The A's never had a winning record. . . . They very rarely had a winning *month*." Before acquiring the Athletics, Kansas City had hosted a New York Yankee farm club. During the late 1950s the Athletics appeared to maintain that role. Whenever the club developed a good player like Roger Maris or Ralph Terry, it traded him to the Yankees, where he blossomed into a star. Many fans blamed owner Arnold Johnson, who had close ties to the Yankee owners. However, the situation did not improve after Johnson died in 1960 and the team fell into the hands of eccentric Chicago insurance man Charles O. Finley. Finley discontinued trading with the Yankees, but the team continued to flounder on the field. The irascible Finley feuded with his players, sportswriters, the league office, and Kansas City itself. Under these circumstances Kansas City fans gave the Athletics surprisingly strong support, but attendance nonetheless fell precipitously during the Finley years.[68]

By 1963 both the Braves and the Athletics had begun to cast about for new homes. Finley, as James notes, "spent his entire time in Kansas City threatening to move." In 1961 he eyed Dallas–Ft. Worth. He considered Denver, New Orleans, Phoenix, and Seattle as well.[69] The American League repeatedly turned down his requests to move. In Milwaukee Lou Perini, who had moved the team in 1953, sold the Braves to a Chicago-based syndicate. Reports circulated that the new owners planned to relocate the team. "We didn't buy the franchise to move it. . . . How do those rumors get started?" asserted Braves Board Chairman William Bartholomay. Shortly thereafter he secretly hired a firm to find a new home for the Braves.[70]

Both the Braves and the Athletics honed in on Atlanta as a potential market. Although the Georgia community had fewer residents than either Milwaukee or Kansas City, it had other charms. A growing metropolis far distant from any major league town, Atlanta boasted the entire South as its hinterland. Revenues from a seven-state television and radio network promised to more than make up for any attendance shortfalls. The Atlanta-based Coca-

Cola Company reportedly was prepared to purchase extensive advertising time. Civic boosters hoping to justify public expenditures to entice a big league team echoed a now familiar refrain. "The true worth of a major league team is what it does for the posture of a city," explained Arthur B. Montgomery of Coca-Cola. "You're either a first-rate or a second-rate city." Atlanta's aggressive Mayor Ivan Allen cited the "national prestige" that he hoped his city would earn. "Is there any other area of activity where a city gets as much national publicity as sports?" asked Allen. With the civil rights movement growing, Allen also saw the acquisition of a big league team as evidence of a new era in southern race relations. Atlanta, the home of Martin Luther King, billed itself as a city "too busy to hate." "Major league sports here are a by-product of equal rights," explained Allen. "The Negro's full citizenship was one reason we (are) looked on with favor and the Negro population swells our potential."[71]

Finley visited Atlanta in 1963 and promised Mayor Allen that if Atlanta built a stadium, he would move his team there. The American League, however, refused to grant Finley permission to move and forced him to sign a four-year lease guaranteeing that he would remain in Kansas City. Mayor Allen nonetheless secured approval for the construction of a downtown stadium and began negotiations with the Braves, whose owners registered at Atlanta hotels under false names to hide their involvement. In March 1964, Bartholomay and Allen shook hands on an agreement to move the Braves to Atlanta. One month later Bartholomay, amid a concerted season-ticket selling push designed to save the team for Milwaukee, again blatantly lied about his intentions. "We are positively not moving," he told reporters. "We are playing in Milwaukee, whether you are talking of 1964, 1965 or 1975. I hope this is the last time anyone tries to link us with Atlanta or any other city."[72]

The Sporting News exposed Bartholomay's chicanery in July 1964. Milwaukee exploded with livid anger. The *Milwaukee Journal* decried the "greed, ingratitude, deception, and betrayal" that characterized the Atlanta coup. Baseball, charged Mayor Henry W.

Maier, had become "a traveling flea circus." The city feared losing the $3.5 million that major league baseball purportedly added to the economy, explained *Sports Illustrated*, and furthermore it did not "relish the colossal loss of face it would suffer. Milwaukee, scornfully called Bushville when the Braves arrived in 1953, would be right back where it started."[73] One letter writer captured the controversy in a parody of classic baseball verse:

This is the worst of all possible deeds,
From Boston to Bushville to South. . . .
Hopping around where the outlook's more sunny,
Clutching and grasping for big TV money,
Changing their names till it ain't even funny,
From Boston to Bushville to South.[74]

Both Milwaukee County and the state of Wisconsin filed antitrust suits to block the Braves' flight. The city, they argued, had expended millions of dollars to construct the stadium and support the team. The Braves would be the first team to abandon a publicly funded stadium and Milwaukee would be the first major league city to be left entirely without a baseball franchise. "How a ball club is permitted to come into a city like this, milk it for a dozen years and then jump elsewhere, I can't understand," protested Milwaukee County Executive John Doyne. Under these circumstances, argued the city attorney, "The denial of major league baseball . . . constitutes a denial of a substantial and significant right to the city."[75] Milwaukee won an injunction preventing the Braves from moving in 1965, but the National League granted the team permission to switch to Atlanta in 1966.

The Braves played three exhibition games in their new Atlanta stadium ("the happiest occasion since we got General Sherman headed back north in 1864," stated Mayor Allen) and then settled in for an unhappy lame-duck season in Milwaukee. The Wisconsin Supreme Court dashed any hopes of permanently blocking the move when it declared itself "powerless" to act against a major league team.[76]

In 1966 the Braves opened the season in Atlanta, where they drew 1.5 million fans in their inaugural season. More significantly, the Braves collected $2.5 million in television and radio revenues, five times what they had earned in Milwaukee. Georgia sportswriter Furman Bisher hailed these developments, without any sense of irony, as the "Miracle in Atlanta." *The Sporting News*, on the other hand, called them a "sorry chapter in baseball history."[77]

The loss of Atlanta to the Braves infuriated Charlie Finley. When his lease to play in Municipal Stadium expired in 1967, Finley announced that he would move the Athletics to Oakland, California, where the city had built a new ballpark, and threatened to sue the American League if they again blocked his plans.[78] The people of Kansas City expressed mixed reactions to the departure of the Athletics. Although bitter over the abandonment, they seemed relieved to see Finley leave. "The loss of the A's is more than recompensed by the pleasure of getting rid of Mr. Finley," commented U.S. Senator Stuart Symington, "Oakland is the luckiest city since Hiroshima."[79]

Both Kansas and Milwaukee now called for another expansion to win back their major league status. "We can't steal a team from another city after what we've been through," explained one potential Milwaukee investor. A group called Teams, Inc., headed by local Ford dealer Bud Selig, set out to convince Organized Baseball to add more teams. In Kansas City an advertisement in the local newspaper congratulated the community on losing the A's, predicting, "the real excitement, the real fun that comes with solid, year-in, year-out major league baseball is just around the corner. . . . In two years we will be back and will field a team that will truly represent Kansas City."[80]

The major leagues, arguing that the available talent pool would not support expansion, targeted 1971 as the earliest possible date to add new teams. The delay infuriated Missouri's Senator Symington. Symington, reportedly using "picturesque language similar to dock hands," convinced baseball owners to accelerate their timetable rather than succumb to a new congressional investigation.[81] Big league officials agreed to a new expansion for the 1969 season. When announced, the lineup of new teams included Kansas City, Seattle, San Diego, and Montreal. Baseball had bypassed Milwaukee, the erstwhile home of the Braves.

The latest round of reshuffling again yielded disappointing results. Although the Atlanta Braves drew well in the late 1960s, the Athletics did not catch on in Oakland. Finley had brought with him to California not the sad sack Athletics who had demoralized Kansas City, but a squad of exciting young players destined for greatness. The 1968 roster included Reggie Jackson, Rollie Fingers, Jim "Catfish" Hunter, Bert Campaneris, Sal Bando, and Joe Rudy. The Athletics won more games than they lost for the first time since 1952. But after 50,000 fans turned out for the home opener, the crowds never materialized. Finley, writes Norman Macht, "gave them fan appreciation days, but very few came out to be appreciated." The Athletics drew only 111,000 more fans in Oakland than they had in Kansas City.[82]

If the Athletics' invasion of Northern California failed to significantly improve Finley's financial fortunes, it nonetheless shattered the idyll of the crossbay San Francisco Giants. When Horace Stoneham had moved the Giants to San Francisco, he had assumed he would maintain a monopoly in the region. "We thought there'd always be one club in the vicinity and we'd be it," he explained. The arrival of the A's "certainly . . . will hurt us," predicted Stoneham. "It is a question whether both of us can survive."[83] From 1958 to 1967 the Giants had been one of baseball's great success stories, averaging almost 1.5 million patrons a year, despite playing in the ill-conceived Candlestick Park. In 1968 Giant attendance dropped to 837,220. With the exception of 1971, when the team won a division championship, the Giants failed to attract over 900,000 fans until 1978. The Athletics, meanwhile, became the best team in baseball, winning the World Series in 1972, 1973, and 1974, but only once drawing over 1 million people to the Coliseum.

Of the four expansion teams added in 1969, only the Montreal Expos drew particularly well. The Expos attracted 1.2 million fans while winning fewer than a third of their games, but Kansas City fans displayed lukewarm affection for their replacement team. Only

902,414 turned out to watch the new Royals play. In San Diego the Padres lost 110 games and drew a meager 512,970 people. The Seattle Pilots, who, according to *Sports Illustrated*, "charged some of the highest prices in baseball to watch one of the sport's worst teams," declared bankruptcy after one season.[84] The American League hastily moved the Pilots to Milwaukee, where, under the stewardship of Bud Selig, they became the Brewers.

Since 1961 expansion teams had demonstrated a mixed record. Before 1969 none of the teams, with the exception of the third-place 1962 Los Angeles Angeles, fared well in the standings. Nonetheless, the National League teams, thanks to the construction of new stadiums, had flourished at the box office. In Houston the 1965 opening of the Astrodome, baseball's first indoor arena, lured 2.1 million people to see the recently renamed Astros finish in ninth place. Dubbed the "Eighth Wonder of the World," the Astrodome continued to be an attraction even as the club foundered. The New York Mets moved to Shea Stadium in 1964, where they regularly drew in excess of 1.7 million fans a year despite their perennial last-place finishes. Suddenly, in 1969, the Mets, behind a young pitching staff bolstered by Tom Seaver, miraculously won the World Championship. Mets fans, jubilant in defeat, grew ecstatic in victory. Attendance climbed to over 2 million fans.

One final shift would close out baseball's era of movable franchises. In Washington the second incarnation of the Senators had proven no more successful than the first. Other than in 1969, the American League expansion team had finished repeatedly at or near the bottom of the standings. Attendance had only occasionally topped 700,000 fans. Team owner Robert Short blamed the lack of support on the proximity of the Orioles, Washington's high crime rate, and the District's predominantly black population. But the Senators' perpetually laggard performance and the highest ticket prices in baseball kept even willing fans at bay. Short, wrote Arthur Daley, had "bought a franchise that was overpriced. He was underfinanced. Acting as his own general manger, he was hornswoggled in every trade."[85]

But, as Daley observed, "There is a reward for mismanagement in modern baseball. . . . The delinquent is given permission by the lodge brothers to seek instant prosperity elsewhere." After the 1971 season Short moved the Senators to Dallas–Ft. Worth, where city fathers promised him a new stadium and a $7.5 million radio-television deal. Many people suspected that Short had deliberately orchestrated the Senators' failure. Short had previously owned the Minneapolis Lakers of the National Basketball Association. After a few years he had moved the Lakers to Los Angeles, where he sold the team for a substantial profit. He had repeated a similar scenario in Washington. "Bob Short committed the perfect crime. He stole our team," complained one Senator fan.[86]

The Senators, renamed the Rangers, debuted in Texas in 1972. Nearly two decades had passed since the Braves had left Boston. The baseball map now bore little resemblance to the traditional contours that had defined the pre-1953 era. Expansion had introduced eight new teams; nine cities had lost teams to other communities. Washington, D.C., had lost two teams. The result was a truly more national pastime, played in many more cities and regions. Yet a sense of restiveness, resistance, and skepticism had replaced the enthusiasm that had greeted the earlier franchise shifts. "Now, as never before," commented Congressman Emanuel Celler after the second flight of the Senators, "there is growing recognition that the owners . . . occasionally exhibit precious little concern for the community welfare." The owners, complained Senator Sam Ervin, "demonstrate a 'public be damned' attitude."[87]

Nor had baseball's haphazard, unplanned approach to franchise placement necessarily benefited the game. Total major league attendance had jumped from 14.4 million in 1952 to 27 million in 1972, but average team attendance in 1972 was less than it had been in the post-World War II boom years, despite a dramatic national population increase and a longer season. Several teams appeared poised to move yet again. The San Francisco Giants seemed destined for Toronto. Charlie Finley began eyeing New Orleans. The Twins reportedly had soured on Minnesota, and Washington, D.C., hoped to fill its baseball void with the San Diego Padres. The outward path, however, would be strewn with legal barriers.

Ever since the Braves had left Milwaukee, noted *The Sporting News*, "No club has moved without facing political heat, legal action, or the threat of lawsuits. Now the penalty for moving a team in distress is a multimillion dollar damage suit."[88]

The impending chaos that seemed so imminent in the 1970s never came to pass. The 1972 exodus of the Senators marked the last franchise shift of the twentieth century. Baseball would add six more teams through expansion, extending its domain into Florida, Colorado, Arizona, Toronto, and returning to Seattle, but the teams that existed in 1972 remained in place. An age of stability replaced an era of uncertainty, and fans rewarded the teams with a new outpouring of support that would drive baseball attendance to unprecedented heights. Although few realized it in the mid-1970s, baseball stood on the brink of a new golden age.

Populist Baseball

Baseball Fantasies
in the 1980s

Baseball's postmodern era began fittingly in a French restaurant on Manhattan's East Side in January 1980. Thirty-one-year-old writer Dan Okrent assembled a group of friends at La Rotisserie Français to suggest a way to make the upcoming season "a little more fun." Okrent's proposition was a simple one. "It wasn't enough to watch baseball, or to study it in the box scores and leaders list," he told his colleagues. "We all [wish] in some way to possess it, to control it." As lifelong baseball fans, they had honed the skills necessary to run a baseball team. "Hadn't we been appraising talent all our lives?" asked Okrent. Can't we run a team better than Al Campanis, the general manager of the Los Angeles Dodgers, or Tal Smith of the Houston Astros? But as Okrent knew, "Lacking twenty million bucks, memberships in the right country clubs, and a pair of plaid pants, I was clearly never going to own a major league baseball club." Okrent suggested that the group create its own major league: form teams, draft real major league players, and keep track of the progress of their squads based on how the players performed in several statistical hitting and pitching categories. Unlike the real majors, each team would have an identical amount of money to spend, thus leveling the playing field. They dubbed their creation the Rotisserie League and over the next several weeks hammered out a league constitution and rules. By the start of the season, the group had grown to eleven—ten men and one woman—and on the first Sunday of the season they gathered to hold an auction, placing dollar values on players from the rosters of the National League.[1]

The game began as a whimsical lark. The owners, predominantly writers and advertising executives, thought up clever names for their teams. Okrent called his club the Okrent Fenokees, after the swamp in the Pogo comic strip; Michael Pollet's charges became the Pollet Burros; Rob Fleder's team, the Fleder Mice. But the competition quickly took a serious turn. The Rotisserie League came to dominate their lives. "Each morning, all of us ran to the box scores, manically searching the agate type for news," reported Okrent. The "owners" made daily calls to major league teams to check out the health of their players. Bruce McCall began publishing a newsletter about his McCall Collects. Okrent, the commissioner of the league, compiled the weekly standings from statistics in *The Sporting News*. Unable to wait for the journal to arrive in the mail on Friday, he would drive twenty miles each way to a newsstand that received the paper on Thursday.[2]

The owners developed a schizophrenic rooting style that transcended traditional baseball loyalties. They might root in one inning for a batter on the Mets, in the next for a pitcher on the Dodgers. The Rotisserie League had, in effect, deconstructed baseball, breaking down the game from its normative team emphasis, and reconstituting it on an individual statistical basis. This fantasy now assumed its own reality. "You could say these teams are imaginary," wrote Rotisserie Leaguer and *Sports Illustrated* reporter Steve Wulf, "but we prefer to think of them as real and the Chicago Cubs as imaginary." The Rotisserie Leaguers made trades, waiver moves, and placed players on the disabled list. They teased, bantered, argued, and bonded. "They're animals, thieves, liars, and cheats. And I don't say that lovingly," charged Valerie Salembier, the league's only woman owner, who clawed her way to a fourth-place finish. At the start of the season many of the owners hardly knew each other, but, as Steve Wulf later wrote, they had learned that solid friendships could be "formed out of knowing Biff Pocoroba's vital statistics." By the end of the season, most agreed with Glen Waggoner's repeated cry, "This is the best thing that ever happened to me."[3]

During the 1980 season Okrent had formed a second circuit, the Bush League, based in New England and drafting players from the American League. In Spring 1981 Okrent published an article in *Inside Sports* chronicling the Rotisserie League's inaugural season. A second feature, "How To Own A Baseball Team" by Conn Nugent of the Bush League, appeared in *Harvard Magazine*.[4] Both pieces included rules for playing the game. Suddenly Rotisserie Leagues and other fantasy loops began popping up throughout the nation. By 1984, when Okrent and the other founding fathers and mother published *Rotisserie League Baseball*, an "official how to play guide," the game had become, according to *People* magazine, "the hottest craze to hit the national pastime since trading cards." Soon hundreds of thousands of people played Rotisserie League baseball and its variants. Celebrity participants included Congressman Fred Gandy, New York Governor Mario Cuomo, and *Today* Show host Bryant Gumbel, who when in China regularly called New York to monitor his team's progress. The term Rotisserie League became a part of the national sports language. "I'm convinced," joked Okrent, "that if I bring about world peace and find a cure for cancer, the headline on my obituary will still be, 'Okrent Dies—Invented Rotisserie.' "[5]

Writing in 1981, Nugent referred to his Bush League as "populist baseball." "We have reinvented baseball," boasted original Rotisserie League member Lee Eisenberg.[6] Indeed, the Rotisserie League was only one manifestation of an explosion of vicarious fan participation in the 1980s. Fans not only rediscovered baseball, they attempted to redefine and reclaim it in their own image. The Rotisserie creators had inadvertently tapped into several broad currents of change coursing through the game and nation in the 1980s: resentment over soaring baseball salaries, the binding of the nation's psychological wounds after the divisive 1960s, the maturity and affluence of the postwar baby boom generation, and the emergence of a new information age triggered by the personal computer, satellite communications, and cable television. Many baseball fans perceived an opportunity to indulge themselves in an illusory form of empowerment. They flocked to ballparks in record numbers. They rejuvenated childhood dreams by becoming owners of fantasy teams and players at "fantasy camps," where aging baby boomers worked out with and played against the baseball heroes of their youth. They reconstructed baseball statistics, devising new ways to measure player productivity and assess conventional strategies. Many invested the game with a new baseball romanticism. Intellectuals wrote scholarly articles and books and penned soppy paeans to baseball's ethos. Filmmakers evoked the game's mystique in movies like *The Natural, Bull Durham*, and *Field of Dreams*. These efforts were neither coordinated nor necessarily conscious, but Americans in the 1980s attempted, in Okrent's words, to "possess" and "control" baseball, to reshape it to fit the contours of the computer and consumer age of late twentieth-century America.

Baseball attendance had remained relatively static during the 1960s and early 1970s. Despite infusions generated by franchise shifts and expansion, average game attendance hovered between 14,000 and 15,500, well below the post–World War II peak. In the mid-1970s patronage began to rise. Some have attributed this surge to the remarkable 1975 World Series that pitted the Cincinnati Reds against the Boston Red Sox. Five of the seven contests were decided by one run. In the sixth game, regarded by many as the greatest ever played, the Red Sox staved off elimination with Bernie Carbo's game-tying three-run home run in the eighth inning and then won it in the twelfth on Carlton Fisk's majestic home run down the left-field foul line. Amid protests from traditionalists, most World Series games had been shifted from afternoon to evening to accommodate the television audience. On the night of the seventh game a record 76 million people tuned in to watch the grand finale.[7] The Reds came from a 3–0 deficit to tie the game in the seventh and win it, 4–3, in the ninth. The following year major league attendance soared over the 30-million mark for the first time in baseball history. Real growth escalated, however, in 1977, when total attendance (sparked in part by expansion into Toronto and Seattle) jumped to 38,709,780 and the game average reached an unprecedented 18,380. In 1979 teams averaged over 20,000 patrons per game. Ten years later the figure topped 26,000, as over 55 million people turned out for major league games.

Baseball's sudden prosperity, achieved in an unstable economic environment, reflected several factors.[8] New stadiums with easier automobile access attracted suburban fans. A series of close divisional races invigorated interest. Perhaps most significantly, the vast postwar generation, raised in the 1950s, the last era in which professional baseball would reign as the nation's undisputed favorite sport, had reached maturity and returned to its roots. Moving into their thirties and settling down with jobs and families, male baby boomers, many of whom had allowed their baseball allegiances to ebb during the tumultuous sixties, once again appeared at games. With the Vietnam War over in 1975 and the countercultural impulse on the wane, many former protesters staged a symbolic homecoming through baseball. The sheer numbers and growing affluence of the postwar cohort fueled baseball's resurgence.

Ironically, the new interest in baseball coincided with a controversial transformation of the baseball industry. Beginning in the late 1960s the Major League Baseball Players' Association, led by veteran union organizer Marvin Miller, had steadily chipped away at baseball's venerable reserve clause, the contract stipulation that bound players to one team and prevented them from selling their services to the highest bidder. In December 1975, as baseball basked in the afterglow of the Reds–Red Sox World Series, a federal arbitrator ruled that players could only be reserved for one year at the end of their contracts, after which they would become free agents. The decision transformed baseball's economic structure and sent team payrolls skyrocketing. The average salary jumped from $45,000 in 1975 to $144,000 in 1980 and $891,000 in 1991.[9] A new

breed of high-spending team owners, symbolized by George Steinbrenner of the New York Yankees and Ted Turner of the Atlanta
Braves, fueled the bidding frenzy. Attempts by team owners to
stem the rising tide led to a long player strike in 1981 and a shorter
work stoppage in 1985. Fans grew increasingly frustrated by the
constant labor-management warfare and alarmed by the escalating
player incomes.

The economic strife, however, failed to deter people from going
to the ballpark. Indeed, free agency stimulated attendance by ending the age of baseball dynasties. In earlier decades a few teams,
most notably the New York Yankees, had dominated competition.
The new baseball marketplace allowed teams to quickly rebuild and
contend, ushering in an era of competitive balance. Between 1976
and 1991 nine different teams won the National League pennant
and eight triumphed in the American League.[10] Six other teams
won divisional titles. Not even the bitter seven-week shutdown in
1981 seriously dented fan enthusiasm. Attendance in 1982 established a new major league record.

Okrent's Rotisserie League captured both the upsurge in enthusiasm and the growing resentment over rising player salaries and
overbearing owners. In the fantasy league competitors bid for players in much the same way that the modern baseball magnate did.
Okrent entitled the 1981 *Inside Sports* article that launched the phenomenon "The Year George Foster Wasn't Worth $36," a pointed
contrast to the hundreds of thousands of dollars a player of Foster's
stature might draw as a free agent. "There being no Marvin Miller
present, we quickly agreed to a form of price fixing," explained
Okrent of the decision to cap spending at $250 per team. Although
Okrent in 1981 focused on the challenge of being a general manager, subsequent accounts more frequently emphasized the fantasy
of ownership. *Playboy* called the competitors "Armchair Steinbren-
ners," a sentiment shared by Jim Battles of the Pacific Ghost
League. "I feel like an owner, like George Steinbrenner," commented Battles in 1983. " 'I paid good money for you guys,' I feel
like saying, 'and you're dogging it.' "[11]

The illusion of ownership, however, paled before the fantasy of playing in the major leagues. Former Chicago Cubs catcher Randy Hundley and longtime Cubs fan Alan Golding ran summer baseball camps for children. Why not, they wondered, a camp for "middle-aged kids," where men over thirty-five could practice and play against Hundley and his former teammates? Their 1982 brochure promised, "We won't just take you out to the ball game. We'll put you in it—against the 1969 Chicago Cubs." The price tag was a hefty $2,195 plus meals for a one-week camp, but sixty-three aspiring, if over-the-hill, athletes, ranging in age from thirty-six to fifty-six, responded. They included a corn farmer, a jet pilot, an engineer, a psychiatrist, a Chicago policeman, a law professor who canceled his classes to attend, and a host of other professionals. In January 1983 they traveled to the former Cubs spring training facilities in Scottsdale, Arizona, where they were greeted by the stars of the 1969 Cubs, including Hall of Famer Ernie Banks, future Hall of Famers Billy Williams and Ferguson Jenkins, all-star third baseman Ron Santo, and Hundley. The real Cubs ushered the Cub-wanna-bes into the locker room where they donned genuine Cubs uniforms. "Most of us would have been willing to die at that point," reported camper and *Sports Illustrated* writer Roy Blount, Jr.[12]

The novices received instruction from the former ballplayers. "Williams showed me that I'd been holding a bat wrong all my life," revealed Blount. "I've [also] been holding the glove wrong all my life. [Jim] Hickman and Jenkins also explained to me that I'd been holding the ball wrong all my life."[13] The faux-Cubs dressed, showered, and sat in the whirlpool with the real Cubs who regaled them with tales of their legendary manager Leo Durocher and the team's storied collapse in 1969 before the oncharging Miracle Mets. After a week of training, the middle-aged pretenders played a game against the Cubs, batting and pitching against their onetime heroes, in front of a crowd of 4,200 people, including Durocher himself.

Like all fairy tales this one had its dark side. The campers pulled hamstrings and discovered aches in deltoids, quadriceps, and other muscles they had never known existed. "The only part of me that doesn't hurt is my fingernails," moaned one amateur. A thirty-eight-year-old real estate developer required knee surgery. And the play on the field could leave one feeling, in Blount's description "overpowered" and "lost." "It was never my boyhood dream to miss a pop-up in front of thousands of people," confessed Blount. The 1969 Cubs crushed the upstarts 23–6 in the final contest. Nonetheless, the uncommon venture proved an outrageous success. Television networks glorified these "historic first middle-aged campers" on national news reports. Blount's raucous *Sports Illustrated* article, entitled, fittingly, "We All Had a Ball," glamorized the "fantasy camp" for millions of potential participants. "The reality," affirmed *New York* Magazine, was "better than the fantasy."[14]

Other entrepreneurs moved quickly to sate the reawakening of adolescent baseball hormones. In 1984 a company called Baseball Fantasies Fulfilled offered a Los Angeles Dodgers camp. Another packaged a Yankees/Dodgers version, wherein "you play the game with your heroes and against your enemies." By 1985 a half-dozen promoters ran operations featuring players from fifteen different teams, including baseball idols Willie Mays and Mickey Mantle. Several major league clubs sponsored their own camps. The training junkets became popular gifts from wives on their husband's fortieth birthdays. Acquisitive child-men carted home baubles and souvenirs: camp T-shirts, replica big league contracts, videotaped highlights of the week's play, group camp photos, personalized bats, baseball trading cards with their photos and personal information, and uniforms bearing their names. Costs soon soared as high as $3,400, but the high price did not diminish the ardor of the affluent clientele. In 1990 the Big League Sports Medicine Conference in Reno staged a physicians' baseball camp, where doctors interspersed medical seminars with workouts led by former San Francisco Giants Orlando Cepeda and Vida Blue, while receiving twenty credit hours of continuing medical certification.[15]

The popular camps allowed aging fans to indulge a variety of baseball fantasies. "This is one place where I can completely immerse myself in a fantasy world and not think of anything else but baseball," observed a Canadian corporate president. The men could "think, smell, and eat baseball for seven days," noted one of the rare female participants.[16] With few exceptions the camps were a male preserve. Grown men revived childhood visions and aspirations long since left behind, though not forgotten. The play actors imagined themselves as their boyhood heroes. "I'm on third base, dancing down the line like Jackie Robinson," marveled a Dodger camp partisan, moments before stealing home. Others spoke of dashed hopes. "My dream was to be a professional baseball player," confessed one participant. "I had to settle for being a doctor."[17] Most endured considerable physical agony to complete the camps. An Arkansas neurosurgeon broke two ribs diving into second base. He wired himself with an electronic device to block the pain and played out the week. A lawyer pitched two innings with a broken hand. A fifty-two-year-old from Los Angeles discovered on returning home, "Both of my shoulders had self-destructed . . . but I didn't realize it at the time. I was on an emotional high all week." Nonetheless, he confessed, "I am ready to go back to Dodgertown again and go through the paces one more time."[18]

The chance to fraternize with real baseball players, with whom, observed a pair of sociologists, the campers had "sustained imaginary social relations since adolescence" proved the most satisfying fantasy. "These guys represent the best years of our lives," remarked a nostalgic neurosurgeon. As Blount noted, "Take away the Cubs and the camp would have degenerated into middle-aged doctors, lawyers, brokers and businessmen, rolling around on the ground fighting over whose bat it was."[19] Meeting the heroes of one's youth could at times be less than exhilarating. Financial consultant Robert Grossman described meeting the always-charming Enos Slaughter at a Yankee camp. As Grossman walked to the plate, bat in hand, Slaughter called him over as if to give him a batting tip. "He stops six feet in front of me and deposits a gallon of tobacco juice on my right cleat," Grossman recorded in his diary. "The guy scares me." But when Grossman met former Yankee first baseman Bill "Moose" Skowron in the hotel lobby, Skowron asked to join him for dinner. "He would like to join *me*?"

marveled Grossman. "I spend two hours talking to the Moose. . . . This is one of my main heroes. . . . Just me and the Moose. . . . Who is going to believe this? He pays for dinner over my objections. I would have bought him a car for those two hours and he pays for my dinner." If that was not enough, Grossman later found himself "nose to nose" with Mickey Mantle. "I walk into the elevator and turn to jelly. . . . I drool and twitch. My voice is strangely high-pitched and hoarse at the same time," wrote the adoring acolyte. Mantle also awed a White Plains attorney. "I hope my wife understands this," said the lawyer after meeting Mantle. "I can die now and go to heaven."[20]

The onset of a new information age further enhanced the ability of baseball fans to vicariously participate in the game. The emergence of computers had generated a fascination with numbers not unlike what had swept the nation in the era of Henry Chadwick. Baseball, with its rich statistical heritage and ongoing analytical possibilities, became a showpiece and testing ground for the new technology. Computers offered the possibility of amassing data and generating simulations to establish probabilities based on large numbers of occurrences. As early as 1959 statisticians used early mainframe computers to construct models of play based on thousands of theoretical games. In 1965 General Electric demonstrated a new computer model by analyzing American League clutch hitting. Two years later Macmillan Publishing employed Information Concepts, Inc. (ICI) to create a massive database of baseball records. Under the guidance of David Neft, a professional statistician, ICI researchers painstakingly compiled a player-by-player, season-by-season accounting of the game's history. ICI entered the information into a computer data bank and Macmillan typeset the resulting volume entirely by computer—the first such book ever prepared in this manner. *The Macmillan Baseball Encyclopedia* appeared in 1969 and established a milestone in baseball and computer applications. Its hundreds of pages of minute statistical information placed the answers to myriad baseball questions at any fan's fingertips and opened new vistas for serious researchers.[21]

Others also grasped the potential of the computer for baseball analysis. Brothers Eldon and Harlan Mills recorded every play from the 1969 and 1970 seasons into a computer in order to determine the possible outcomes of each batter's plate appearance. A Canadian statistician simulated 200,000 games to determine a team's best possible batting order. Pete Palmer embarked on an even more ambitious project. Palmer created a computer model based on all major league games played since 1901, incorporating the result of every at bat, enabling him to measure the significance of every possible offensive event.[22]

In the 1960s and early 1970s only those with access to powerful mainframe computers could engage in this level of inquiry. But a growing number of fans, with and without computers, became interested in challenging baseball's antiquated reliance on traditional statistics. In 1971 Bob Davids gathered sixteen fellow baseball enthusiasts at Cooperstown, New York, to form the Society for American Baseball Research (SABR). Dedicated to promoting the study of both baseball history and statistics, the organization grew slowly but steadily. SABR's committee on statistical analysis, chaired by Pete Palmer, attracted a core of partisans who questioned the sanctity of batting average as the dominant measure of baseball prowess and devised new methods to gauge performance. They exchanged ideas about baseball statistics and published their results in SABR's *Baseball Research Journal*.[23]

Among the new breed of rebels was a shy, intensely curious Kansan named Bill James. A baby boomer born in 1948, James had developed a facility for numbers and a fascination for baseball undimmed by his boyhood allegiance to the woeful Kansas City Athletics. At the University of Kansas in the 1960s, James majored in English and economics, learning mathematical modeling techniques and the rudiments of graceful writing. Upon graduation he served in the army and then briefly as a high school teacher. But James's true passion remained baseball. In the mid-1970s he abandoned the classroom and took a job as a boiler room attendant at a food packing plant. The pay was poor and the prospects dim, but the position allowed James to "spend five minutes an hour making sure the furnaces didn't blow up and 55 minutes working on my numbers."[24]

His numbers came from the *Macmillan Baseball Encyclopedia* and daily box scores. James counted them, reconfigured them, recalculated them into new statistics, and recorded his findings in endless notebooks. He worked without a computer or even a calculator. A self-confessed "eccentric" and "stat freak," James counted "all kinds of stuff that lots of people are sort of interested in, but nobody in his right mind would actually begin to count." He tallied the number of stolen bases recorded against each catcher and pitcher. He recorded how many people paid to see each starting pitcher. James considered himself a "baseball agnostic," making "it a point to never believe anything just because it is widely known to be so." He developed a technique of "listening very carefully to the things that baseball people said and then asking the question: If this is true, what would be the consequences of it? If it was false, what would be the consequences of that?" Sportscasters might comment that a ballplayer had his prime years between the ages of twenty-eight and thirty-two or a manager might credit a defensive player with saving his team 100 runs a year. James would spend tedious hours poring over box scores, checking out these assertions. He had also learned to doubt many of the statistical assumptions that had governed the game since Chadwick's day and sought to develop new measurements of batting, pitching, and fielding.[25]

Standing tall and darkly bearded, James bore a cursory resemblance to the nineteenth-century father of baseball statistics. He also shared Chadwick's crusading zeal, if not in the direction of social reform, at least regarding the uses and abuses of baseball numbers. To James, baseball statistics had "the powers of language" constituting "a literature and poetry accessible to millions." Some numbers evoke power, others speed. They "define skills, they draw limits," wrote James. Furthermore, baseball possessed an unparalleled historical record, compiled across the decades to allow a level of analysis and interpretation unavailable in almost any other field. Yet commentators relied on unverified traditional wisdom and oft-repeated clichés. Sportswriters, protested James, used baseball statistics selectively not to understand baseball, but to "decorate their articles" and force conclusions by "arranging . . . evidence so that it points in the direction desired." James, on the other hand, wanted to develop tools and measures to establish the validity of these assertions, "to teach people . . . to cut toward the truth."[26]

James discovered kindred spirits in SABR and dubbed the work of the upstart statisticians "sabermetrics." He wrote articles based on the new science for *Baseball Digest* and authored a regular column for the small-circulation *Baseball Bulletin*. Although he believed that an audience existed for his work, most editors did not agree. "The articles I thought were really good, the articles that made a contribution toward one's understanding of the subject, would not sell," he learned.[27] In 1977 James decided to self-publish his work, offering unorthodox statistics unavailable anywhere else. Operating out of "a tiny bedroom in one of the tiniest houses" in Lawrence, Kansas, James calculated monthly records for batters and pitchers, counted the stolen bases allowed by individual catchers and pitchers, and introduced the concept of range factor (counting all the plays each defensive player successfully participated in) as a replacement for fielding average. He photocopied, collated, and stapled the sixty-eight-page typewritten manuscript between two cover pieces and tossed in instructions for a table baseball game. James entitled his effort the *Baseball Abstract*, priced it at four dollars a copy, and advertised in *The Sporting News* and other baseball publications. Seventy-five people responded.[28]

James's first *Abstract* relied heavily on numbers interrupted only occasionally by exposition. He lacked, he later explained, "the self-confidence to write about the material." With his second *Abstract*, published in 1978, James began to hit his stride. Weighing in with 115 pages, James introduced a team-by-team format and supplemented his statistics with lengthy analytical essays.[29] A graceful and often witty writer, James adopted an informal conversational style. His *Abstracts*, as he later wrote, had "no true beginning, no middle or end, no natural order, any more than a series of conversations that you might have with a friend would have a beginning, a middle, or an end." He encouraged his readers to follow his thought processes and engage in their own analysis. He introduced new statistics as "tools" to equip them to explore these issues on their own. He aimed his writing not at the average baseball supporter, but at the intense, intelligent, educated elite at the peak of the fan pyramid. The 1978 edition sold 325 copies.[30]

By 1981 James had emerged as a cult figure to a small but growing group of followers who shared his disdain for conventional baseball wisdom. His early subscribers included Roger Angell, the *New Yorker's* popular baseball writer nonpareil, novelist Norman Mailer, baseball agent Randy Hendricks, and Rotisserie League creator Dan Okrent. Through Okrent's intervention James became a regular contributor to *Esquire*. In 1980 Angell recounted an afternoon at the ballpark with James in the *New Yorker*, describing the *Abstract* as "invaluable" and James's use of statistics as "dazzling." In 1981 Okrent made James the focus of a long, laudatory feature in *Sports Illustrated*. "He finds things in [baseball statistics] that most people don't know are there," crowed Okrent. That year, the *Abstract*, still self-published, but now a bound volume complete with graphics, sold 2,200 copies.[31] In 1982 Ballantine Books began producing *The Bill James Baseball Abstract* for a mass audience.

The years in the wilderness had allowed James to hone his craft and emerge on the national scene as a polished talent. The first *Abstract* introduced several fundamental concepts that underscored James's work: batting averages overrated players like Bill Buckner, who rarely walked or hit home runs, and underrated others like Gene Tenace, who had low batting averages, but nonetheless reached base frequently and hit for power; hitter-friendly ballparks like Fenway Park inflated offensive statistics, while Shea Stadium and others favored pitching, resulting in statistical illusions in judging players; and, most significantly, players could be evaluated using "Runs Created," a formula that James had developed that combined "all of the known elements of a player's batting record" into a reliable measure of offensive production. James presented his "tool shack," a collection of a dozen original measures of player performance with esoteric names like "Isolated Power," "Value Approximation Method," and "Pythagorean Method." He promised that forty more tools lay waiting to be unveiled in future editions. James also evaluated teams, managerial strategies, and, in what would become his most popular and controversial feature, ranked major league players at every position.[32]

James's sharp wit and pungent opinions elevated the *Baseball Abstracts* from a technical treatise into an entertaining excursion. "The starting eight of the Phils has nearly 100 years of professional experience, which would be wonderful if they were in the real estate business," he wrote in 1980. "There is a tunnel at the end of the light, and it is not far off." He described Cleveland second baseman Duane Kuiper as "a pathetically inept offensive player," commenting, "It's absolutely incredible that a player this bad could be given 3,000 at bats in the major leagues." His engaging digressions into relatively meaningless topics like the "Birthday effect" (batters hit better on their birthdays) and Reggie Jackson's performances before large crowds further spiced the *Abstracts*. When Joe Morgan, one of James's favorite performers, stated that "I don't think that I've ever had a bad September," James checked it out and concluded, "I think I've finally found Joe's weakness. The man has no memory. He has probably had more bad Septembers than any great player in history."[33]

The *Baseball Abstract* took off. The 1982 and 1983 editions sold a total of 150,000 copies. His eighth annual *Abstract*, published in 1984, rose to number four on the *New York Times* best-seller list. Articles featuring James appeared in nonsports journals like *Atlantic Monthly, Psychology Today*, and *Discovery*. *Sport* magazine hailed James in 1984 as "arguably the most influential baseball writer in America."[34]

James remained, however, a "designated outsider." His sudden success, blunt assessments, and inevitable miscalls offered ample ammunition for critics. "I think we — the media — have created a monster," worried sportswriter Tracy Ringolsby in 1984. "James has gotten carried away with himself. He sets himself up as a godlike figure. . . . He's trying to make absolute judgments in a game that has no absolutes." After James described Detroit Tiger utilityman Enos Cabell as a player who "can't play first, can't play third, can't hit, can't run and can't throw," Cabell responded, "I think he knows as much about baseball as I do about writing." Cabell's manager Sparky Anderson, a frequent James target, added, "I don't think anyone in baseball takes him very seriously."[35] Others noted that James's forecasts were often erroneous. The eloquently disparaged 1980 Phillies, after all, won the World Series.

Far more important than the accuracy of James's predictions was his impact on baseball statistics and reporting. By 1984 James had become the central figure in a virtual baseball revolution in which fans wielding personal computers and sophisticated and often complex new statistics sought to wrest control of baseball's numerical soul from the sport's traditional record keepers. The introduction of the personal computer in the late 1970s and its rapid proliferation in the 1980s empowered thousands of people to engage in a type of analysis previously available to a select few. By 1985 SABR itself had grown to almost 6,000 members. The success of the *Abstract* opened the doors of publishing houses to scores of books on baseball statistics. These works ranged from the truly significant, like *The Hidden Book of Baseball* by John Thorn and Pete Palmer, which became the basis for *Total Baseball*, the definitive compendium of the game's history and statistics, to the superficial and inconsequential.

Major league baseball and the people who reported on the game were characteristically slow to recognize the potential of the computer and the rising statistical sophistication of its fans. "Computers are coming. They are ready for us, but we are not quite ready for them," commented Cleveland Indian general manager Gabe Paul back in 1965. Two decades later baseball remained largely unprepared. Like many other people confronted with the new technology, baseball remained leery of its applications and consequences. No teams used computer technology in any meaningful way before 1983. *Discovery Magazine* reported only a quarter of the teams employed computers in 1987. Baseball people "think they know it all and would like to keep everything in their heads. They wouldn't dream of turning game decisions over to a computer," explained one entrepreneur trying to sell baseball computer systems to reluctant buyers. Most rejected and resented the work of James and other "stat freaks." "People who have spent their lives in baseball tend to distrust the ideas of people who haven't played," observed sabermetrician Gary Gillette.[36]

Newspapers had also failed to recognize the increased demand for statistical information. In 1981, when Bill James and Rotisserie Leagues first burst on the scene, the daily press reported only the most rudimentary elements of baseball information in their weekly summaries: batting average, at bats, runs scored, home runs, hits and runs batted in for hitters; wins, losses, innings pitched, walks, strikeouts, and earned run average for pitchers. Players who did not have the requisite number of at bats or pitching decisions never appeared. Early Rotisserie Leagues turned to *The Sporting News*, the "Bible of Baseball," for more complete statistics for all players. But, as a weekly, *The Sporting News* presented stale, outdated numbers and omitted key information like walks for batters and increasingly popular statistics like on base percentage and slugging average. The original Rotisserie League omitted fielding from its calculations because *"The Sporting News* doesn't publish weekly fielding stats, and without weekly stats you've got no way to compute weekly standings, and without weekly standings you've got nothing to live for."[37]

The new communications revolution, however, provided a solution. On September 15, 1982, Gannett Newspapers launched *USA Today*, the nation's first national daily newspaper. Assembled in Washington, D.C., and then distributed via satellite to printing plants throughout the nation, *USA Today* made an expanded "results-oriented" sports section one of its prime features, "the immediate hook to get people into the paper," according to one editor. The mandate for the sports section, according to in-house historian Peter Prichard, was "to cover every game, every score, and every statistic." *USA Today* offered expanded league standings and box scores, which included up-to-date batting and earned run averages, home runs, runs batted in and stolen base counts, and other pertinent information. A box with details on "how they scored" accompanied each game account. To the delight of Rotisserie Leaguers, *USA Today* published complete up-to-date major league batting and pitching statistics each Wednesday and Thursday. Although the newspaper as a whole received generally unflattering assessments from media critics, the sports section garnered instant raves. "If what matters are results, old-fashioned scores and averages and standings, and more of them than you can get anywhere else, *USA Today* routs its rivals," commented the *Washington Journalism Review*. "And it is just what hardcore sports fans have been craving for years—but not getting."[38]

The *USA Today* sports section became, along with its colorful weather map, its most emulated feature. Local dailies, according to *Sports Illustrated*, "started paying more attention to nuts and bolts," increasing the space allotted to sports and publishing enhanced standings, box scores, and statistical summaries. The "endless columns of stats . . . whetted the public appetite for even more." *USA Today* replaced *The Sporting News* as the primary source for Rotisserie Leagues. The fantasy circuits, claimed *Time* Magazine in 1987, sent *USA Today* circulation soaring each spring.[39]

For those who could not wait until the following morning, the information revolution offered other options. By 1984 Dan Okrent had hooked into a computer service that allowed him to check National League box scores each night on his home computer. The spread of cable television, pioneered by Ted Turner who broadcast Atlanta Braves games as a staple of his innovative national channel, allowed Rotisserie Leaguers to watch a seemingly never-ending flood of nationally televised games and catch nightly scores and details on ESPN, a twenty-four-hour cable sports network. "I once loved baseball as normal men do," wrote fantasy league enthusiast Kevin Cook. Now, "I watch the Cubs on WGN, the Braves on WTBS, the Dodgers on KTTV, and everyone else on [ESPN] SportsCenter, Sports Latenight, and George Michael's Sports Machine."[40] The constant stream of sports results became a precursor for the split screen format, offering an ongoing flow of business and news information that became commonplace in American newspapers and on cable and network television in the 1990s.

Although the early Rotisserie Leagues usually did not rely on computers, by the mid-1980s personal computers were becoming an essential element of fantasy play. In 1985 Ghost League Baseball sold a computer program that instantly calculated Rotisserie standings and a weekly modem service that downloaded current statistics. Other software packages soon followed. "The Rotisserie phenomenon has a lot to do with the development of the personal computer," reported the *Sporting News* in 1989, when fantasy players numbered an estimated half million people. "The computer makes it easier for everyone to get involved."[41]

Fans also became involved on an even more esoteric level, weaving a baseball romanticism out of folklore and nostalgia. Baseball novels proliferated during the 1980s. Major twentieth-century American literary figures like Bernard Malamud, Robert Coover, and Philip Roth had long ago discovered that baseball offered a fertile setting for serious fiction.[42] Their works, most notably Malamud's *The Natural* and Coover's *The Universal Baseball Association*, tended to be foreboding explorations of the limitations of the American dream. The prototypical baseball novel of the 1980s, however, struck a different chord.

The best-selling and most influential baseball novel of the decade, *Shoeless Joe* by W. P. Kinsella, appeared in 1982, roughly the same time that Bill James, Rotisserie Leagues, and Fantasy Camps gained notice. Kinsella's central character, Ray, a baby boomer and former English major, had become a particularly unsuccessful Iowa corn farmer. One day he hears a voice, telling him, "If you build it, he will come." Ray instinctively understands that "it" is a baseball diamond in his cornfield, and "he" is Shoeless Joe Jackson, the disgraced star of the 1919 Chicago Black Sox. In Kinsella's fantasy Ray builds the ball field, conjures up not just Jackson, but the other Black Sox as well, and lures reclusive novelist J. D. Salinger, author of the countercultural prophecy *Catcher in the Rye*, to Iowa, where he discovers America's lost soul. Ray is reunited with his father, a former minor league catcher, who died when Ray was young. *Shoeless Joe* unabashedly paid homage to baseball as the key to a reawakening of the American spirit. "The play reaffirms what I already know," Jackson tells Ray. "That baseball is the most perfect of games, solid true, pure and precious as diamonds. If only life was so simple."[43]

In 1984 film director Barry Levinson and star Robert Redford brought Malamud's *The Natural* to the screen. As a novel, *The Natural* had merged baseball history and the Arthurian legend into a dark, depressing vision of human fallibility. Roy Hobbs, possessor of almost superhuman baseball skills, repeatedly fails to achieve his full potential because of his inability to learn from experience. Like the real Joe Jackson, he succumbs to temptation and accepts money to throw a crucial playoff game. Hollywood's version remained relatively faithful to the original until the grand finale. Amid inspirational music and colorful fireworks, Hobbs, portrayed by the preternaturally handsome, golden-haired Redford, defies the fixers and hits the game-winning home run. He then returns to his midwestern home, reunited with a son he never knew (nor had in the novel), to play catch among waving fields of golden wheat.

The movie version of *The Natural* horrified many critics and viewers. "This may or may not be a good picture, but it . . . certainly isn't my book," Malamud reportedly commented. *Time* magazine critic Richard Shickel lamented that "Malamud's intricate ending is vulgarized . . . [They] transform something dark and open-ended—truly fabulous into something eccentrically sentimental." Malamud's novel, complained Shickel, "was sacrificed on the altar of a happy Hollywood ending." But if the filmmakers had tampered with a literary masterpiece, they had produced a baseball classic. The movie struck a chord among contemporary Americans. Screenwriter Robert Towne explained, "The duties of a screenwriter are not just as a technician to adapt a book. In large part they are to reflect the attitude of his time. Malamud wrote the book following a catastrophic war. . . . From the vantage point of 1984 . . . I'm writing about the ability of man to overcome defeat."

The Natural, as a movie, captured not Malamud's vision, but the sensibilities of 1980s America, risen from the ashes of Vietnam and the uncertainties of the 1960s and 1970s.[44]

Before 1984 baseball films had been considered box office poison. The popular success of *The Natural* opened the floodgates to a stream of baseball cinema, most of it idyllic and romanticized, with uplifting and happy endings. Modern day movie Caseys rarely struck out. Unlike *The Natural*, the most popular of these movies focused around fans, not players. In *Bull Durham*, former minor league player Ron Shelton's bawdy, knowing tribute to small-town baseball, the most memorable character is Annie Savoy, an attractive, intelligent woman who each year selected a player on the team to expose to her special brand of sexual and spiritual enlightenment. "I believe in the Church of Baseball," intones Susan Sarandon as Annie in the movie's memorable opening. "I've tried all the major religions and most of the minor ones. And the only church that feeds the soul, day-in, day-out, is the Church of Baseball."[45] In 1989 *Shoeless Joe* came to the screen as *Field of Dreams*, and Kinsella's hypnotic incantation, "If you build it, he will come," entered the nation's cultural language. Kinsella's message of regeneration through baseball permeated the film. "The one constant through all the years has been baseball," spoke the Salinger character, renamed Terence Mann. "Baseball has marked the time. The field, this game, is part of our past . . . It reminds us of all that once was good, and that could be again."[46]

This type of sentimentality dominated the vast outpouring of baseball writing during the decade, as journalists, academics, and intellectuals offered their thoughts on the game. Poet Donald Hall, echoing themes offered in the movie version of *The Natural* and in *Shoeless Joe*, celebrated baseball in a collection of essays entitled *Fathers Playing Catch with Sons*. Pulitzer Prize–winning newspapermen George Will and David Halberstam wrote best-selling books on the game.[47] Baseball history and literature became the subject of scholarly studies and university courses.

No figure epitomized the romantic elevation of fan and game more than A. Bartlett Giamatti. A scholar of Renaissance literature and lifetime Boston Red Sox rooter, Giamatti had written a lyrical paean to the game entitled "The Green Fields of the Mind" in the *Yale Alumni Magazine* in 1977. "You rely on it to buffer the passage of time, to keep the memory of sunshine and high skies alive," rhapsodized Giamatti. Baseball for Giamatti was "the last place where Americans dream . . . the last great arena, the last green arena, where everybody can learn the lessons of life." When named president of Yale University, he confessed, "All I ever wanted to be was president of the American League."[48] He became instead in 1986 the President of the National League and then, in 1989, the Commissioner of Baseball. Giamatti, the ultimate fan, had achieved the ultimate fan fantasy.

The idealization of baseball in the 1980s might easily be interpreted as a reflection of the era of Ronald Reagan, a reassertion of traditional verities and values in a conservative decade. But remnants of 1960s countercultural thinking ran through much of the fan-based reinvention of baseball. James attributed his dogged independence to his "sixties youth." Much of the rhetoric of "populist" baseball revolved around issues of empowerment. "Where once slouched a slavish fan, dependent on the judgement and money of others, there now stands a Jeffersonian squire with his own team and destiny," wrote Conn Nugent of the Bush League.[49] *Bull Durham's* Annie Savoy embodied the free-spirited, sexually liberated truth seekers of the 1960s, who dabbled in religions seeking fulfillment. *Field of Dreams* transformed Kinsella's incarnation of J. D. Salinger into the fictional Terrence Mann, a former black radical and sixties icon portrayed by James Earl Jones. Disillusioned, Mann had become embittered and dropped from sight. None of these characters, real or fictional, completely surrender their social ideals or spirit of rebellion, but they discover a form of reentry into the American mainstream through the healing power of baseball.

The trend culminated in 1994 when the Public Broadcasting Service (PBS) presented *Baseball: A Film by Ken Burns*. Televised nightly over the course of a week, the eighteen-and-a-half-hour documentary combined magnificent historical baseball footage with the romantic ruminations of celebrity fans about baseball's role in American life. Burns, a baby boomer, veteran of the antiwar movement, and lifelong baseball fan, encapsulated the excessive idealization of the game. Baseball, he argued, "encodes and stores the genetic material of our civilization," offering "the comfort of continuity, the generational connection of belonging to a vast and complicated American family, the powerful sense of home . . . and the great gift of accumulated memory."[50]

The blatant excesses, rhetorical overkill, and obvious self-indulgence of the fan movement of the 1980s invited a critical skewering. For many the quest for vicarious participation epitomized what historian Christopher Lasch called a "culture of narcissism." "What we have here, I'm afraid," complained one sportswriter about Rotisserie Leagues in 1990, "is the worst of the '70s Me Decade (how can I use this thing to validate myself?) and the '80s Greed Decade (how can I cash in without actually doing anything?) creating the baseball fan of the '90s." Rotisserie baseball, protested another critic, "seems like total bourgeois individualism run amuck. It hasn't reinvented the game so much as buried it under the manipulation of stats and the exertion of wills."[51] The obsessive popularity of fantasy baseball posed problems in many workplaces. "In their drive to keep up with the stupefying stream of statistics they need . . . many Rotissereans will make use of the office computer, fax machines, long-distance lines and photocopier," reported *USA Today* in 1993. Some dedicated up to an hour of their workday to their fantasy teams. The Iowa Racing and Gaming Commission suspended its executive secretary for using office facilities and time to manage his club. Even the Rotisserie pioneers seemed appalled by their creation. "Now I know how Dr. Frankenstein must have felt," wrote Steve Wulf in 1989. Dan Okrent agreed. "I'm with the people who say, 'Get a life.' This has just gotten to be nuts," exclaimed Okrent in 1993.[52]

A similar backlash had set in against the new statistics. The game, wrote Roy Blount in 1991, had become "staturated." "Bat, ball and glove have been replaced by computer [and] calculator

. . . or so it seems in this age of statistical overkill," remonstrated George Vass in *Baseball Digest*. Bill James pulled the plug on the *Baseball Abstract* in 1988. In an uncharacteristically churlish farewell, James remarked on "an unchecked explosion" of meaningless numbers, "a Chernobyl of statistics, polluting nearly every discussion." James, who had always encouraged the give-and-take with his readers, wrote, "I get more and more letters that irritate the hell out of me. . . . I am encountering more and more of my readers that I don't even like."[53] James's mission to provide a better breed of baseball statistics and to revamp traditional thinking had been only partially successful. Statistics offered in newspapers and on game broadcasts were now more plentiful and modestly more sophisticated. But the broader messages conveyed by James and his fellow sabermetricians had changed the game minimally. Game strategies remained governed by the traditional wisdom, rather than statistical analysis, and few teams paid any attention to ballpark or other statistical illusions in making personnel decisions.

Indeed, the subconscious, quixotic, often idiosyncratic quest to reclaim and reinvent the game in the 1980s had never been more than a fantasy. Although fans might contend for spiritual dominance, control rested firmly in the hands of the players and owners, who remained embraced in a deadly serious economic struggle. Americans continued to celebrate baseball in the early 1990s. A staggering 70,256,456 fans, an average of almost 31,000 a game, attended major league games in 1993. Baseball seemed on a record pace again in 1994. But on August 12, prodded by intractable owners determined to control salaries, players again went on strike. Unable to reach agreement, the antagonists canceled the World Series, violating a ninety-year-old trust. The strike dragged on into the 1995 season, carrying with it much of the romantic enthusiasm of the preceding decade. Sales of baseball books plummeted from their consistently high prestrike levels. When the labor conflict finally ended, fans returned hesitantly.

Baseball, however, once again demonstrated the resilience and technological adaptability that had carried it through its earlier crises. The Internet offered new ways for fans to follow their teams, both real and fantasy. The democratic vehicles of personal web pages and online discussion lists reinvigorated fan participation. In 1998 Mark McGwire of the St. Louis Cardinals and Sammy Sosa of the Chicago Cubs staged a mesmerizing race to establish a new seasonal home run record, and the resurgent New York Yankees won 125 total games to establish a new standard for excellence. Interest and attendance rose anew as baseball stood poised on the brink of the twenty-first century. Despite the perennial warnings of baseball Cassandras, time has yet to pass baseball by. What remains to be seen is not whether the game will survive, but how Americans in a rapidly changing world will again reinterpret and reinvent their national pastime.

Notes

Chapter 1: The National Game

1. The Currier & Ives print *The National Game* has been reproduced in many histories of baseball. See, for example, John Bowman and Joel Zoss, *Diamonds in the Rough: The Untold History of Baseball* (New York: Macmillan, 1989), 234.

2. Allen Guttmann, *From Ritual to Record: The Nature of Modern Sports* (New York: Columbia University Press, 1978), 100; A. Bartlett Giamatti, "The Green Fields of the Mind," *Yale Alumni Magazine* (November 1977); Michael Novak, *The Joy of Sports: End Zones, Bases, Baskets, Ball* (New York: Basic Books, 1976), 62; Ralph Andreano, *No Joy in Mudville: The Dilemma of Major League Baseball* (Cambridge, Mass.: Shenkman, 1965), 3; Warren Jay Goldstein, *Playing for Keeps: A History of Early Baseball* (Ithaca, N.Y.: Cornell University Press, 1989); Steven M. Gelber, "Their Hands Are All Out Playing: Business and Amateur Baseball, 1845–1917," *Journal of Sport History* 21 (1984), 5–27; Steven M. Gelber, "Working at Playing: The Culture of the Workplace and the Rise of Baseball," *Journal of Social History* 11 (Summer 1983), 3–22.

3. On variations on townball, see George B. Kirsch, *The Creation of American Team Sports: Baseball and Cricket, 1838–1872* (Urbana: University of Illinois Press, 1989), 53–54; and Harold Seymour, *Baseball: The Early Years* (New York: Oxford University Press, 1960), 7.

4. David Quentin Voigt, *American Baseball: From the Gentleman's Sport to the Commissioner System* (University Park: Pennsylvania State University Press, 1983), 4.

5. R. M. Lewis, "Cricket and the Beginnings of Organized Baseball in New York City," *International Journal of the History of Sport* 4 (December 1987), 315; Seymour, 24; Terry R. Furst, "The Image of Professional Baseball: The Sport Press and the Formation of Ideas About Baseball in Nineteenth Century America" (Ph.D. diss., New School for Social Research, 1986), 3; Kirsch, 92; Geoffrey C. Ward and Ken Burns, *Baseball: An Illustrated History* (New York: Knopf, 1994), 6.

6. James M. DiClerico and Barry Pavelec, *The Jersey Game: The History of Modern Baseball from Its Birth to the Big Leagues in the Garden State* (New Brunswick, N.J.: Rutgers University Press, 1991), 25–26; Kirsch, 62–63.

7. Melvin L. Adelman, *A Sporting Time: New York City and the Rise of Modern Athletics, 1820–1870* (Urbana: University of Illinois Press, 1986), 136.

8. Seymour, 35; Adelman, 135.

9. *New York Times*, February 12, 1991; James W. McPherson, *What They Fought for, 1861–65* (New York: Anchor Books, 1995), 30.
10. On the spread of baseball from 1857 to 1860, see Seymour, 26, 29, 40, 43; Bowman and Zoss, 49–52; Kirsch, 70; and Adelman, 132.
11. Seymour, 50; Bowman and Zoss, 366–67.
12. Kirsch, 40–42; Lewis, 317; Seymour, 30; Kirsch, 97; Adelman, 110–14.
13. Kirsch, 97.
14. Guttmann, 95, 97; Bowman and Zoss, 67.
15. Guttmann, 107–8; Novak, 57.
16. David Lamoreaux, "Baseball in the Late Nineteenth Century: The Source of Its Appeal," *Journal of Popular Culture* 11 (Winter 1977), 598; Goldstein, 102; Novak, 57.
17. Gelber, "Working at Playing," 8–10; Goldstein, 162n.
18. Adelman, 293; Novak, 58.
19. Kirsch, 58–62.
20. Adelman, 291.
21. On the debate over the fly rule, see Goldstein, 48–56, and Adelman, 130.
22. Seymour, 30; Chadwick quoted in Goldstein, 49.
23. Adelman, 131, 148.
24. Stephen Freedman, "The Baseball Fad in Chicago, 1865–1870: An Exploration of the Role of Sport in the 19th Century City," *Journal of Sport History* 15 (Summer 1978), 42; DiClerico and Pavelec, 38; Guttmann, 97; Adelman, 156–57; Seymour, 44.
25. Kirsch, 210; Goldstein, 87.
26. Seymour, 42; Henry Chadwick, "Baseball," *Outing* 12 (May 1888), 117.

Chapter 2: The Mortar of Which Baseball Is Held Together
1. *The Echo*, March 20, 1889 (item 128 in the Edwin Chadwick Papers). With thanks to Anthony Brundage.
2. For discussions of Chadwick, see Ralph Andreano, *No Joy in Mudville: The Dilemma of Major League Baseball* (Cambridge, Mass.: Shenkman, 1965), 49–53; Frederick Ivor Campbell, "Via: Henry Chadwick," *Harvard Magazine* 90 (September–October 1987), 60–61; Jacob C. Morse, "In Memory of Henry Chadwick," *Baseball Magazine* 1 (June 1908), 9–11; Mac Sounders, "Henry Chadwick," *Baseball Research Journal* 15 (1986), 84–85; Edwin P. Tanner, "Henry Chadwick," in Allen Johnson and Dumas Malone, eds., *The Dictionary of American Biography*, Volume 2 (New York: Scribners, 1930), 587; Albert G. Spalding, *America's National Game* (Lincoln: University of Nebraska Press, 1992), 339–44; John Thorn and Pete Palmer, *The Hidden Game of Baseball: A Revolutionary Approach to Baseball and Its Statistics* (New York: Doubleday, 1984), 9–19; and Frederick Ivor-Campbell, "Henry Chadwick," in Frederick Ivor-Campbell, Robert L. Tiemann, and Mark Rucker, *Baseball's First Stars* (Cleveland: Society for American Baseball Research), 26–27.
3. Anthony Brundage, *England's "Prussian Minister": Edwin Chadwick and the Pol-*

itics of Government Growth, 1832–1854 (University Park: Pennsylvania State University Press, 1988), 4.

4. Ibid.
5. Andreano, 49.
6. Henry Chadwick, *The Game of Baseball: How to Learn It, How to Play It, How to Teach It, with Sketches of Noted Players* (New York: George Munro, 1868), 9.
7. On Chadwick's early career, see Morse, 10, and *Reach Baseball Guide* (1909), 158.
8. Chadwick, *The Game of Baseball*, 10.
9. Biographies of Edwin Chadwick include Brundage, *England's "Prussian Minister"*; S. E. Finer, *The Life and Times of Sir Edwin Chadwick* (London: Methuen, 1952); and R. A. Lewis, *Edwin Chadwick and the Public Health Movement* (London: Longmans, 1952).
10. Biographical portraits of Henry Chadwick, including those in the *Spalding Baseball Guide* that he edited, often mentioned his brother. See also the favorable comments on Edwin Chadwick's call for exercise in the *New York Clipper*, August 4, 1860.
11. The best discussion of the antebellum reform movement is Ronald G. Walters, *American Reformers, 1815–1860* (New York: Hill and Wang, 1978). On sports and reform, see Melvin L. Adelman, *A Sporting Time: New York City and the Rise of Modern Athletics, 1820–1870* (Urbana: University of Illinois Press, 1986).
12. Adelman, 269–86.
13. Chadwick, *The Game of Baseball*, 10.
14. Henry Chadwick, *Hanley's Baseball Book of Reference* (1866), vii.
15. Warren Jay Goldstein, *Playing for Keeps: A History of Early Baseball* (Ithaca, N.Y.: Cornell University Press, 1989), 34.
16. Chadwick, *The Game of Baseball*, 112.
17. *Spalding Baseball Guide* (1889), 54.
18. Spalding, 341.
19. *Spalding Baseball Guide* (1889), 58. See also Goldstein, 139.
20. Ivor-Campbell, "Via: Henry Chadwick," 60.
21. Spalding, 341; John Bowman and Joel Zoss, *Diamonds in the Rough: The Untold History of Baseball* (New York: Macmillan, 1989), 70; Voigt, 67; Harold Seymour, *Baseball: The Early Years* (New York: Oxford University Press, 1960), 69.
22. Patricia Cline Cohen, *A Calculating People: The Spread of Numeracy in Early America* (Chicago: University of Chicago Press, 1982), 225.
23. Ibid., 175, 12.
24. Victor C. Hilts, "Statistics and Social Science," in Ronald N. Giere and Richard S. Westfall, *Foundations of the Scientific Method: The Nineteenth Century* (Bloomington: Indiana University Press, 1973), 211.
25. Cohen, 176, 219.
26. Chadwick, *The Game of Baseball*, 11.
27. George B. Kirsch, *The Creation of American Team Sports: Baseball and Cricket, 1838–1872* (Urbana: University of Illinois Press, 1989), 27; Chadwick, ibid.
28. Chadwick, ibid.
29. Cohen, 225.

30. Chadwick, *The Game of Baseball*, 11-12.
31. Ibid., 10.
32. Ibid., 11; Paul Dickson, *The Joy of Keeping Score* (New York: Walker and Company, 1996), 54.
33. Dickson, 15.
34. Henry Chadwick, ed., *Beadle's Dime Base Ball Player: Comprising the Proceedings of the Annual Baseball Convention* (1861), 58.
35. Dickson, 15; John J. Evers and Hugh S. Fullerton, *Touching Second: The Science of Baseball, the History of the National Game, Its Development Into an Exact Mathematical Sport, Records of Great Plays and Players, Anecdotes and Incidents of Decisive Struggles on the Diamond, Signs and Systems Used by Championship Teams*, 2nd ed. (Chicago: Reilly and Britton Co, 1910), 300; Andreano, 50-51.
36. Branch Rickey and Robert Riger, *The American Diamond: A Documentary of the Game of Baseball* (New York: Simon and Schuster, 1965); Thorn and Palmer, 4; Roger Angell, *The Summer Game* (New York: Viking Press, 1972), 3-5.
37. Thorn and Palmer, 9; Adelman, 124.
38. Thorn and Palmer, 11.
39. For a copy of this box score, see ibid., 13.
40. For a copy of this box score, see *Baseball Magazine* 18 (October 1925).
41. *Spalding Base Ball Guide* (1894), 37.
42. Thorn and Palmer, 11; Adelman, 175; Henry Hecht, "A Box Full of Goodies," *Sports Illustrated* 58 (April 4, 1983), 89.
43. Margo Anderson Conk, *The United States Census and the New Jersey Urban Occupational Structure, 1870-1940* (Ann Arbor: UMI Research Press, 1980), 1, 9-14; John Koren, ed., *The History of Statistics, Their Development and Progress in Many Countries* (New York: B. Franklin, 1970), 244. See also Helen Mary Walker, *Studies in the History of Statistical Method* (New York: Arno Press, 1975), 151-153 and H. Scott Gordon, "Alfred Marshall and the Development of Economics as a Science," in Giere and Westfall, 234-35.
44. Goldstein, 145.
45. Chadwick, 58; Thorn and Palmer, 14; Goldstein, 68-69.
46. Chadwick, *Beadle's Dime Baseball Player* (1864), 59-60.
47. Thorn and Palmer, 11-14; Goldstein, 175-76.
48. Chadwick, *The Game of Baseball*, 68.
49. Thorn and Palmer, 17.
50. Ibid., 28, 14.
51. Chadwick, *The Game of Baseball*, 67.
52. Ibid., 66.
53. *Spalding Base Ball Guide* (1894), 60.
54. *Baseball Magazine* 45 (November 1942); see, for example, Chadwick, *The Game of Baseball*, 112.
55. Thorn and Palmer, 36; Thomas R. Heitz, "Rules and Scoring," in John Thorn and Peter Palmer, ed., *Total Baseball* (New York: Warner Books, 1989), 2244; *Baseball Magazine* 44 (November 1942).
56. *Spalding Official Base Ball Guide* (1878-1883); *DeWitt Base Ball Guide* (1885), 117.
57. *Baseball Magazine* 45 (November 1942).

58. Ibid.
59. Heitz, 2245.
60. *Spalding Baseball Guide* (1889), 21.
61. *The Sporting News* (July 26, 1886).
62. Voigt, 67.
63. Peter Levine, *A. G. Spalding and the Rise of Baseball: The Promise of American Sport* (New York: Oxford University Press, 1985), 53, 62; Voigt, 158, 162; Spalding, *America's National Game*, 289–92; Ivor-Campbell, "Henry Chadwick," 27.
64. Ivor-Campbell, "Henry Chadwick," 27; *Baseball Magazine* 1 (June 1908).
65. Albert Bartlett, *Baseball and Mr. Spalding* (New York: Farrar, Star and Young, 1951), 289; Benjamin Rader, "Introduction," *The National Game* (Lincoln: University of Nebraska Press, 1992), xiii.
66. On Chadwick's final years, see Ivor-Campbell, 27; *Baseball Magazine* 1 (June 1908); *Reach Baseball Guide*, 1909.
67. *Baseball Magazine* 1 (June 1908).
68. Bartlett, 289; Rader, xiii.
69. John Heydler, "How the Batting Records Could Be Made More Accurate," *Baseball Magazine* 22 (January 1919), 140–43; Frank C. Lane, "The Faulty Foundations of Batting Averages," *Baseball Magazine* 42 (January 1929), 347–49.
70. Thorn and Palmer, 22–23.

Chapter 3: Incarnations of Success
1. Connie Mack, "Clean Living and Quick Thinking," *McClure's Magazine* 43 (May 1914), 53; Gustav W. Axelson, *"Commy": The Life Story of Charles A. Comiskey* (Chicago: Reilly & Lee, 1919), 290; William A. Phelon, "The Great American Magnate," *Baseball Magazine* 9 (January 1913), 17–23; Charles C. Alexander, *John McGraw* (New York: Viking, 1988), 7, 3.
2. Frank B. Hutchinson, Jr., "Charles Albert Comiskey—the Man," *Baseball Magazine* 2 (April, 1909), 52–55.
3. Frederick G. Lieb, *Connie Mack, Grand Old Man of Baseball* (New York: G. P. Putnam, 1945), 16–17; Connie Mack, *My 66 Years in the Big Leagues: The Great Story of America's National Game* (Philadelphia: Winston, 1950), 1–10, 21; "Connie Mack as Baseball Manager and Civic Servant," *Literary Digest* 104 (March 1, 1930), 41; Connie Mack, "The Bad Old Days," *Saturday Evening Post* 208 (April 4, 1936), 16–17.
4. Alexander, 9–14, 66.
5. Ed Fitzgerald, "Clark Griffith, the Old Fox," *Sport* 16 (May 1954), 45; Bob Considine and Shirley Povich, "The Old Fox, Baseball's Red-Eyed Radical and Arch-Conservative, Clark Griffith," *Saturday Evening Post* 208 (April 13, 1940), 15.
6. Alexander, 12; Mack, *66 Years*, 16; Hugh S. Fullerton, "Interesting People," *American Magazine* 71 (March 1911), 605; Axelson, 10–11.
7. Hugh C. Weir, "The Real Comiskey," *Baseball Magazine* 7 (February 1914); Axelson, 46.
8. Alexander, 17.
9. Mack, *66 Years*, 17.
10. Benjamin Rader, *Baseball: A History of America's Game* (Urbana: University of

Illinois Press, 1992), 67. On the Irish in baseball, see also Stephen A. Riess, *Touching Base: Progressive Baseball and American Culture in the Progressive Era* (Westport, Conn.: Greenwood Press, 1980), 184–85; and Alexander, 35.

11. David Quentin Voigt, *American Baseball: From the Gentleman's Sport to the Commissioner System* (University Park: Pennsylvania State University Press, 1983), 186; Eugene Converse Murdoch, *Ban Johnson: Czar of Baseball* (Westport, Conn.: Greenwood Press, 1982), 24; Harvey Frommer, *Primitive Baseball: The First Quarter Century of the National Pastime* (New York: Atheneum, 1988), 106.

12. Alexander, 4, 55.

13. Considine and Povich, 98, 127–30.

14. Bob Considine, *"Mr. Mack," Life* 25 (August 9, 1948), 50; Mack, "The Bad Old Days"; Harold Seymour, *Baseball: The Early Years* (New York: Oxford University Press, 1960), 182; Ed Fitzgerald, "The Truth About Connie Mack," *Sport* 10 (July 1948), 63; Lieb, 45.

15. Fitzgerald, "Clark Griffith," 72; "Clark (Calvin) Griffith," *Current Biography Yearbook, 1950* (New York: H. W. Wilson Co., 1950), 198–200.

16. Alexander, 38–39.

17. William G. Fullerton; "Connie Mack and His Athletics," *Harper's Weekly* 59 (September 12, 1914), 259; Axelson, 104, 74; Seymour, 179; Tiemann, SABR, 36.

18. Considine and Povich, 49.

19. *Current Biography Yearbook 1950*; Alexander, 39–40; Bill James, *The Bill James Historical Baseball Abstract* (New York: Villard Books, 1986), 112.

20. Charles C. Alexander, *Our Game: An American Baseball History* (New York: Henry Holt, 1991), 40; Seymour, 61.

21. Axelson, 112.

22. Dean A. Sullivan, ed., *Early Innings: A Documentary History of Baseball 1825–1908* (Lincoln: University of Nebraska Press, 1995), 187; Fitzgerald, "The Truth About Connie Mack," 64.

23. Mack, *66 Years*, 78–79.

24. Axelson, 113.

25. Fitzgerald, "Clark Griffith," 70.

26. Alexander, *John McGraw*, 20–22.

27. Ibid, 44–45.

28. Voigt, 284; Robert Burk, *Never Just a Game: Players, Owners and American Baseball to 1920* (Chapel Hill: The University of North Carolina Press, 1994), 147; Murdoch, 46.

29. Axelson, 128–29.

30. Alexander, 53, 63, 68–70.

31. Fitzgerald, "Clark Griffith," 72.

32. Voigt, 225.

33. On the founding of the American League, see Murdoch, 45–49; Bruce Kuklick, *To Every Thing a Season: Shibe Park and Urban Philadelphia* (Princeton, N.J.: Princeton University Press, 1991), 15–17; and Axelson, 141–42.

34. Francis C. Richter, *Richter's History and Records of Baseball, The American Nation's Chief Sport* (Philadelphia: F. C. Richter, 1914), 282.

35. Weir; William G. Evans, "Comiskey, Prince of Magnates," *Baseball Magazine* 20 (December 1917), 209–13.
36. Murdoch, 46.
37. Lieb, 65.
38. Fitzgerald, "Clark Griffith," 73
39. On the conflicts between McGraw and Johnson, see Alexander, 85–93.
40. Fitzgerald, "Clark Griffith," 74
41. Edward T. Collins, "Connie Mack and His Mackmen," *American Magazine* 77 (June 1914), 13–18; Riess, 161–62.
42. Henry B. Needham, "Connie Mack," *American Magazine* 72 (June 1911), 181–83.
43. Evans, "Comiskey, Prince of Magnates"; Weir; George C. Rice, " 'The Old Roman,' " *Baseball Magazine* 1 (June 1908), 47–50.
44. Rader, 86.
45. On the construction of new stadiums, see Robert F. Bluthhardt, "Fenway Park and the Golden Age of the Baseball Park, 1909–1915," *Journal of Popular Culture* 21 (Summer 1987), 43–52; G. Edward White, *Creating the National Pastime: Baseball Transforms Itself, 1903–1953* (Princeton, N.J.: Princeton University Press, 1996), 10–46; and Kuklick.
46. Axelson, 190–91.
47. Fitzgerald, "Clark Griffith," 74; Phelon.
48. White, 17–23. Kuklick, 15, 17.
49. Axelson, 130; Evans, "Comiskey, Prince of Magnates."
50. Burk, 159, 62; Kuklick, 50.
51. Axelson, 302; Burk, 159; Ring Lardner, *You Know Me Al* (New York: Scribner, 1960).
52. Marc Okkonen, *The Federal League of 1914–1915: Baseball's Third Major League* (Garrett Park, Md.: Society for American Baseball Research, 1989).
53. Considine and Povich, 91.
54. Fitzgerald, "The Truth About Connie Mack," 66.
55. Ibid; Murdoch, 79; Kuklick, 35–36; Mack, *66 Years*, 36.
56. Collins, 13–18.
57. Burk, 206.
58. Evans, "Comiskey, Prince of Magnates."
59. Ibid.; Axelson, 218, 318.
60. Eliot Asinof, *Eight Men Out* (New York: Holt, Rinehart, 1963), xi, 16.
61. James, 111–12.
62. Alexander, *Our Game*, 128–29; Burk, 233–34.
63. Ronald Story, "The Black Sox Scandal," in William Graebner, ed., *True Stories from the American Past* (New York: McGraw-Hill, 1993), 121; William P. Hayes, "Anecdotes of Charles Comiskey," *Baseball Magazine* 48 (January 1932), 345–47.

Chapter 4: New Ways of Knowing

1. Quoted in Warren Susman, *Culture as History* (New York: Pantheon, 1984), 105.
2. H. G. Salsinger, "The Glitter, The Gloss and the Glamor of It All," *Baseball*

Magazine 29 (November 1922), 539–40; Frank C. Lane, "Flashing the World Series to Waiting Millions," *Baseball Magazine* 28 (November 1922), 533–35.

3. Wilmer Thomson, unnamed, undated flyer found at a hamburger stand in Pennsylvania.

4. Quoted in Nick Curran, "How World Series Broadcasts Were Started in 1922," *Baseball Digest* (October 1964), 47–51.

5. Quoted in Curt Smith, *Voices of the Game* (South Bend, Ind: Diamond Communications, 1987), 9.

6. Susman, 111.

7. Walter Lippmann, *Public Opinion* (New York, Harcourt, Brace, 1922), 60–61.

8. Salsinger, 539–40

9. The following discussion is drawn primarily from Norman L. Macht, " 'Watching' the World Series," *American History Illustrated* (September–October 1991), 48–50.

10. Lane, 533–35; Salsinger; Irving E. Sanborn, "Flashing the Series to 50,000,000 People," *Baseball Magazine* 25 (November 1920), 517.

11. For the early history of radio, see Red Barber, *The Broadcasters* (New York: Da Capo Press, 1986), 8; Wayne M. Towers, " 'Gee Whiz!' and 'Aw Nuts!': Radio and Newspaper Coverage of Baseball in the 1920's," unpublished paper presented at the 62nd Annual Meeting of the Association for Education in Journalism, Houston, Texas, 1979; Smith, 6.

12. Smith, 8.

13. For details on the 1922 broadcast, see Towers, 13; Curran, 47; Smith, 9; G. Edward White, *Creating the National Pastime: Baseball Transforms Itself, 1903–1953* (Princeton, N.J.: Princeton University Press, 1996), 208–9; and Charles Fountain, *Sportswriter: The Life and Times of Grantland Rice* (New York: Oxford University Press, 1993), 196.

14. Towers, 13; Graham McNamee, *You're on the Air* (New York and London: Harper & Brothers, 1926), 58–59; White, 209; Smith, 11.

15. Lane, 533–35.

16. McNamee, 52–53.

17. Ibid., 58–59.

18. Barber, 11–12, 15; McNamee, vi.

19. Barber, 25; Gordon H. Fleming, *Murderers' Row* (New York: Morrow, 1985), 373.

20. Raymond F. Yates, "How Radio Magnifies the World Series," *Baseball Magazine* 35 (November 1925), 555–56.

21. McNamee, 184.

22. N. J. Abodaher, "Baseball Via the Ether Waves," *Baseball Magazine* (November 1929), 551–53; White, 211–17; Smith, 12.

23. Abodaher, 551–53; *Sporting News* quoted in White, 214–17.

24. Quoted in White, 216.

25. Quoted in Fleming, 355.

26. Smith, 21–24, 14.

27. Thomson flier.

28. Lane, 533–35; Thomson flier; McNamee, 55.

29. Paul Dickson, *Baseball's Greatest Quotations* (New York: HarperCollins, 1991), 64.

30. Marshall Smelser, *The Life That Ruth Built: A Biography* (New York: Quadrangle Books, 1975), 376; "The New Hero of the Great American Game at Close Range," *Current Opinion* (October 1920), 477–78; *Literary Digest* 73 (October 4, 1922), 58–62.

31. Quoted in Fleming, 86–87.

32. Ken Sobol, *Babe Ruth and the American Dream* (New York: Random House, 1974), 125; Richard Crepeau, *Baseball: America's Diamond Mind, 1919–1941* (Orlando: University Presses of Florida, 1980), 104; Benjamin G. Rader, "Compensatory Sports Heroes: Ruth, Grange and Dempsey," *Journal of Popular Culture* 16 (Spring 1982), 11–22; Susman, 146.

33. Smelser, 560; Roger Kahn, "The Real Babe Ruth," *Baseball Digest* 18 (October 1959), 23.

34. Frank C. Lane, "Why Babe Ruth Has Become a National Idol," *Baseball Magazine* 28 (October 1921), 483–85.

35. James K. Fitzpatrick, *Builders of the American Dream* (New Rochelle, N.Y.: Arlington House, 1977), 263.

36. Gerald Holland, "The Babe Ruth Papers," *Sports Illustrated* 11 (December 21, 1959), 111–17; Crepeau, 94; Fleming, 246.

37. Fleming, 121.

38. Sobol, 23, 141.

39. Silas Bent, *Ballyhoo: The Voice of the Press* (New York: Boni and Liveright, 1927), 190, 196.

40. Kal Wagenheimer, *Babe Ruth: His Life and Legend* (Maplewood, N.J.: Waterfront Press, 1990), 62–64.

41. F. C. Lane, "Baseball Takes the Air," *Baseball Magazine* 59 (June 1936), 293.

42. Laurence S. Ritter and Mark Rucker, *The Babe: A Life in Pictures* (New York: Tickner and Fields, 1988); Bent, 124.

43. Raymond Fielding, *The American Newsreel, 1911–1967* (Norman: University of Oklahoma Press, 1972).

44. Lippmann, 216; Sobol, 121.

45. Robert Creamer, *Babe: The Legend Comes to Life* (New York: Simon and Schuster, 1974), 205; Smelser, 201.

46. Reviews quoted in Fleming, 146–67, 283; Sobol, 19–20.

47. Smith, 8.

48. Grantland Rice, *The Tumult and the Glory* (New York: Barnes, 1954), 112–13.

49. Bent, 122, 133–24.

50. Quoted in Lippmann, 217–28.

51. Creamer, 186; Smelser, 109.

52. Christy Walsh, *Farewell to Heroes* (New York, 1937), 1–2.

53. Sobol, 139; Fleming, 286–87.

54. Walsh, 11–12.

55. Sobol, 122; Smelser, 200; Walsh, 25.

56. Fleming, 286–87.

57. Ibid., 52.

58. Sobol, 168–69, 190–91.
59. Roland Marchand, *Advertising the American Dream: Making Way for Modernity, 1920–1940* (Berkeley: University of California Press, 1986), 96.
60. Sobol, 168–69, 209; Wagenheimer, 86; Ritter and Rucker.
61. Walsh, 2, 14–16; Creamer, 273.
62. Walsh, 25; Sobol, 174–75; Fleming, 52.
63. Wagenheimer, 87; Fleming, 52; Walsh, 43.
64. Creamer, 333.
65. Quoted in White, 214–15.

Chapter 5: Adjusting to the New Order
1. Bill Rabinowitz, "Baseball in the Great Depression," in Peter Levine, ed., *Baseball History* (Westport, Conn.: Meckler, 1989), 49–50.
2. Ibid., 50.
3. G. H. Fleming, *The Dizziest Season: The Gashouse Gang Chases the Pennant* (New York: Morrow, 1984), 19; Rabinowitz, 50.
4. Gerald Holland, "The Great MacPhail," *Sports Illustrated* 11 (August 31, 1958), 58–64.
5. For an excellent discussion of these matters, see G. Edward White, *Creating the National Pastime: Baseball Transforms Itself, 1903–1953* (Princeton, N.J.: Princeton University Press, 1996), Chapters 5 and 7.
6. Rabinowitz, 52–54.
7. *Baseball Magazine* 50 (January 1933).
8. On Mack and the Athletics, see Charles C. Alexander, *Our Game: An American Baseball History* (New York: Henry Holt, 1991), 164; and Bruce Kuklick, *To Every Thing a Season: Shibe Park and Urban Philadelphia* (Princeton, N.J.: Princeton University Press, 1991), 62.
9. Rabinowitz, 52; White, 170; J. G. Taylor Spink, *Judge Landis and 25 Years of Baseball* (New York: Crowell, 1947), 172; Roland Marchand, *Advertising the American Dream: Making Way for Modernity, 1920–1940* (Berkeley: University of California Press, 1986), 305; Fleming, 22.
10. Bill James, *The Bill James Historical Baseball Abstract* (New York: Villard Books, 1986), 170; White, 121; James Vlasich, *A Legend for the Legendary: The Origin of the Baseball Hall of Fame* (Bowling Green, Ohio: Bowling Green State University Popular Press, 1990), 228–29.
11. Robert Rice, "Thoughts on Baseball," *New Yorker* 27 (May 26, 1950).
12. Harold Seymour, *Baseball: The Golden Age* (New York: Oxford University Press, 1971), 413–14; Neil J. Sullivan, *The Minors: The Struggles and the Triumph of Baseball's Poor Relation from 1876 to the Present* (New York: St. Martin's Press, 1990), 97; Robert Gregory, *Diz: Dizzy Dean and Baseball During the Great Depression* (New York: Viking, 1992), 39.
13. Seymour, 414; Paul Dickson, *Baseball's Greatest Quotations* (New York; HarperCollins, 1991), 357.
14. Benjamin Rader, *Baseball: A History of America's Game* (Urbana: University of Illinois Press, 1992), 134; Seymour, 413; Murray Polner, *Branch Rickey, A Biography* (New York: Atheneum, 1982), 81.

15. Rader, 134; Kevin Kerrane, *Dollar Sign on the Muscle: The World of Baseball Scouting* (New York: Simon and Schuster, 1989), 24, 27, 231–32; Gregory, 39.
16. Sullivan, 99–100.
17. Seymour, 417; Rader, 135.
18. Polner, 83; *Baseball Magazine* 44 (January 1930) and 75 (July 1946); David Quentin Voigt, *American Baseball*, Volume 2 (University Park: Pennsylvania State University Press, 1983), 161.
19. Polner, 110, 113.
20. Arthur Mann, *Branch Rickey: American in Action* (Boston: Houghton Mifflin, 1957), 156–57; Seymour, 414.
21. Kerrane, 57; Branch Rickey, *Branch Rickey's Little Blue Book* (New York: Macmillan, 1995), 123.
22. Polner, 103.
23. Kerrane, 176, 143.
24. Don Warfield, *The Roaring Redhead: Larry MacPhail—Baseball's Great Innovator* (South Bend, Ind.: Diamond Communications, Inc., 1987), 3–26.
25. Ibid., 26–27.
26. Ibid., 26–32.
27. Fleming, 223; Warfield, 59.
28. White, 164.
29. Gerald Eskenazi, *The Lip* (New York: Morrow, 1993), 96; Robert L. Taylor, "Borough Defender: MacPhail and the Dodgers," *New Yorker* 18 (July 12, 19, 1941).
30. Mann, 174; Warfield, 31–32.
31. Polner, 106; Arthur Mann, "The Larry MacPhail Story," *Sport* 21 (April, 1956).
32. Roger Kahn, *The Era* (New York: Ticknor & Fields, 1993), 18; Warfield, 48.
33. Warfield, 50–52.
34. Ibid., 52.
35. Ibid., 57–58.
36. Ibid., 58–59; Walter (Red) Barber, "The Night the Lights Came on in Baseball," *Modern Maturity* 26 (October–November 1983), 36.
37. Warfield, 60; Rader, 138.
38. Stanley B. Frank, "That MacPhail!" *Baseball Digest* 4 (April 1945), 7–10; Barber, 36.
39. Warfield, 61.
40. Harold Parrott, *The Lords of Baseball* (New York: Praeger, 1976), 103; Lee MacPhail, *My Nine Innings: An Autobiography of Fifty Years in Baseball.* (Westport, Conn.: Meckler Books, 1989), 4.
41. Leo Durocher, with Ed Linn, *Nice Guys Finish Last* (New York: Simon and Schuster, 1975); Holland, 58–64.
42. Warfield, 72–73; Holland, 58–64;
43. Warfield, 73; Mann, "The Larry MacPhail Story."
44. Warfield, 73; Ray Fitzgerald, "Larry MacPhail Deserves His Niche in the Hall of Fame," *Baseball Digest* 35 (May, 1978).
45. Warfield, 76–77.

46. Warfield, 78; Tommy Holmes, *Dodger Daze and Knights: Enough of a Ball Club's History to Explain Its Reputation* (New York: McKay, 1953), 141; Dickson, 262.
47. White, 182.
48. Mann, "The Larry MacPhail Story."
49. Red Barber, *Rhubarb in the Catbird Seat* (Garden City, N.Y.: Doubleday, 1968), 56–58; Warfield, 90–91.
50. Warfield, 95; Esknazi, 118–119.
51. Taylor, "Borough Defender"; Warfield, 138, 257.
52. Taylor, "Borough Defender."
53. Warfield, 89–90; Polner, 114–15; MacPhail, 23.
54. Warfield, 85–88; Parrott, 125–26.
55. Warfield, 85–88; Parrott, 125–26.
56. Eskenazi, 11; Polner, 119; Taylor, "Borough Defender."
57. Warfield, 265, 88; Parrott, viii, 71, 112, 117; Polner, 114–115.
58. Warfield, 139.
59. Ibid., 144.
60. Eskenazi, 105; Holmes, 176; Parrott, 117; Mann, "The Larry MacPhail Story."
61. Jack McDonald and Charles Dexter, "The Fall of the House of MacPhail," *Saturday Evening Post* 215 (April 17, 1943); Parrott, 141.
62. Parrott, 139.
63. Warfield, 257; Jules Tygiel, *Baseball's Great Experiment: Jackie Robinson and His Legacy* (New York: Oxford University Press, 1983), 50.
64. Tygiel, 51.
65. Warfield, 167; Kahn, 19.
66. Tygiel, 42–46, 57–58.
67. Tygiel, 69.
68. Ibid., 81, 83–85.
69. Ibid., 52; Warfield, 167–68.
70. Warfield, 174–77.
71. Mann, "The Larry MacPhail Story" and Arthur Mann, *Baseball Confidential: Secret History of the War Among Chandler, Durocher, MacPhail, and Rickey* (New York: McKay, 1951).
72. Mann, "The Larry MacPhail Story."
73. Gerald Holland, "The Great MacPhail," *Sports Illustrated* 11 (August 17, 1958), 62–68; Kahn, 139; Warfield, 219–20.
74. Tygiel, 81; Holland, "The Great MacPhail" (August 31, 1958).
75. Dickson, 336; Warfield, 126, 250.

Chapter 6: Unreconciled Strivings

1. On Rube Foster, see Peterson, 103–15; Rogosin, 33; Bruce 31–32; Lanctot, 29; and Jules Tygiel, "Black Ball" in John Thorn, Pete Palmer, Michael Gershman, and David Pietrusza, *Total Baseball*, 5th ed. (New York: Viking, 1991), 435.
2. The literature on black baseball is extraordinarily rich. The pioneering works in this field include Robert Peterson, *Only the Ball Was White: A History of the Legendary Black Players and All-Black Professional Teams* (Englewood Cliffs, N.J.: Prentice-Hall, 1970) and Donn Rogosin, *Invisible Men: Life in Baseball's Negro*

Leagues (New York: Atheneum, 1983). An impressive body of team and community studies has supplemented these overviews. This chapter relies heavily on Richard Bak, *Turkey Stearnes and His Detroit Stars: The Negro Leagues in Detroit, 1919–1933* (Detroit: Wayne State University Press, 1994); Janet Bruce, *The Kansas City Monarchs: Champions of Black Baseball* (Lawrence: University Press of Kansas, 1985); Paul Debono, *The Indianapolis ABCs: History of a Premier Team in the Negro Leagues* (Jefferson, N.C.: McFarland, 1997); Neil Lanctot, *Fair Dealing and Clean Playing: The Hilldale Club and the Development of Black Professional Baseball, 1910–1932* (Jefferson, N.C.: McFarland, 1994); James Overmyer, *Effa Manley and the Newark Eagles* (Metuchen, N.J.: Scarecrow Press, 1993); and Rob Ruck, *Sandlot Seasons: Sport in Black Pittsburgh* (Urbana: University of Illinois Press, 1987). Two photographic histories of black baseball, Bruce Chadwick, *When the Game Was Black and White: The Illustrated History of the Negro Leagues* (New York: Abbeville Press, 1992) and Phil Dixon, with Patrick J. Hannigan, *The Negro Baseball Leagues: A Photographic History* (New York: Amereon House, 1992), were also very helpful as was Jim Reisler, *Black Writers/Black Baseball: An Anthology of Articles from Black Sportswriters Who Covered the Negro Leagues* (Jefferson, N.C.: McFarland, 1994). For those interested in learning more about the stars of black baseball, the oral histories of John Holway and the reference works of James A. Riley are indispensable.

3. W. E. B. DuBois, *Souls of Black Folk* (New York: Vintage Books/Library of America, 1990).
4. Overmyer, 111; Lanctot, 23; Bruce, 44.
5. Bruce, 42, 49.
6. Bak, 135.
7. James H. Bready, *Baseball in Baltimore* (Baltimore: The Johns Hopkins University Press, 1998), 174; Lanctot, 61; Bruce, 45–47.
8. Rogosin, 32–33; Reisler, 49.
9. Debono, 2, 44–48.
10. Lanctot, 23.
11. On the Negro National League, see Debono, 49, 84; Bak, 71.
12. Bruce, 88; Reisler, 60.
13. Lanctot, 66; Bruce, 24, 45; Overmyer, 266.
14. Debono, 101.
15. Overmyer, 15–17, 59, 215.
16. Overmyer, 5, 59–60, 167–68, 174; Bruce, 45; Lanctot, 176.
17. Debono, 74; Steven J. Ross, *Black Diamonds, Blues City* (film); Overmyer, 86;
18. Bak, 183; James Bankes, *The Pittsburgh Crawfords: The Life and Times of Baseball's Most Exciting Team* (Dubuque, Iowa: Wm. C. Brown, 1991).
19. James M. DiClerico and Barry Pavelec, *The Jersey Game: The History of Modern Baseball from Its Birth to the Big Leagues in the Garden State* (New Brunswick N.J.: Rutgers University Press, 1991), 146.
20. Imamu Amiri Baraka, *The Autobiography of LeRoi Jones/Amiri Baraka* (New York: Freundlich Books, 1984), 35.
21. Bak, 126; Bready, 166; Bruce, 42.
22. Baraka, 35; Overmyer, 66.

23. Bankes, 104–5; Ross, *Black Diamonds;* Chadwick, 54; Overmyer, 112; Bruce, 44.
24. Bruce, 3.
25. Debono, 73.
26. Bruce, 44–45.
27. Chadwick, 50; Debono, 180.
28. Overmyer, 34, 64, 97; Reisler, 99–100; Ruck, 157; Bready, 181; Bruce, 47.
29. Bak, 87; Ross, *Black Diamonds;* Overmyer, 63.
30. Overmyer, 63.
31. Brad Snyder, Senior Thesis, Duke University, 1994.
32. Chadwick, 55; Peterson, 113; Ross, *Black Diamonds*.
33. Bruce, 58.
34. Charles E Whitehead, *A Man and His Diamonds: A Story of the Great Andrew (Rube) Foster, the Outstanding Team He Owned and Managed and the Superb League He Founded and Commissioned* (New York: Vantage Press, 1980), 180.
35. Lanctot, 112–20; Overmyer, 107.
36. Lanctot, 40, 62–63.
37. Lanctot, 121; Overmyer, 113–14.
38. Debono, 22, 42; Lanctot, 62; Bruce, 44–45.
39. Overmyer, 166; Reisler, 60, 61.
40. Lanctot, 184; Ross, *Black Diamonds*.
41. Lanctot, 183–84.
42. Reisler, 36–37.
43. Bruce, 29, 51–52; Lanctot, 184; Snyder, 4.
44. Reisler, 61; Dixon and Hannigan, 176.
45. Debono, 20; Lanctot, 20, 23.
46. Lanctot, 60; Overmyer, 104–5; Bready, 167.
47. Lanctot, 37; Bruce 52–53; Bak, 57, 186.
48. Bankes, 25; Bruce, 51.
49. Debono, 66–67.
50. Lanctot, 99.
51. Overmyer, 122.
52. Bready, 175; Snyder, 2–9; Bruce Kuklick, *To Every Thing a Season: Shibe Park and Urban Philadelphia, 1909–1976* (Princeton, N.J.: Princeton University Press, 1991), 146–47.
53. Chadwick, 121.
54. Bruce, 11.
55. Ruck, 116.
56. On Nat Strong, see Lanctot, 29, 62.
57. Lanctot, 29.
58. Overmyer, 269.
59. Lanctot, 73–74.
60. Lanctot, 66.
61. Bruce, 31; Lanctot, 145, 162.
62. Lanctot, 96.

63. Ruck, 221; Bruce, 21–22.
64. Bak, 55–57, 202; Lanctot, 37–38; Peterson 113–14.
65. Dixon, 99; Ruck, 123; Peterson 113.
66. Bruce, 29.
67. Lanctot, 198–200.
68. Bak, 186–87, 192.
69. Lanctot, 200.
70. Overmyer, 10, 272–77; Bankes, 91–92.
71. Rogosin, 104.
72. Bankes, 94.
73. Overmyer, 9–10; Ruck, 149–50.
74. Rogosin, 107.
75. Overmyer, 268–69.
76. Bruce, 90.
77. Overmyer, 135, 139.
78. Overmyer, 134, 138–39.
79. Bruce, 90; Lanctot, 95.
80. Lanctot, 132; Bankes, 115.
81. Overmyer, 113–14, 140.
82. Snyder, 2–24.
83. Overmyer, 204.
84. Dixon, 241–42; Peterson, 59.
85. Dixon, 242; H. B. Webber and Oliver Brown, "Play Ball!" *Crisis* 45 (May, 1938), 137; Bruce, 111.
86. Reisler, 16. 13.
87. Reisler, 80–81.
88. Reisler, 13; Overmyer, 244.
89. Overmyer, 108–9; Debono, 121; Chadwick, 165; Dixon, 252.
90. Overmyer, 235.
91. Bruce, 116.
92. Reisler, 143.
93. Bruce, 116.
94. Geoffrey C. Ward and Ken Burns, *Baseball: An Illustrated History* (New York: Alfred A. Knopf, 1994), 413.

Chapter 7: The Shot Heard 'Round the World

1. George W. Hunt, "Of Many Things," *America* 162 (January 27, 1990); *USA Today*, October 3, 1991; Don DeLillo, *Underworld* (New York: Simon and Schuster, 1997), 59–60.
2. *New York Daily News*, October 4, 1951; *New York Times*, October 4, 1951.
3. For biographical information on Thomson and Branca, see Ron Fimrite, "Side by Side," *Sports Illustrated* 75 (September 16, 1991), 66–77; Bobby Thomson with Lee Heiman and Bill Gutman, *The Giants Win the Pennant, The Giants Win the Pennant* (New York: Zebra Books, 1991); John Drebinger, "Bobby Thomson, Scotland's Gift to Baseball," *Baseball Magazine* 89 (October 1947), 379–81; Ros-

coe McGowen, "Branca, Boy Behemoth of the Brooks," *Baseball Magazine* 89 (October 1947), 365–67; Roger Kahn, "The Day Bobby Hit the Home Run," *Sports Illustrated* 13 (October 10, 1960).

4. Carl Prince, *Brooklyn's Dodgers: The Bums, The Borough, and The Best of Baseball, 1947–1957* (New York: Oxford University Press, 1996), 120–22; Peter Levine, *From Ellis Island to Ebbets Field: Sport and the American Jewish Experience* (New York: Oxford University Press, 1992), 124–25.

5. Peter Gammons, "1950 vs. 1990: A Tale of Two Eras," *Sports Illustrated* 70 (April 16, 1990), 26–32.

6. Harvey Rosenfeld, *The Great Chase: The Dodgers–Giants Pennant Race of 1951* (Jefferson, N.C.: McFarland, 1992), 105.

7. Ibid., 74.

8. Benjamin Rader, *Baseball: A History of America's Game* (Urbana: University of Illinois Press, 1992); Charles C. Alexander, *Our Game: An American Baseball History* (New York: Henry Holt, 1991), 220.

9. On average attendance figures, see Rader, 173.

10. Roger Kahn, *The Era: When the Yankees, New York Giants, and the Brooklyn Dodgers Ruled the World* (New York: Ticknor & Fields, 1993), 286.

11. Russell P. Hodges and Al Hirschberg, *My Giants* (Garden City, N.Y.: Doubleday, 1963), 112; Curt Smith, *Voices of the Game* (South Bend, Ind.: Diamond Communications, 1987), 65.

12. *New York Times*, October 1, 1951.

13. Cecil Powell, "Of Willie Mays, Joe McCarthy, and Bobby Thomson," *Massachusetts Review* 32 (Spring 1991), 106; Smith, 117–27.

14. Thomson, 354–55.

15. Smith, 128.

16. Kahn, *The Era*, 288; Dave Berkman, "Long Before Arledge . . . Sports and TV: the Earliest Years, 1937–1947 as Seen by the Contemporary Press," *Journal of Popular Culture* 22 (Fall 1988), 49–63; Rosenfeld, 253–54.

17. Red Smith, "What It's Like On Color TV," *Baseball Digest* 10 (October 1951), 23–25.

18. Rader, 160; Curt Smith, 136–38; *New York Times*, October 1, 1951.

19. Curt Smith, 138.

20. Ibid., 116–27.

21. Ibid., 112; Jim Harper, "Gordon McLendon: Pioneer Baseball Broadcaster," *Baseball History* 1 (Spring 1986), 42–51.

22. Smith, 127; Harper, 45–46.

23. Dan M. Daniel, "Television Opens Up Fantastic Avenues for Baseball Revenue," *Baseball Magazine* 80 (May 1948); Branch Rickey and Robert Riger, *The American Diamond: A Documentary of The Game of Baseball* (New York: Simon and Schuster, 1965), 194; Kahn, *The Era*, 285.

24. Grantland Rice, "Is Baseball Afraid of Television?" *Sport* 12 (April 1951), 12–13; Dan Daniel, "TV Must Go—Or Baseball Will," *Baseball Magazine* 89 (November 1952), 6–8; William Veeck, Jr., "Don't Let TV Kill Baseball," *Sport* 14 (June, 1953), 10–14.

25. Thomson, 54; Bob Oates, "Thomson's Homer Just a Single in L.A.," *Baseball Digest* 18 (October 1959), 59–61; "The World Series Stare," *Look* (October 1951); Ray Robinson, *Home Run Heard 'Round the World* (New York: HarperCollins, 1991), 16.
26. *Time* (October 15, 1951).
27. *Look* (October 1951).
28. Thomas Kiernan, *The Miracle at Coogan's Bluff* (New York: Crowell, 1975), 61.
29. Irving Rudd and Stan Fischler, *The Sporting Life* (New York: St. Martin's, 1990), 99–102; Ron Briley, "Amity Is the Key to Success: Baseball and the Cold War," *Baseball History* 1 (Fall 1986), 10.
30. *Time* (April 28, 1952); Rosenfeld, 30, 210; Charley Dressen, as told to Stanley Frank, "The Dodgers Won't Blow It Again," *Saturday Evening Post* 224 (September 13, 1952); Powell, 106.
31. *New York Times*, October 4, 1951.
32. Ron A. Smith, "The Paul Robeson–Jackie Robinson Saga and a Political Collision," *Journal of Sport History* 6 (Summer 1979).
33. Jules Tygiel, *Baseball's Great Experiment: Jackie Robinson and His Legacy* (New York: Oxford University Press, 1983), 334–35.
34. Thomson, 182–83.
35. Rosenfeld, 84.
36. Tygiel, 263.
37. Thomson, 179.
38. Gerald Eskenazi, *The Lip* (New York: Morrow, 1993), 249; Hodges, 98; Rosenfeld, 54; Kahn, "The Day Bobby Hit the Home Run"; Tygiel, 305.
39. *New York Post*, October 1, 1951; *New York Times*, October 4, 1951.
40. Thomson, 164–65, 169; Kiernan, 68; Rosenfeld, 184–89.
41. Rosenfeld, 36; Thomson, 254.
42. Gammons, 26–32; Rader, 163.
43. Curt Smith, 133; Harper, 48.
44. Frank Graham, Jr., *A Farewell to Heroes* (New York: Viking, 1981), 231.
45. Thomson, 266, 307.
46. Rudd, 105.

Chapter 8: The Homes of the Braves
1. Howard Cosell, "Great Moments in Sports: Milwaukee Makes the Majors," *Sport* 31 (April 1961), 72.
2. *U. S. News and World Report* (May 18, 1958).
3. *New York Times*, March 19, 1953; David Quentin Voigt, *American Baseball*, Volume 3 (University Park: Pennsylvania State University Press, 1983), 87.
4. Joe King, *The San Francisco Giants* (Englewood Cliffs, N.J.: Prentice-Hall, 1958), 3; Geoffrey C. Ward and Ken Burns, *Baseball: An Illustrated History* (New York: Knopf, 1994), 307.
5. H. D. Robins, *American Baseball Needs Four Major Leagues* (Los Angeles, Calif.: Western Technical Press, 1947).
6. Dyer Braven, "Is the West Coast Ready for Big League Baseball?" *Sport* 17 (May

1947), 11–13; On the Pacific Coast League bid, see Andy McCue, "Open Status Delusions: The PCL Attempt to Resist Major League Baseball," *Nine* 5 (Spring 1997), 288–304.

7. Neil J. Sullivan, *The Dodgers Move West* (New York: Oxford University Press, 1987), 92; McCue, 296; William Marshall, *Baseball's Pivotal Era, 1945–1951* (Lexington: University of Kentucky Press, 1999), 259–62.

8. Voigt, xix.

9. Daniel M. Daniel, "Yankees, Red Sox Take to the Air: Baseball Visions Vast Implications," *Baseball Magazine* (July 1946), 267–69; *The Sporting News* (August 31, 1949); G. Edward White, *Creating the National Pastime: Baseball Transforms Itself, 1903–1953* (Princeton, N.J.: Princeton University Press, 1996), 308.

10. White, 305; Lee Lowenfish, "A Tale of Many Cities: The Westward Expansion of Major League Baseball in the 1950s," *Journal of the West* 71 (July 1978), 73–74.

11. White, 305; James Edward Miller, *The Baseball Business: Pursuing Pennants and Profits in Baltimore* (Chapel Hill: The University of North Carolina Press, 1990), 14.

12. For Veeck's version of these events, see Bill Veeck and Ed Linn, *Veeck as in Wreck* (New York: Simon and Schuster, 1962), 279–90. See also *Life* (March 30, 1953) and Bob Allen, "Unthinkable: Whoever Heard of a Baseball Team Moving to Another City?" *The Diamond* (July 1993), 23.

13. Harold Kaese and Russell G. Lynch, *The Milwaukee Braves* (New York: G. P. Putnam, 1954), 287; Tim Cohane, "None But the Braves," *Look* (August 25, 1953), 87–88.

14. Allen, 23–25; Kaese and Lynch, 288.

15. Allen, 23; Gavin Astor, "Home Are the Braves in Atlanta," *Look* (May 3, 1966), 21–22; Lowenfish, 76.

16. *Life* (March 30, 1953); Gilbert Millstein, "More Brooklyn Than Brooklyn: Milwaukee and Its New Ball Team," *New York Times Magazine* (July 5, 1953), 10, 89; W. C. Heinz, "Baseball Players' Dream Town: Milwaukee and Her Braves," *Cosmopolitan* (May 1954), 90; Cohane, 87, 89; Kaese and Lynch, 289.

17. Heinz, 90; Kaese and Lynch, 292.

18. Al Hirschberg, "Can Milwaukee Keep It Up?" *Sport* 16 (February 1954), 79; Cohane, 87–88; Thomas Meany, *Milwaukee's Miracle Braves* (New York: A. S. Barnes, 1957), xi.

19. Hirschberg, 79; Millstein, 10.

20. Shirley Povich, "Now Milwaukee's Really Become Big League," *Baseball Digest* 14 (July 1955), 29–31.

21. Hirschberg, 89; Millstein, 10.

22. Kaese and Lynch, 283; *Life* (July 6, 1953).

23. Kaese and Lynch, 291; Heinz, 90–93.

24. Millstein, 26; *Life* (July 6, 1953).

25. Heinz, 91.

26. *U. S. News and World Report* (May 18, 1958).

27. Stuart McIver, "Will Baltimore Be Another Milwaukee?" *Sport* 16 (April 1954),

82; James H. Bready, *Baseball in Baltimore* (Baltimore: The Johns Hopkins University Press, 1998), 216; Miller, 69.

28. Miller, 39.
29. John McNulty, "Back in the Big League: Baltimore Orioles," *New Yorker* (May 1, 1954); Miller, 32, 25, 43; Edgar Williams, "The Lowdown on Baltimore," *Baseball Digest* 13 (May 1954), 60.
30. McNulty; Gilbert Millstein, " 'Let's Back Up Them Birds,' " *New York Times Magazine* (May 9, 1954), 34.
31. *Life* (April 26, 1954); Miller, 36; Millstein, "Let's Back . . . ," 34; McNulty.
32. Millstein, "Let's Back . . . ," 17.
33. *U. S. News and World Report* (May 18, 1958).
34. Arthur Mann, "How to Buy A Ball Club for Peanuts," *Saturday Evening Post* 227 (April 9, 1955), 108.
35. *Saturday Evening Post* 226 (June 12, 1954); White, 313.
36. Hall of Fame clipping, February 21, 1969; Gerald Holland, "The A's Find Friends in Cowtown," *Sports Illustrated* 2 (April 25, 1955).
37. Charles C. Euchner, *Playing the Field: Why Sports Teams Move and Cities Fight to Keep Them* (Baltimore: Johns Hopkins University Press, 1993), 17; White, 312.
38. Sullivan, 115–17.
39. Dick Young, "To Hell with the Los Angeles Dodgers," *Sport* 24 (August 1957), 83.
40. Sullivan, 87.
41. *San Francisco Independent*, October 14, 1997; Arnold Hano, "Sudden Success at San Francisco," *Sport* 26 (December 1958), 63.
42. Vincent X. Flaherty, "Miracle Move of the Dodgers—From Flatbush to Fantasia" in J. G. Taylor Spink, ed., *Baseball Register, 1960* (St. Louis, Mo.: Sporting News, 1960), 3–4.
43. Steve Bitker, *The Original San Francisco Giants: The Giants of '58* (Champaign, Ill.: Sports Publishing, 1998), 5–6; Flaherty, 6.
44. Bitker, 6.
45. Young, 83.
46. Bitker, 14; John W. Noble, "What They Say in the Dugouts About: The San Francisco Giants," *Sport* 25 (June 1958), 18, 79; *Sports Illustrated* 8 (June 16, 1958), 15.
47. Sullivan, 159; James Murray, "Coining Gold in the Cellar," *Sports Illustrated* 8 (June 30, 1958), 32.
48. Tim Cohane, "West Coast Produces Baseball's Strangest Story," *Look* (August 19, 1958), 50.
49. Arthur Daley, "Will the Giant-Dodger Gold Rush Pan Out?" *New York Times Magazine* (May 11, 1958), 37; Cohane, "West Coast . . .", 50; Charles C. Alexander, *Our Game: An American Baseball History* (New York: Henry Holt, 1991), 240.
50. Daley, 37; Bitker, 7, 13; Robert W. Creamer, "Smash Hit in San Francisco," *Sports Illustrated* 8 (June 16, 1958), 31–32.
51. On Chavez Ravine, see Cary S. Henderson, "Los Angeles and the Dodger War,

1957–1962," *Southern California Quarterly* 6 (Fall 1980), 261–89; T. S. Hines, "Housing, Baseball, and Creeping Socialism—The Battle of Chavez Ravine, Los Angeles, 1949–1959," *Journal of Urban History* 7 (1982), 123–143; and Sullivan, 83–87.

52. Sullivan, 138, 144–60; Cohane, "West Coast . . . ," 50–53; Henderson, 278.

53. Buzzie Bavasi with John Strege, *Off the Record* (Chicago: Contemporary Books, 1987), 89; Alexander, 243.

54. Sullivan, 161–68.

55. Daley, 39.

56. Henderson, 280–84; Sullivan, 172, 178–81.

57. Sid Ziff, "Incredible Year for the Dodgers," *Baseball Digest* 18 (December 1959), 8–9; Sullivan, 188.

58. Alexander, 243; Bitker, 18.

59. Sullivan, 197, 191.

60. Lowenfish, 74.

61. *New York Times*, November 14, 1958.

62. *New York Times*, July 7, 1968.

63. Clark Nealon, et al., "The Campaign for Major League Baseball in Houston," *Houston Review: History and Culture of the Gulf Coast* (1985), 19, 26–27; Voigt, III–12.

64. Nealon et al., 26.

65. Walter Bingham, "No Feud Like an Old Feud," *Sports Illustrated* 14 (May 1, 1961), 50–51.

66. Nealon, 3, 16; George Kirksey, "Houston—The Next Major League City," *Baseball Digest* 18 (March 1959), 21–27; Danny Peary, *We Played the Game: 65 Players Remember Baseball's Greatest Era, 1947–1964* (New York: Hyperion, 1994) 398.

67. Astor, 22; John Shulian, "National Pastime," *Sports Illustrated* 48 (June 1, 1998), 112.

68. Bill James, *The Bill James Baseball Abstract, 1986* (New York: Ballantine Books, 1986), 39–42.

69. Ibid., 41–42; Hall of Fame clipping, February 21, 1969; Norman L. Macht, "Philadelphia Athletics–Kansas City Athletics–Oakland A's" in Peter Bjarkman, ed., *Encyclopedia of Major League Baseball Team Histories: Volume II, the American League* (Westport, Conn.: Meckler, 1991), 331–32.

70. Huston Horn, "Bravura Battle for the Braves: Milwaukee Braves Fast Becoming the Atlanta Braves," *Sports Illustrated* 21 (November 2, 1964), 32–33; *The Sporting News* (October 30, 1965).

71. Astor, 24; Horn, 32–33;

72. Horn, 32–33; Ron Briley, "Milwaukee and Atlanta, A Tale of Two Cities: Eddie, Hank, and the 'Rover Boys' Head South," *Nine* 6 (Fall 1997), 34; Astor, 22.

73. Briley, 38; Horn, 21–22; *The Sporting News* (August 7, 1965).

74. *The Sporting News* (December 12, 1964).

75. Briley, 35–38;

76. William Leggett, "Atlanta, You Can Have the Rest: Leave Us Eddie Mattress, Our Hero," *Sports Illustrated* 22 (April 26, 1965), 24–25; *The Sporting News* (August 18, 1966).

77. Furman Bisher, *Miracle in Atlanta: The Atlanta Braves Story* (New York and Cleveland: World Publishing Company, 1966); *The Sporting News* (August 18, 1966).

78. Voigt, 113; Macht, 333.

79. Tom Clark, *Champagne and Baloney: A History of Finley's A's* (New York: Harper & Row, 1976), 38–39.

80. Leggett, 24–25; undated Hall of Fame clipping.

81. *The Sporting News* (November 4, 1967).

82. Macht, 334; Clark, 46.

83. Hall of Fame clipping, November 4, 1967.

84. *Sports Illustrated* (January 10, 1977).

85. Alexander, 278; *New York Times*, October 1, 1971.

86. *New York Times*, October 1, 1971; Hall of Fame clipping, February 23, 1971; *The Sporting News* (October 16, 1971).

87. *New York Times*, December 2, 1971, September 23, 1971.

88. *The Sporting News* (October 23, 1971, February 28, 1976); *Atlanta Constitution*, December 5. 1974.

Chapter 9: Populist Baseball

1. Daniel Okrent, "The Year George Foster Wasn't Worth $36," *Inside Sports* (March 31, 1981), 89–90; The Rotisserie League, *Rotisserie League Baseball* (New York: Bantam Books, 1984), 4.

2. Ibid.

3. Ibid.; Steve Wulf, "For the Champion in the Rotisserie League, Joy Is a Yoo Hoo Shampoo," *Sports Illustrated* 60 (May 14, 1984), 8; Debbie Becker, "Fan at Her Best," *Women's Sports and Fitness* (August 1985), 17.

4. Conn Nugent, "How To Own a Baseball Team," *Harvard Magazine* (March–April 1981), 54–56.

5. Jack Friedman, "The Most Peppery Game Since the Hot Stove League," *People*, 21 (April 23, 1984), 40; Michael Walsh, "In New York: Major League Fantasies," *Time* (May 4, 1987), 10–11; Nathan Cobb, "Rotiss: The Greatest Game for Baseball Fans Since Baseball," *Smithsonian* 21 (June 1990), 100–9.

6. Nugent, 54; Marcia F. Coburn, "Men Will Be Boys," *Chicago* 39 (June, 1990), 77–80.

7. Charles C. Alexander, *Our Game: An American Baseball History* (New York: Henry Holt, 1991), 293.

8. For a good discussion, see Bill James, *The Bill James Historical Baseball Abstract* (New York: Villard Books, 1986), 258.

9. Benjamin Rader, *Baseball: A History of America's Game* (Urbana: University of Illinois Press, 1992), 194.

10. Ibid., 201.

11. Okrent, 89–90; Kevin Cook, " 'I Signed Nolan Ryan for $8,' " *Playboy* 35 (May 1988), 126–29; *San Francisco Examiner*, June 30, 1983.

12. M. Demarest, "The Boys of Winter," *Time* (February 7, 1983), 66; Roy Blount, Jr., "We All Had a Ball," *Sports Illustrated* 74 (February 21, 1983), 56–60; Philip Ross, "Days of Heaven," *New York* 46 (February 7, 1983), 17–19.

13. Blount, 60.
14. Demarest, 66–67; Ross, 17; Blount, 56–60.
15. Brian Cahn, " 'The Day I Batted Against the Dodgers,' " *Los Angeles* 29 (March, 1984), 195; Gerard A. Brandemeyer and Luella K. Alexander, " 'I Caught the Dream': The Adult Baseball Camp as Fantasy Leisure," *Journal of Leisure Research* 19 (1986), 28–29; Debra Michals, "Living a Fantasy: Playing Ball with Mantle and Mays," *Business Week* (March 18, 1985), 151–52; Ira J. Dreyfuss, "Physician's Fantasy: Baseball Camp for Grown-Up Kids," *Physician and Sports Medicine* 18 (March 1990), 168–70.
16. Paul McLaughlin, "Play Ball!" *Canadian Business* 61 (July 1988), 54–56; Ellen Karasik, " 'Me, 83 Men, and Baseball,' " *Philadelphia Inquirer Magazine* (March 18, 1990), 29.
17. Cahn, 302; Dreyfuss, 168.
18. Brandemeyer and Alexander, 33; William McNeill, *Dodger Diary* (Woodside, N.Y.: Celtic, 1986).
19. Brandemeyer and Alexander, 26, 31; Blount, 60.
20. Brandemeyer and Alexander, 34–37.
21. John Thorn and Pete Palmer, *The Hidden Game of Baseball: A Revolutionary Approach to Baseball and Its Statistics* (New York: Doubleday, 1984), 46–47.
22. Ibid, 47–48; John Thorn et al., *Total Baseball*, 6 ed. (New York: Total Sports, 1999), 632.
23. Thorn and Palmer, 48.
24. Michael Lenehan, "An Eye on All the Records," *Atlantic Monthly* (September 1983), 58–63, 66; Daniel Okrent, "He Does It by the Numbers," *Sports Illustrated* (May 25, 1981), 45.
25. Bill James, "Confessions of a Stat Freak," *Sport* (September 1979), 1989; Bill James, *The Bill James Baseball Abstract, 1983* (New York: Ballantine Books, 1983), 1; Bill James, *The Bill James Baseball Abstract, 1984* (New York: Ballantine Books, 1984), 3; Bill James, *The Bill James Baseball Abstract, 1988* (New York: Ballantine Books, 1988), 232.
26. James, "Confessions of a Stat Freak," 89; Lenehan, 70; James, *Baseball Abstract, 1988*, 232.
27. James, *Baseball Abstract, 1988*, 231;
28. Okrent, "He Does It by the Numbers," 45, 48; Susan McCarthy, "Looking Backward at Ten" in Bill James, *Baseball Abstract, 1986*, 328–29.
29. James, *Baseball Abstract, 1988*, 231; McCarthy, 329.
30. James, *Baseball Abstract, 1983*, 1; James, *Baseball Abstract, 1988*, 231–32; Okrent, "He Does It by the Numbers," 48.
31. James, *Baseball Abstract, 1984*; James, *Baseball Abstract, 1988*, 23–32; Roger Angell, "Pluck and Luck" in *Late Innings: A Baseball Companion* (New York: Simon and Schuster, 1982), 301; Okrent, "He Does It by the Numbers," 45.
32. Bill James, *The Bill James Baseball Abstract, 1982* (New York: Ballantine Books, 1982), 328–29.
33. Okrent, "He Does It by the Numbers," 42; James, *The Baseball Abstract, 1982*, 9, 132; James, *Baseball Abstract, 1984*, 200.
34. Lenehan, 59; Joe Klein, "The Media Guide," *Sport* 75 (October 1984), 15–16; Sy

Weissman, "The Microchipped Diamond," *Psychology Today* (17 August 1983), 44–51; Bob Cipher, "Square Root, Root, Root for the Home Team: Stalking the Ultimate Baseball Statistic Is Now Serious Business," *Discovery* 8 (October 1987), 87–88, 90–92.

35. R. Zoglin, "Holy R.B.I.—It's Statman!" *People* (June 3, 1991), 93–94; Klein, 16.
36. Thorn and Palmer, 47; Cipher, 90; Weissman, 44–51.
37. The Rotisserie League, 36.
38. Peter S. Prichard, *The Making of McPaper: The Inside Story of USA Today* (New York: St. Martin's, 1989), 1, 187, 327–29, 369; William Taafe, "The Sports Fan's Daily Spread," *Sports Illustrated* 77 (October 6, 1986), 44–48.
39. Taafe, 44–48; *Time* (May 4, 1987).
40. Wulf, 8; Cook, 126–29.
41. *The Sporting News* (April 3, 1989).
42. Bernard Malamud, *The Natural* (New York: Harcourt, Brace, 1952); Robert Coover, *The Universal Baseball Association, Inc., J. Henry Waugh, prop.* (New York: Random House, 1968); Philip Roth, *The Great American Novel* (New York: Holt, Rinehart, 1973).
43. W. P. Kinsella, *Shoeless Joe* (Boston: Houghton Mifflin, 1982).
44. Cited by Darryl Brock, SABR-List, April 13, 1999; Stephen C. Wood, J. David Pincus, and J. Nicholas Den Bonis, "Baseball: The American Mythos in Film, *The Natural*," *Nine: A Journal of Baseball History and Social Policy Perspectives* 4 (Fall, 1995), 149–51.
45. Thorn et al., 2504.
46. Ibid., 604.
47. Donald Hall, *Fathers Playing Catch with Sons* (San Francisco: North Point Press, 1985); George Will, *Men at Work* (New York: HarperPerennial, 1991), 17; David Halberstam, *Summer of '49* (New York: Morrow, 1989).
48. Paul Dickson, *Baseball's Greatest Quotations* (New York: HarperCollins), 155–56.
49. James, *The Baseball Abstract, 1988*, 234; Nugent, 54.
50. Geoffrey C. Ward and Ken Burns, *Baseball: An Illustrated History* (New York: Knopf, 1994), xviii.
51. Steve Rosenbloom and Kelly Garrett, "Why Rotisserie Leagues Are the Best/ Worst Thing That Ever Happened to Baseball Fans," *Sport* 81 (March 1990), 48– 49; Coburn, 77–80.
52. *USA Today*, April 6, 1993; *Sports Illustrated*, 73 (September 10, 1990); Steve Wulf, "Rotisserie Revisited," *Sports Illustrated* 71 (August 7, 1989), 78.
53. Roy Blount, Jr., "Staturated," *Sports Illustrated* 74 (April 15, 1991), 133–34; George Vass, "Some of Baseball's Valued Statistics Can Be Deceiving," *Baseball Digest* (June 1987), 41–49; James, *Baseball Abstract, 1988*, 234.

Index